AN EMERGENT MANIFESTO OF HOPE

edited by DOUG PAGITT + TONY JONES

Published by Baker Books
a division of Baker Publishing Group
P.O. Box 6287, Grand Rapids, MI 49516-6287
www.bakerbooks.com

Paperback edition published 2008

ISBN 978-0-8010-7156-0

Printed in the United States of America

The Library of Congress has cataloged the original edition as follows:
An emergent manifesto of hope / Doug Pagitt and Tony Jones, editors.
p. cm.
Includes bibliographical references.
ISBN 10: 0-8010-6807-X
ISBN 978-0-8010-6807-2
1. Postmodernism—Religious aspects—Christianity. 2. Non-institutional churches. 3. Church renewal. 4. Christianity—Forecasting. I. Pagitt, Doug, 1966– II. Jones, Tony, 1968–
BR115.P74E44 2007
262.001′7—dc22 2006035282

In keeping with biblical principles of creation stewardship, Baker Publishing Group advocates the responsible use of our natural resources. As a member of the Green Press Initiative, our company uses recycled paper when possible. The text paper of this book is comprised of 30% post-consumer waste.

ēmersion is a partnership between Baker Books and Emergent Village, a growing, generative friendship among missional Christians seeking to love our world in the Spirit of Jesus Christ. The ēmersion line is intended for professional and lay leaders like you who are meeting the challenges of a changing culture with vision and hope for the future. These books will encourage you and your community to live into God's kingdom here and now.

The first of these books, ***An Emergent Manifesto of Hope***, brings you the voices of those who are shaping the emergent conversation. Some are men and women who have been working out an emerging theology for decades. Others represent the next wave of Christian thought and practice. Both the veterans and the up-and-comers represent the essence of the Emergent Village—optimistic, passionate, hard-to-ignore.

Through their discussions of topics such as reconciliation, humanity, sexuality, and evangelism, these pastors and practitioners give you a glimpse of the ways in which the people of Emergent Village are changing what it means to live as a Christian in this age. You might not agree with everything they have to say, but you will come away from this conversation with a deeper understanding of the hopeful imagination that drives the emerging church.

Emergent Village resources for communities of faith

Contents

INTRODUCTION

Friendship, Faith, and Going Somewhere Together

TONY JONES

To answer the question, "What is Emergent Village?" I often go back to the beginning. When I jumped on board Emergent Village, I really didn't know what I was getting into. I was invited to a meeting in a crummy hotel meeting room in Arlington, Texas, in August of 1998. And, as so many have found, being in a room with these individuals was an exhilarating experience. The energy in the room was palpable. The room positively crackled. I think that's because we had the feeling, even back then, that we were on to something.

Even as we struggled to determine what that "something" was, we talked about an element of the connection that was seemingly even more important, and surely more elusive, and that was and is *friendship*.

To be sure, there are words in English that have been overused to the point of confusion. *Love* is one. And *friend* is another. Yet as we searched for ways to identify ourselves, other appellations didn't fit. We were more than a "network," and we surely weren't a "denomination." We didn't want to be a "club" or a "society." Some people have called us a "think tank," but that doesn't quite fit either.

We just kept coming back to the word *friend*. We wanted to recover that word and to invest it with theological meaning. We knew this wouldn't be easy, for not only were we fighting the meaninglessness of a word that had been overused, but we also had the creeping suspicion that many of us didn't really know how to be true friends.

It doesn't take long to figure out that friendship is hard. Most of us find this out by, say, kindergarten. Recently I had to walk with Tanner, my five-year-old son, to his friend's house a couple blocks away and watch him apologize for something he'd said on the bus. There, standing in the driveway, watching with his friend's mom, I experienced vicariously through Tanner how it felt to discover for the first time that a friendship is a fragile thing, something that needs great care.

By the time I was first getting involved in Emergent (before it was even called Emergent), I had had about two and a half decades of struggling through friendships—enough to keep me quite humble about the prospect of more and better and longer-lasting friendships. Like most everyone, I suppose, I had a wake of ex-friends (not to mention ex-girlfriends!) in my past as I encountered Emergent.

Yet I did immediately sense that there was something different about this group. We talked about ideas we had for the church and for developing a deeper life with Christ, but we almost always talked about doing it together. In fact I had the growing sense that *this* was the group of men and women who would take the church into its next iteration, and I became convinced that we were going to do it *together*.

In the beginning we came together under the auspices of Leadership Network (LN), a church-assisting foundation in Dallas. LN had hired Doug Pagitt, a former evangelical youth pastor and proven networker, to develop a network of innovative, young pastors. Doug began this work in 1997, making a point to fly around the country and connect with any young church leader about whom he had heard good things.[1] With that kind of energy in the room, there was excitement every time we met. Persons flowed in and out of the group—the boundaries of the "us" were quite porous.

From the beginning one of the things that we were committed to doing was throwing parties. We often called them "events" or "conferences," but everyone knew that in reality they were parties for the church and for our common life in God. Regardless of the invited speakers or the musicians playing on stage, the real premium was placed on relational connection—that's our technical term for friendship.

As with any friendship, I suppose, some folks didn't jibe with what we were about. I was sitting in the Baghdad Café in the Castro neighborhood of San Francisco a few months ago. It was 2 a.m., and I was there with Mark Scandrette, Karen Ward, and Lilly Lewin. We had been speaking all day at an event, and there we were, ordering pancakes and hamburgers in the middle of the night, still talking a mile a minute. In a moment of insight, Mark said, "We really are a relationally manic people."

That maniacal style has been a struggle for some, and understandably so. Our kind of friendship is a high-demand friendship. Folks give a lot and they expect a lot in return. But this friendship bears much fruit. This soil has been worked thoroughly, and good stuff has sprung up from it. What you hold in your hands is an example of the good stuff, and I'm talking about "good" in several ways.

First of all, it is a "good" as in "goods and services." Most likely, you paid for this book. It's a good that has somehow been produced and delivered to you. Friendships often produce goods, items that become an extension of the friendship. In that sense, Emergent Village has been producing goods for a while. Events, conferences, even new churches that have been inspired by the Emergent friendship can be considered goods that have come about through it.

But in another way, we consider this kind of "good" differently than others might. The books that have been produced from the soil of the Emergent Village friendship are not to be considered be-all and end-all books on any subject. Instead, they should be considered discussion starters—part of the conversation about what it is to be Emergent, friends, Christians. Like a coffee-table book, this book (and the others that come from Emergent Village) is meant to sit at the middle of a relationship, to provoke conversation, and consequently to deepen the friendship. So this "good" works in a cyclical way in the friendship. It both *comes from* the friendship and *deepens* the friendship.

In another sense, we hope this book is a "good," and that's the philosophical sense. Aristotle's definition of *good* comes at the beginning of his *Nicomachean Ethics*: "Every skill and every inquiry, and similarly, every action and choice of action, is thought to have some good as its object. This is why the good has rightly been defined as the object of all endeavor."[2] In other words, every human enterprise is done with some end, some result in mind. That result is the "good" of the endeavor. The "highest good," according to Aristotle, is that good at the end of the line, the good that is desirable exclusively for its own sake.

In his well-known definition of a practice, neo-Aristotelian philosopher Alasdair MacIntyre relies on this understanding of a "good":

> By a "practice" I am going to mean any coherent and complex form of socially established cooperative human activity through which *goods* internal to that form of activity are realized in the course of trying to achieve those standards of excellence which are appropriate to, and partially definitive of, that form of activity, with the result that human powers to achieve excellence, and human conceptions of the ends and *goods* involved, are systematically extended.[3]

So when we get together and do things together, the things we do together are the "goods" internal to that enterprise. The striving toward excellence, together, achieves goods, and the goods subsequently result in more striving and more goods.

I can't say that we knew exactly what we were getting into in 1998, when we planned our first event together. But it does seem that we were engaging in some sort of "socially established cooperative human activity," as MacIntyre calls it. To say it in a less philosophical way, we've rolled up our sleeves and done stuff together. It has involved everything from debating leading theologians and biblical scholars (live and in print) to literally digging in the dirt together to get God's goodness under our fingernails. As a result, we've achieved some "goods."

One of those goods, I think, is this polyphonic text. In a variety of voices, this group of friends is attempting to sing a song together. There are times, I'm sure, when the harmonies don't match, when someone seems to be singing out of tune. But that's really not the point for us. The point is that we're singing and we're singing together. We get better at singing only by doing it and listening to those around us. You might think of Emergent Village in general, and this book in particular, as a choir with no conductor.

Of course the Christian faith is based on a sacred text that has a similar trajectory. At times the Bible seems contradictory, out of harmony with itself. But on the whole, it is beautiful in its grand sweep, and those disharmonious parts, in fact, help establish the beauty of the whole. Our hope is that this book, in a small way, is a reflection of the disharmonious beauty of the Christian Story.

Finally, we hope that this book is "good" in the sense that when you read it you don't hear a giant sucking sound. I have found these essays to be compelling and brilliant, each in its own way.

Be mindful that in this book a wide variety of authors are gathered, not unlike Emergent Village itself. And each author comes from a different field and values a different expertise. One is a missionary, another a philosopher, another a beat poet, and another a writer. Each of these activities carries its own rationality—that is, its own internal way of thinking and doing—and as such, each has its own way of judging what is good (and what is bad). So it's a bit artificial for us to ask each of these individuals to write three thousand words of prose to be fitted into this book. How do you explain where you fit in the Emergent friendship in three thousand words? Or, worse yet, how do you describe your hopes and dreams for the future of God's kingdom and your cooperation in it in as many words?

Obviously, that's really an impossible task. However, the impossibility of it hasn't daunted these authors one bit. And as a result, you hold a thing of beauty in your hands, something that's "good" in the sense of being favorable, bountiful, and fertile—like a field that is "good" for planting. When I look at my backyard garden in the spring, it isn't the least bit orderly or systematic, but it sure is beautiful and good. It's full of leftover weeds from last fall, some old leaves, and not a few rocks that have been heaved to the surface by the winter frost. But as I turn the soil, spread a year's worth of compost over it, and ready it for planting, I know that this good garden will, by August, produce good fruit. It won't be perfect. There will be weeds and bugs, some plants won't make it, and the dog might get in and dig a bit. But on the whole, the outcome will be good, and we'll be eating homegrown tomatoes by the middle of August.

I hope that you can see the beauty in the mess that is this book. It's not one, univocal message. But, seriously, who would want a garden of all green beans? No, you've got to have variety, and that's what you'll find in the pages that follow.

What is Emergent Village?

A mess. A beautiful, *good* mess.

HOPE

PART 1

A People of Hope

Emergent—a Generative Friendship of Missional Christians

Doug Pagitt

I am the vine; you are the branches. If a man remains in me and I in him, he will bear much fruit; apart from me you can do nothing. If anyone does not remain in me, he is like a branch that is thrown away and withers; such branches are picked up, thrown into the fire and burned. If you remain in me and my words remain in you, ask whatever you wish, and it will be given you. This is to my Father's glory, that you bear much fruit, showing yourselves to be my disciples.

As the Father has loved me, so have I loved you. Now remain in my love. If you obey my commands, you will remain in my love, just as I have obeyed my Father's commands and remain in his love. I have told you this so that my joy may be in you and that your joy may be complete. My command is this: Love each other as I have loved you. Greater love has no one than this, that he lay down his life for his friends. You are my friends if you do what I command. I no longer call you servants, because a servant does not know his master's business. Instead, I have called you friends, for everything that I learned from my Father I have made known to you. You did not choose me, but I chose you and appointed you to go and bear fruit—fruit that will last. Then the Father will give you whatever you ask in my name. This is my command: Love each other.

John 15:5–17

There is something compelling and something scary about the notion of being invited into a friendship. We may well know the benefits of friendship—how life is designed for friendship and even requires it. We know that no one can live alone. We need and are changed by our friends.

And as great as the rewards of friendship are, there is also concern. Friendship involves openness, vulnerability, and risk. We have all been involved in friendships that didn't work. Sometimes people change; other times circumstances change. There is no doubt that friendships are often volatile relationships. They come with great possibility—for life and for struggle.

So the idea of entering into friendship can be intimidating. This may be especially true of being friends with Jesus. For some people the idea of being a friend of Jesus is what their faith is based on—a relationship with a loving Friend. For others it is almost a sacrilege to consider Jesus as a "mere Friend"; Lord, Savior, Creator are words many are comfortable with, but Friend, well, it can seem so trite, so "buddy Jesus," so irreverent. To still others the notion of Jesus as a Friend implies a connection with Jesus that is just too close and intimate. It is easier to keep an appropriate distance.

When Jesus invited his disciples into friendship, they may have responded in these same ways, and for some it must not have set very well. That may be the reason Jesus explained this friendship, as he did in John 15, with ideas such as "Greater love . . . I no longer call you servants . . . What is mine is yours . . ." The stakes are raised even higher with the ending line in this passage: "Love each other." It is as if Jesus were saying, "Lay down your life for each other. Obey one another. Be more than servants to each other. What is yours should be others' as well." Not only are we called to love God and be friends with Jesus, we are also called to love and be friends of one another.

For too many people, life is a lonely experience. We are tormented by our own choices and the choices of others. We put our passions or insecurities above people and live with the isolated consequences. In short, many of us are just bad friends. But we don't want to be. We want to be friends in the Jesus way, and we need others to transform us so that we may find and join in God's hopes and dreams for the world.

The Emergent imagination is at its most basic level a call to friendship—friendship with God, with one another, and with the world. This has implications in the way Emergent is structured, in the way people relate to each other with differences and agreement, and in the way the Emergent Village forms and influences communities.

This call comes with all the normal pressures and fears of friendship. There is deep recognition of how hard friendship can be, especially when this friendship pulls us beyond our culturally influenced understanding of *friendliness*. The Emergent concept of friendship is more than professional relationships of like-minded peers, it is an invitation to the Jesus way of life as partners with each other and colaborers in the work of God in the world.

Friendship is more than being friendly. Friendship means vulnerability, risk, struggle, and pain. It means welcoming the "other" and the familiar. It means putting aside our agendas for the passions of another. It means being right but being quiet. It means being right and speaking up. It means being more concerned about the other than oneself. It means joining in life and death. It means time.

As in many friendships, our desire is greater than our lived reality. Most friendships are held together by a hope of what can be as much as a history that has been created. But even in the midst of these hope-filled failings, there is a realization that we need to pursue this friendship not as an addition to faith but as a necessity of it.

For all the good that has come from the servant leadership model of church leadership, which has gained well-deserved acceptance in recent decades, there are those of us who want to move beyond servanthood as the model for our engagement with one another and take the dangerous leap into friendship as the way of understanding one another.

Because participants in this friendship are from varied walks of life, live in different places, and speak different languages, much attention has been paid to creating ways of connecting. For the better part of a decade, the Emergent way of being friends has included the notion of pilgrimage. While technological ways of communicating are key to maintaining connections, nothing can replace face-to-face meeting. Certainly reading and writing have their place, but they cannot accomplish for a friendship what sharing a meal can.

The motley friendships that develop are hard for many to understand and hard to control or evaluate, but they seem right. We think that, just as the collection of Jesus's disciples was an odd group (men and women, Zealots and Pharisees, tax collectors and temple guardians, the wealthy and the poor, and so on), the friendships of the friends of Jesus ought to look odd. So the Emergent friendship desires to bring together, not pull apart. To create something new, not rehash old divisions.

The following chapters serve as a call into a friendship, are the result of friendship. So read with this invitation in mind, and read with the grace needed by those who seek friendship through faith, hope, and love.

1

GROWING PAINS

The Messy and Fertile Process of Becoming

MARK SCANDRETTE

I'm a thirty-four-year-old riding on a toy, the last person on earth who still rides a Razor kick-scooter, I think, as I glide down the street to meet Bob. At the café I order a decaf Americano and toasted whole wheat bagel and notice Bob already seated at a table listening to his iPod and keying on his laptop. Bob and I are occasional walking buddies, having met a few years ago at an Emergent event in San Diego during a time when Bob was rethinking his vocation, spirituality, and life goals. Shortly before we met, he had quit a lucrative career in publishing to pursue a more integrated life, more family time, work with the local Episcopal diocese, and theological study in Berkeley.

Once Bob suggested to me, "The emerging church is like junior high students and sex—a lot of people talking about it, but not a lot of people actually doing it—and those that are doing it are messy—and fertile as hell!" Bob is right. Though exploration of ideas and dialogue can be helpful, it is critical that we move from conversation to action. The true measure of our critical success is our ability to create generative contexts and a growing capacity to love in fidelity with the example of Jesus.

Emergent. The emerging church. It is unfortunate, and yet inevitable, that words used to describe a phenomenon have so quickly become a label and brand name. Some of us chafe under the loss of independence and "street cred," which results from becoming identified with a particular group—what some have called a "movement." Others among us clamber to be included and huddle under the banner of what is perceived to be the hip new thing. For many of us the discovery that we are not alone,

---

Mark Scandrette is a writer, spiritual teacher, and executive director and cofounder of ReIMAGINE, a center for spiritual formation in San Francisco. ReIMAGINE sponsors city-based learning experiences, peer learning groups, and The Jesus Dojo—a yearlong intensive formation process inspired by the life and teachings of Jesus. Mark is also a founding member of SEVEN, a monastic community working as teachers and advocates for holistic and integrative Christian spirituality. He is an Emergent Village Coordinating Group participant, having served on the planning team for the Emergent conventions and the annual Emergent Gathering. A dilettante poet and chef, Scandrette lives with his wife, Lisa, and their three children in an old Victorian in San Francisco's Mission District.

and the solidarity we find in the shelter of each other, has been life-giving and at times lifesaving.

The terms *Emergent* and *emerging church*, like the word *Christian*, have quickly become catchall phrases to which people and groups bring their independent meanings. The result is that we are each misrepresented and misunderstood. The increasing visibility, perceived credibility, and for some, scandal, of the emerging church are threats to the spirit of what we mean by *emerge*—the primal humility, vulnerability, and passion of a search for a way with God together in the world we live in.

Finding Companions in the Wake of Change

Some among us, like the animals of the forest, have sensed a storm on the horizon. We have had a premonition of the torrent of change that will affect general culture and the church—shifts in social consciousness, globalization, economics, increasing mobility, plurality, and societal fragmentation. These are examples of the many changes that determine the landscape of our journey of navigating faithfulness in the way of Jesus in the world we live in—changes that are coming and have now come.

People seem to be affected by these shifts with varying levels of intensity, depending on region, personality, and social location. A common result is a great desire for conversation with other people who are also struggling to make sense of things. The emerging church is a place where people have felt the freedom to explore questions and experiment with new forms of lifestyle and corporate practice. Often the questions have been about the essence of the Christ-message, vocation, the nature and form of the church, cultural and philosophical analysis, and the present agenda of God in the world.

We resonate with the story of two friends walking along the road to Emmaus, discussing the significance of the life and teachings of Jesus. During their conversation, a stranger met them, and in his presence their hearts were strangely warmed. Many of us have felt the presence of Jesus in the midst of our conversations with one another. For people in our time, conversation may be the first step toward entering the Way. Conversation is also a path toward a greater sense of authentic relationship than some have experienced in more formal structures. Whatever the emerging church becomes, it began as a generative friendship among younger entrepreneurial leaders and seekers—an improvised support system for people desperate for connections with others experimenting with new ideas about faith and community.

If nothing else, we find ourselves in a time when old categories and traditional boundaries are breaking down and new connections are being made. I think of the fifty-eight-year-old suburban bricklayer I met for lunch last year who ventured into the city to talk about the stirrings of his heart and his search for a way of life with Jesus beyond the dogmas of his conservative church tradition. "I can't believe I'm sitting here in this neighborhood with you," he kept saying, as we talked about the Bible and life.

Often observers comment about the socially extroverted personality of the Emergent "conversation," and we've recently seen an explosion in the number of local, self-styled Emergent cohorts. Once a month our community hosts a conversation in various Bay Area locations. I am constantly surprised by the diversity and intensity of people who participate—many who defy typical stereotypes: young women, a middle-aged Korean pastor, suburban housewives. At a recent gathering thirty people packed into our house for an evening of food and conversation—families, students, business professionals, pastors, and nonprofit workers. They come from various traditions, including Greek Orthodox, Pentecostal, Presbyterian, Episcopal, evangelical, and even one person from our neighborhood with no Christian background who was drawn to the idea of conversation about spiritual matters.

One of my favorite expressions of generative friendship has been the Emergent Gathering in Santa Fe, New Mexico, which for some has become a pilgrimage of sorts. We stay in cabins near the mountains, feasting, hiking, and talking together over three days. Often near the beginning of a social movement, people will travel long distances to connect with others who share similar passions. These national and regional gatherings have become a movable feast, a mobile local/global community where solidarity is strengthened.

We are challenged to preserve our conversational and relational dynamics as interest in emerging church issues escalates. The transferability and economy of words and ideas can easily eclipse genuine dialogue and relationship. Fascination with celebrity and vicarious experiences poses an additional challenge to the integrity of what we hope are generative friendships.

Many who had experienced a profound sense of aloneness have discovered courage and solidarity through reading what others have written, traveling to events, and initiating new friendships. At their best, interactions via written words, distant events, and high-profile personalities will progress to more local conversations and community making.

You should not think that the "real" emergence is happening elsewhere. You are invited to embrace your own celebrity—recognizing the importance of your own journey over simply being a fan of others'—and cultivate a local culture of faith-seeking. To address spectator tendencies, I give this unsolicited advice: no one can emerge for you. Make your own life. Host your own emergence. Stop reading so many books and blogs. Start your own conversations, and be a caring friend. The most important conversations happen between people who have the potential to live out their story together.

The Energy and Awkwardness of Transformation

It is fascinating how quickly outsiders become insiders, and the dispossessed become the owners of the farm. It remains to be seen whether we will resist the temptations to seize the power and positions easily offered by desperate institutions that would domesticate our adventures for the masses. Simultaneously we criticize and crave the affirmation, credibility, respectability, power, and resources of various institutions and organizations. Many of us are frankly conflicted about our role in the body of Christ. Is the most effective way of change from the center or at the margins? When do we stay and when do we go?

We should acknowledge that for many of us the door was opened to reimagine faith and the church through pain, disappointment, failure, burnout, public or private humiliation, or a sense of personal alienation. It can be argued that any social movement attracts anomalies, extremists, and crazies—and the emerging church phenomenon is no exception. We have brought along our peculiarities, unhealthy pathologies, and shadow sides. Explorations into emerging faith have created tension in marriages. In isolated cases the emerging church community has been the stage on which people have played out their personal disintegration.

At times I'm fearful that permission to be deconstructive has attracted personalities that are prone to criticism, angst, and melancholy. Sometimes we conceal our unresolved personality issues, organic depressive tendencies, and relational troubles under the veil of a "spiritual crisis." We need encouragement and support to face our personal difficulties more directly, rather than attributing too much of our struggles to ecclesiological or philosophical issues. Hopefully together we learn to cultivate an environment of honesty, transparency, and support that brings greater wholeness to both individuals and communities.

But even a healthy rethinking of faith can still produce a profound sense of disequilibrium. My friend Craig Burnett suggests that deconstruction and reconstruction are regular rhythms in a life of apprenticeship to Jesus. We should not be too quick to dismiss or expect people to just "get over" their deconstruction—as if to graduate sequentially onto reconstruction. But concurrently we should encourage one another to imagine and enact proactive communal solutions and reconstructions.

Author and spiritual director Evan Howard suggests that spiritual conversion, rather than being a singular event, is more accurately described as a series of distinctive epiphanies (for example, a conversion to the role of the Spirit, a conversion to social justice, a conversion to contemplative practices, and so on). These are not conversions from one system to another; they make up the gradual complementary and holistic renewal of the soul. These progressive awakenings can sometimes create a sense of grief and regret. For anyone who is not experiencing such a conversion, the criticism and doubts expressed by such a seeker may sound whiny, negative, and pessimistic. When we experience the deconstruction of our faith, we are in good company with many of the characters of ancient Scripture, whose expectations of what it meant to follow God were constantly being challenged and subverted. Our constructions of faith and practice are dismantled and, at times, destroyed so that we can approximate a more coherent and integrative *orthopraxis*—good theology and good living.

A central and reoccurring theme of conversation has been a renewed fascination with the present availability of the kingdom of God. In terms of God's agenda to remake and restore all of creation, "good news" is something that is as much inhabited as it is believed. Therefore, how we live is of equal importance to what we believe or how we practice the rituals of a particular community or tradition. This allows for an experimental approach to Christian faith and practice. In many quarters there is a quest to recover a more primitive understanding of the life and teachings of Jesus and wrestle with how to live according to his teaching in contemporary society. Jesus is taken seriously both as Savior and Teacher for life. An elevated Christology animates participants in emerging conversations and provides the energy for new communities and renewed practices.

Perhaps interest in theologies of the kingdom of God is related to the contemporary quest for holism, integration, and a sense of interconnection. My colleague, Dr. Linda Bergquist, has suggested that renewed popularity of the "kingdom" language is related to the emerging global narrative of the deep ecology movement—a consciousness and awareness that everything matters and is somehow interdependent.

I am sadly perplexed by commentators and media sources who portray, and dismiss, the emerging church phenomenon as merely an attempt at cultural relevancy marketing. Perhaps they presume that the largest and most conventional public manifestations of what is labeled "Emergent" are representative of the whole. I hope that more substantive and radical communities continue to gain momentum.

Living into the Future Together

We live up to the story we live under. We live in a time when many people are waking up to the realization that the work and message of Jesus are about the future and the present, and represent the potential for significant healing in every dimension of life. We are recovering from a legacy in which religious experience and devotion have been significantly separated from the domain of everyday life. Often our legacy habits perpetuate a limited view of what is spiritual, so there is a need for new practices and perspectives. Embracing the reality of the kingdom means that everything matters and that all of life is sacred. Spiritual leaders are being challenged not only to articulate a message or ideas well, but also to live, providing a compelling example to those who follow them.

Many participants in emerging conversations long for a sense of greater integration between belief and practice, local and global, inward and outward, the individual and a sense of place within a local community and culture. We see this longing for integrative theology and practice expressed in various themes within the emerging church phenomenon:

- significant interest in "community," communal living, and renewed monastic practices
- an open-source approach to community, theology, and leadership that encourages flatter structures, networks, and more personal and collective participation
- revitalized interest in the social dimensions of the gospel of Jesus, including community development, earth-keeping, global justice, and advocacy—with a particular emphasis on a relationally engaged approach to these issues
- renewed interest in contemplative and bodily spiritual formation disciplines that have, historically, been important Christian practices
- a renewed emphasis on creation theology that celebrates earth, humanity, cultures, and the sensuous and aesthetic as good gifts of the Creator to be enjoyed in their proper contexts
- cultivation and appreciation of the arts, creativity, artful living, and provocative storytelling
- reexamination of vocation, livelihood, and sustainable economics

While these streams of interest have perhaps always existed within Christian tradition in some form, what may be unique about the church in its current emergence is a desire to be proficient and passionate in multiple dimensions—because we live with a sense that everything matters and that no part of human experience is outside the light cast by the hope of the Good News of God.

Many emerging communities of faith have adopted a radical holistic approach to what it means to be the church. Through ReIMAGINE, our organization in San Francisco, our family is a part of an intentional missional community seeking to follow the teachings of Jesus in every dimension of life. We proclaim that a new way of life is possible. Seeing ourselves as agents of renewal, we ask, "What is the message of Jesus and how might we follow him in the time and place in which we live?" We facilitate a one-year process called The Jesus Dojo that invites participants into communal formation exercises based on seven streams in the life of Jesus: service, simplicity, creativity, obedience, prayer, community and love. As a monastic community we experiment with common life rhythms inspired by Jesus's example. Many of us live together in cohousing, sharing resources and caring for our urban neighborhood.

Looking into the Mirror

I am extremely excited and hopeful about the future and at the same time painfully aware of how together we stumble awkwardly toward our destiny. With this in mind I submit a few observations about how we might proceed together.

In recent days there has been a lot of talk about the kingdom of God, speculation about what Jesus meant by the kingdom of God, and how we might live as seekers of the kingdom of God in the here and now. The term *kingdom of God* has become so popular, and its usage so varied, that it is difficult to know if we are even talking about the same thing. Some of us, on first "discovery" of the message of the kingdom, have tended to entertain a romantic, idealized, externalized, and vague view of what the kingdom of God might be in our world. There is a tendency to see the kingdom of God as whatever is progressive, exotic, foreign, and obscure—at the exclusion of the small and beautiful things that have been part of our normal experience or home culture. By elevating the countercultural, we put ourselves in danger of the same kind of fragmentation of the message of the gospel we have sought to avoid. We are learning that it does not suffice to have vague and romantic notions of the kingdom of God that are disconnected from the details of the life and teachings of Jesus. This is just one example of how we are rightly accused, at some points, of being dilettantes—ambitious dabblers in various life domains that are relatively new to our consciousness.

We are invited to a more mature engagement with the reality of the kingdom of God, taking seriously the ethics, teaching, and authority of Jesus in our struggle toward personal and corporate obedience to his commands. And we are reminded that kingdom love is not so much something to be exhaustively understood as it is a present reality to inhabit through action.

Many of us are rediscovering the social ethics and tangible compassion of Jesus. This is a healthy development, particularly for those of us groomed in traditions in which the social dimensions of Jesus's life were separated from his role as Savior. We are developing a more global awareness of needs and opportunities for compassion, justice, and resource sharing. At our best, inspired by the Spirit and motivated by love, we seek justice, reconciliation, healing, and restoration for those who are sick, hungry, thirsty, naked, lonely, or imprisoned. At our worst, we are satisfied by our more progressive political views and token checks written out to the "right" organizations. As my colleague Nate Millheim often says, "Sometimes we think we are caring for the needs of the poor because we now read about issues of justice."

For some who awaken to the call for healing, the weight of privilege and the weight of probable responsibility for systemic global injustices can be overwhelming. Because of this there is a temptation to believe that everything is wrong—what we buy, how we eat, where we live, the vehicles we drive. An acute sense of free-floating guilt haunts and paralyzes the person. In this state we can become the worst kind of activists or moralists, motivated by shame instead of love and imagination. Our efforts at compassionate action need to go beyond mere sentimentality and translate into daily actions. Perhaps to do something well we must first do it badly—and hopefully we will learn smarter, more effective, and more integrative means of participating in the healing of our world. The mandate to "seek first the kingdom" propels us to take an engaged and experimental approach to what it means to be faithful in our time. The Spirit of God that hovered over creation is still present in our world, inviting us to collaborate with our Maker in the fulfillment of God's reign on earth.

The road ahead leads us toward justice/mercy/love

You Leave Home to Jericho you roam
    through fallow fields and winter trees stripped bare
    skeleton branches reaching for the air
    and they are waiting . . .

Waiting for the sons and daughters to be revealed.
Waiting for the hands that will soothe and heal.
And down the road
We see the Nazarene
Embraced as Messiah and Rabbi King
We see our desperation for substance
become living abundance

Loosening the chains of injustice
Breaking the yoke of oppression
sheltering the stranger
feeding the hungry
clothing the naked
comforting the sick
welcoming the weak

We will no longer turn away from our own flesh & blood
We will be called Repairer of broken walls, restorer of streets
with dwellings.

The Road Ahead is a Damascus Road of blinding light
broken Spirit
sacrifice—of shattered dreams, High jacked schemes
and the warm wet kiss of mystery.

On that road I hear a voice . . .
I hear a voice saying to you and to me:

I am here.
The hidden whisper of love.
That beautiful and terrible story you hunger to hear.
Be still! Be still sacred scared child.
Awake! Awake from your stubborn numb slumber.
Open those sleeping eyes to my morning day light.
It will not burn away any good it finds
in that humble cracked heart.
Weep! Weep while you can.
While you still feel.
While the pain is still real.
While my love still heals.

The road ahead is a pilgrim Path of Faithful Mystic Wandering
a way enlivened by Rhythm & Simplicity

She is a way of Shema Oneness
Integrated love for Creator and Creation

She is a Way of Benedictine Habits in rotation
work, play, rest, contemplation.

She is a way of Sacred Awareness
Body, Earth, beings, Sensations

She is a way of grateful receptivity—
tasting, touching, seeing, smelling, hearing
the syncopation of eternal arias.

The road ahead is a companion journey of conversation

More quest than destination

because sometimes the question
and the answer
are one and the same

So down that Emmaus Road we go together
and we are met
and in the presence of a stranger
our hearts are strangely warmed.

Mark Scandrette

2

MEETING JESUS AT THE BAR

Or How I Learned to Stop Worrying and Love Evangelism

HEATHER KIRK-DAVIDOFF

So deeply do we care for you that we are determined to share with you not only the gospel of God but also our own selves, because you have become very dear to us.

1 Thessalonians 2:8 NRSV

I first began to understand "relational evangelism" the night that a woman in a bar told me that she had seen Jesus dressed as a homeless cross-dressing man in an elf costume.

I had gone to the bar with a friend after attending a workshop on GenX ministry. The presenter ended with a simple challenge: make a practice of having conversations with people in your community who don't attend your church. It didn't seem like much of a challenge when we heard it, especially since both of us were GenXers ourselves. But as we stood in the bar, our beers growing warm in our hands, we felt increasingly awkward. After a lot of hesitation, I finally turned to a woman standing near me and said, "Can I leave my coat on the floor next to you? I'm sick of holding it." And to my great relief, a conversation began.

We talked about her work, her boyfriend, the music we liked, and eventually about the musical *Rent*, which she loved. We talked about her favorite character, Angel, a drum-playing homeless gay man who spends most of the show dressed as a drag queen Santa Claus. Partway through the show Angel dies from AIDS, surrounded by an eclectic group of

---

Heather Kirk-Davidoff is the Enabling Minister of the Kittamaqundi Community (an independent church in the tradition of Church of the Savior) located in Columbia, Maryland. She is married to Dan Kirk-Davidoff, a climate scientist, and together they are parents to ten-year-old twin boys and a seven-year-old daughter. With her writing partner, Nancy Wood-Lyczak, Heather is the author of two books, *Talking Faith* (Chalice Press, 2004) and *Dare to Dive In: Strategies and Resources for Involving Your Whole Church in Worship* (Abingdon, 2006). She can be reached at www.kirkwood associates.org.

friends. "What's amazing to me," the woman said, "is how much power Angel's love has in the lives of the other characters in the play. And his love doesn't stop affecting them even after he dies. It's like . . . it's like it's made more perfect in his death."

I realized that all of a sudden we were not just making small talk. "You know, some people say Angel is a Christ figure," I sputtered out. "What do you think?"

"I don't know," she replied, "I guess I just feel a lot closer to Angel than I do to Jesus."

I was stunned. I thought I had gone to the bar that evening to meet people who might need something I could offer—an understanding ear, an invitation to come and worship at my church, or even a testimony about who Jesus is and what his love might mean for their life. I didn't expect to be the one who received an invitation to know Jesus better and to follow him more bravely. But to my surprise, and to my delight, I had.

I was hooked. It became my regular practice to go to the bar one or two times a week and have conversations with people I didn't know. I was astonished by how easy it was to talk about "spiritual" issues. People told me about their hopes and their fears, their relationships and their identity struggles. It was hard to explain to my congregation (or to my family) what I was doing, and so I started inviting people to come along with me. I stopped wondering about how to draw younger folks into my church and started focusing on how to draw my congregation out of its building and into relationship with the world outside its doors.

In short, I became something that I never dreamed of being—an evangelist. I wasn't motivated by a desire to save people from the jaws of hell, and I wasn't motivated by a desire to grow my church. I was motivated by my desire to be in relationship with people who were in many ways different from me. I wanted those relationships because they helped me to understand better what Jesus was doing in the world and how I might follow him, even as he led me out of the church and into the bar.

Human Beings or Marketing Reps

What would evangelism look like if we did as Brian McLaren proposes in his book *More Ready than You Realize* and "counted conversations rather than conversions"?[1] Relational evangelism is not just a change in tactic. It is a change in the reason we engage in evangelism, shifting the focus from recruitment to the cultivation of relationships that are an end in themselves, indispensable to our spiritual journeys.

In my experience of the conversation about the emerging church, the issue of evangelism has often hovered around the edges. When I first started attending Emergent conventions, I was acutely aware of being one of a small group of mainline Christians in a sea of evangelicals. I felt excited (and a bit transgressive) finally to be able to talk to Christians who really wanted to reach out to the community and not just wait for people to show up at their church like we mainliners usually do. Each time I met a pastor of an emerging church, I asked about their congregation's approach to evangelism. I was surprised to discover how little they had to say on the topic. A number of pastors I met and admired assured me that they do no intentional evangelizing at all. They put all their effort into building their community—developing relationships with the people in their church and with their neighbors—and they find that their church grows without their even trying.

I had to laugh. Finally I was talking to people whom I identified as evangelicals, and they sounded even more cautious about evangelizing than my mainline friends. I soon realized that, like me, many of the leaders I met through Emergent came from contexts where the evangelism practices they had been taught no longer worked because they were grounded in assumptions that did not fit their current settings.

As a mainline pastor I carried with me some assumptions that I inherited from the tradition in which I was formed. The outreach work I had been trained to do focused on attracting visitors to my church with flyers, programs, and advertisements, and then following up with visits, encouraging them to become members, to make a financial pledge, and to agree to serve on a committee. Behind this work was an assumption that membership in a church was what the people in my community really wanted and needed. My job was to recruit them into the particular church I was leading.

My evangelical colleagues were also trained as recruiters but of a different sort. Evangelism, as they were taught it, is rooted in the assumption that people are (or can easily be led to become) deeply anxious about their fate after they die. Christianity offers a solution to that anxiety because the moment that a person makes a decision to accept Jesus's atoning sacrifice on the cross, his or her eternal fate changes from damnation to bliss. As Dallas Willard insightfully describes in *The Divine Conspiracy*, when Christians focus on recruitment alone, the ongoing nurture of relationships and practices in this life becomes nearly irrelevant.[2]

Whether we come from a mainline Christian or an evangelical Christian background, evangelism has most often focused on recruitment. As I've spoken about evangelism with other emerging church leaders, I've marveled that our different paths have led us to the same conclusion: recruitment kills relationship. Even if your theology is great, even if your church is wonderful, even if your community is the best group of people on earth, as soon as you approach someone with the intention of recruiting them into your theology or church or community, you become a marketer and the other person is the target of your marketing. While GenXers have had a wide range of experience with religion or church or community, we share the experience of being targets of marketing from our earliest days of watching cartoons with product tie-ins. We can spot a sales pitch from a mile away, and we never confuse that with an offer of genuine relationship.

The 1999 movie *The Big Kahuna* made this point brilliantly. Addressing a colleague who turned a sales conversation into an opportunity to witness to his Christian faith, one of the characters says, "It doesn't matter whether you're selling Jesus or Buddha or civil rights or 'How to Make Money in Real Estate with No Money Down.' . . . Because as soon as you lay your hands on a conversation to steer it, it's not a conversation anymore; it's a pitch. And you're not a human being; you're a marketing rep."

Love God, Love Your Neighbor—at the Same Time

Despite our wildly different experiences of evangelism, the thing that connects me to many of the people I've met through Emergent who come from more evangelical backgrounds is that, in the end, we don't want to be marketing reps, even if we are marketing a wonderful Savior or membership in the nicest community you'll ever meet. We want to be human beings, and we want to build relationships with other human beings. Because of that, we're willing to give up just about everything we've ever learned about how to grow a church or spread the gospel.

But we won't give up on relationship. We want to be loved, to be known and understood. But what's more, we want to know other people, to grow in our love and understanding of them. In the context I live and work in—urban and often transient—this desire for relationship is something that people talk about all the time. And it is not the same as the desire to hang around with their friends more (although people feel that too). There is a real desire to build relationship with people we don't yet know, including people who are different from us. In my neighborhood, not only can people eat the food of dozens of different cultures, they can ride the bus or play soccer or go to a concert alongside people who come from dozens of different countries. The vast majority of my peers are curious about the lives, the thoughts, and the dreams of others. They treasure the opportunities they get to meet new people, especially when those people are different from them, and they feel that these opportunities are too few and far between.

If we took these experiences seriously, we would soon realize that developing and tending to relationships are perhaps the key spiritual disciplines of many adults in their twenties and thirties (and often beyond). While we may also pray and read Scripture regularly, while we may chant with monks or do yoga or go on a silent retreat, our relationships with others give us the most insight into who God is and where God is leading us. Just listen to what we are praying for, or look at the creative ways we find to build praying communities with each other on the Web, on the phone, or in huddled bunches at the back of a bar. Look at how we read the Bible, and notice how our study comes alive when we connect it to issues and concerns in our own community. Even at the monastery, the yoga class, the silent retreat, we are looking to connect not only with God but also with others who are on a spiritual path and with whom we might build a relationship.

At the heart of all this hungering and thirsting for relationship is an insight that somehow both mainline and evangelical recruiters seem to have forgotten. When pressed to identify the greatest commandment, Jesus listed two: love the Lord your God, and love your neighbor as yourself. We tend to pull these commandments apart; we make them distinct and often even sequential. Work out your relationship with God, and then your relationships with people will fall into place. But Jesus held these commandments together and said they were alike. He understood something our churches have often forgotten: we grow in our relationship to God and to each other simultaneously. And it is often through learning to love each other that we find ourselves opening to God in new and deeper ways.

Soul-Nourishing Relationships

What if our churches took the practice of building relationships seriously? What if we not only cultivated Christian fellowship through worship and small groups but also held as a high priority the building of relationships with people who are not a part of our church, even people who are very different from us? Far from becoming irrelevant, churches would become essential training grounds for a whole new breed of Christians who want to grow in their understanding of this spiritual path.

How can churches contribute to this discipline? First of all, they can become places where people learn about what a truly soul-nourishing relationship looks like. Not all relationships are positive, and in our hunger to be known we sometimes forget what it means to establish healthy boundaries with each other. In large-group and small-group settings, through explicit teaching and implicit modeling, churches can provide opportunities for people to learn about relationships built on equality and mutual respect, where both parties are willing to listen as well as speak, receive as well as give.

When a network of respectful relationships is in place, churches can become places where people learn to share their faith with honesty and integrity in a way that does not manipulate the relationship into a recruitment possibility. Faith sharing of this sort comes easily for some people, but many of us don't know where to begin. We've had so many negative experiences with evangelism and evangelists that we think twice before we start talking with anyone about being a Christian. We'd rather be silent than risk damaging our relationships because our friends or acquaintances might confuse us with the recruiters we so dislike. We would need to see it done, and done well, before we'd take the risk ourselves.

Many emerging churches are doing this kind of modeling, right in the middle of worship. They strive to make sure the language they use in worship sounds like language we could use in everyday conversation. They connect the biblical story with the stories we talk about during the week—the stories from our newspapers, our favorite movies and television shows, and our lives. In the congregation I serve, we often worship seated around small tables with six or seven other people. At various points in the service, each table group can talk together about Scripture, pray together, or even serve each other communion. I love this practice because it is so similar to other moments we'll find ourselves in during the week—around the dinner table with our families, out to lunch with co-workers, or even seated next to a stranger at a lunch counter, on a park bench, or in an airplane.

If we've practiced building relationships in the church and can share our faith respectfully and without embarrassment, chances are we'll be able to share our faith outside the church as well. But we will not share only what others tell us we should believe. We will share our own commitments, even when they don't fit the "party line." We will share our doubts as well and the things we find funny or peculiar. And we will share our curiosity about the beliefs and commitments, practices and experiences of others, even those who are very different from us. As we do, not only will we bring Jesus to the world, it's likely we'll meet him coming to us from the edges, from the wilderness, where we should never be surprised to find him.

3

WHAT WOULD HUCKLEBERRY DO?

A Relational Ethic as the Jesus Way

NANETTE SAWYER

It was a high school Christmas concert where I first experienced God as light and song and an up-rushing sensation of joy in my body. I was standing with all my choir friends cramped together on risers, the stage lights bright on our cheeks and glittering in all our eyes. I could really only see the hot lights, effectively blinding me, and the dim outlines of auditorium seats where I knew my parents were sitting among the masses.

We were singing of angels we had heard on high, singing "*Gloria in excelsis Deo,*" and I was singing with all the gusto I had. That particular "*Glo-o-o-o-o-ri-a*" seemed to go on into infinity. Singing with no holding back, looking up into the all-embracing lights, sound emanating from the very vibration of my body, nearly touching but not quite touching the other bodies surrounding me, my mind, my heart, my body, and my being all opened out and turned toward something greater than me, greater than that room and all the people in it. I wasn't trying; it just happened. God was there, infinite beauty and joy and happiness, which surrounded me and rushed through me and embraced me. I knew then what the word *glory* meant. God was *gloriously* present with me, for just a moment, a moment that I have never forgotten.

By the time that happened in high school, I had long rejected Christianity. Luminosity had not been part of my childhood experience of church. Although I had encountered God in a variety of places and ways as a child, I didn't have the language to talk about it. It wasn't God or Jesus that I rejected; it was the church's way of thinking and talking about God and Jesus. The language I was given at church tended to

---

Nanette Sawyer is an artist, writer, and minister ordained by the Presbyterian Church (USA). She has a master of theological studies degree in comparative world religions from Harvard Divinity School, and a master of divinity from McCormick Theological Seminary in Chicago. Currently she is pastor of a PC (USA) new church development in Chicago, called Wicker Park Grace (www.wickerparkgrace.net). The Grace community gathers in an art gallery on the west side of Chicago.

make God seem so much smaller than my experience of the Presence, which I felt that day at the Christmas concert. This luminous God was the Presence that I encountered regularly in the sounds and silence of the rural setting where I grew up.

In or Out?

My explicit rejection of Christianity happened when our family minister implicitly rejected me. When I was a preteen, he visited our house, spoke with my parents, then pulled me aside, the eldest, for a chat of our own. He asked me if I was Christian. This is a very interesting question to ask a child who has been raised in a Christian household. Being asked such a question I was, in essence, being told that I might *not* be a Christian. I responded that I didn't know. The conversation went downhill from there and ended with my saying that I guessed I wasn't a Christian. He told me what I had to believe to be a Christian and I didn't believe it.

After that, I spent a good fifteen years defining myself as *not Christian*. Some of the things that I had been taught in Christian contexts, both explicitly and implicitly, were unacceptable to me. I was taught, for example, that there are good people and bad people, Christian people and non-Christian people, saved people and damned people, *and we know who they are.*

I was taught that God wanted and expected women and girls to be submissive and quiet, and that it was the role of men to be in charge, to control the conversation, and to have the smart ideas. I was taught that I was inherently bad, and that I would be judged for that. I was told that the only way out of the judgment was to admit how bad I was, which only reinforced the shame. All of this was light-years away from the luminous *gloria* moment in the high school Christmas concert.

Thinking back on that pivotal interaction with my childhood minister, I believe the whole conversation missed the mark in a big way. He was defining Christian identity as assent to a list of certain beliefs, and he was defining Christian community as those people who concur with those beliefs. This didn't leave any room for questions, doubts, or growth in faith. It made community acceptance of each other completely conditional on having already arrived at a particular intellectual destination. In asking me if I was a Christian, and accepting my preteen answer, he essentially told me that I wasn't part of the community. I wasn't *in*; I was *out*. And so I found myself spiritually homeless.

The Divine Touch through a Human Hand

Nevertheless, I was always looking for ways to encounter God, to feel that luminous Presence in my life. It's interesting that I can say I am a Christian today because of a Hindu meditation master. She taught me some things that Christians had not. She taught me to meditate, to sit in silence and openness in the presence of God. She taught me to love God, which allowed me to experience God's love for me. She also taught me to honor Jesus and suggested that Jesus could teach me. She provided the divine touch through a human hand and showed me how to be an active participant in my own spiritual life. Sitting in meditation, in a technique similar to what Christians call Centering Prayer, I encountered love that is unconditional, yet it called me to responsible action in my life.

I continued to seek, and I practiced opening my awareness to the presence of the Holy in the world, in day-to-day life. Although I didn't have this biblical phrase, I can say now that I was seeking to know the God in whom "we live and move and have our being" (Acts 17:28). I studied and received a master's degree in comparative world religions, and through that process encountered a small urban Presbyterian church in South Boston where my life was again changed.

The minister there invited me into the community by serving me communion without asking if I was a Christian. He embodied the radical welcome of Jesus at the supper table, introducing me to Jesus in a way that no one else had. He didn't ask, "Are you one of us?" He didn't say, "Do you believe?" He simply said, "Nanette, the body of Christ, given for you."

This was the amazing bit. The bread was for me and he told me so. The bread was for nourishment, and Jesus was offering it to me. *To me,* exactly as I was at that very moment. I took the bread, one step toward *gloria*, and a closed door inside me flew open, although my body was still poised to run at the first sign of trouble. Astonished, I peeked through the open door and received again the divine touch through a human hand. And it happened in a church of all places.

Children of God

As I became more deeply involved in that community, I talked with the pastor about the children of the church, about the Sunday school and the Saturday Kids' Club. He said that whether or not the children remembered the Bible stories we taught them, they would always remember that they felt safe and loved while they were at this church. This message of grace was given again and again: *you* are a beloved child of God. At every baptism, of adults or children, we reaffirmed it. We served the neighborhood with meal programs and Baby Basics to show God's love for all God's creation, all God's people, regardless of identity.

With all this background, you may understand the reason my statement of faith, my personal credo, written in seminary and required for ordination in the Presbyterian Church, included the line: "I believe that all people are children of God, created and loved by God, and that God's compassionate grace is available to us at all times."

Imagine my surprise when a particular pastor challenged me on this point. He suggested that "children of God" is a biblical phrase, and that I was using it unbiblically. He believed that not all people are children of God, only Christians. If I'd been quicker on my feet, I would have done a Bible study with him right there; instead, I focused on not letting my jaw hit the floor and mumbled something about God creating all human beings. Back at my seminary desk, I searched for words and understanding about these concepts.

The Rule of Love

In my current ministry in urban Chicago, I talk about Christian grace and compassion and often hear this question from people alienated from the Christianity of their childhood: But what about the Bible? In many places and in many people's lives, the Bible has been used as a tool of judgment and condemnation, wielded as an instrument of separation and segregation rather than reconciliation. Its complexity and moral ambiguity should call us into an active, responsible struggle with moral issues. Instead, it has often been flattened into a simplistic list of rules and regulations. A young man told me, "The Bible is so boring. It has no relevance and no insight, no inspiration for how to live life." Nothing could be further from the truth! It's just that so many of us have lost the art of reaching and seeing into the depths of the Bible.

When it comes to the Bible, tradition, and moral decision making, I've begun to ask myself, "What would Huckleberry do?" Huck Finn worked out something really important on his journey down the Mississippi River with his friend Jim, a runaway slave. When faced with the very real decision about abandoning his recaptured friend to slavery or helping him escape again, Huck was torn up inside. He *knew* that if he helped his friend escape he would burn in the fires of hell for eternity. Huck had a very strong image of what this would be like and decided to do the "right" thing and reveal Jim's location to his slave master. But this didn't seem right either. In a striking moment of clarity, Huck decides to "steal" his friend back out of slavery, and he bursts out, "All right then, I'll go to hell."

As Huckleberry Finn demonstrates, how we interpret and apply the biblical stories and commandments has life-threatening, life-changing, and life-expanding implications and possibilities. Our decisions about biblical interpretation and application can only be strengthened by grounding them in what we know in community with each other. Huck's decision to "steal" Jim was a decision he could make only because he had come to know and love Jim. This kind of real relationship between a white boy and a black man was shocking in the period when this story took place, and it was a major reason Mark Twain took so much heat for writing the book. It is this kind of deep knowing and loving that can change the world, and I believe it's what Jesus modeled for us in the way that he was human. This is what it means to interpret the Bible through the lens of Jesus: we interpret the text through the Rule of Love. As Jesus said, the two most important commandments are that we love God and love our neighbors as ourselves. Our application of anything we find in the Bible needs to be grounded in this essential teaching.

So what about the Bible on this question of the children of God? Is it unbiblical to call all people children of God? It *is* true that there are many places in the New Testament that talk about the children of God as the followers of Jesus. But it is *not* true that this must lead us to the kind of arrogance that asserts that non-Christians are not children of God. In fact, there are three biblical instances undermining such an exclusionary claim.

Paul says in Romans that "we are children of God" (8:16 NRSV) and that we are also waiting for adoption, while the whole creation waits with eager longing for the revealing of the children of God (see vv. 22–23). He indicates that we are *not yet fully* children of God. This metaphor of adoption into the family of God is based on the idea of becoming "conformed to the image" of Jesus, becoming so like him that we become adopted siblings (v. 29). A similar incompleteness and uncertainty is maintained in the first letter of John, which says that we are God's children now, but what we will be has *not yet been revealed* (see 1 John 3:2). And finally, in the Acts of the Apostles 17:28–29, Paul expands the "we" when he affirms to the Greeks, to whom he is preaching, and who are not followers of Jesus, "We are God's offspring."

Even if we could answer the question of who *is* and who *isn't* a child of God, it wouldn't help us be better followers of Jesus; it would only help us divide people into categories. First John answers a different question, I believe, and a more helpful question. Addressed to a community that has just gone through a painful schism, this sometimes rhetorically inflammatory letter seems to be primarily about *how to follow Jesus*, and it pivots on two points: the persistent practice of love and the paradox of human nature in relationship with divine nature.

Paradoxology: Antidote to Arrogance

When that pastor told me I was being unbiblical in calling all people children of God, I wonder if he had this verse in mind: "Those who have been born of God do not sin, because God's seed abides in them; they cannot sin, because they have been born of God" (1 John 3:9 NRSV). Is this a state that any human being can really claim to have attained? Sinlessness? Never do and never have done anything wrong? Never hurt anyone, or taken an unfair advantage? I'm sure that pastor would agree with me that if this is what it is to be a child of God, then none of us are! There's another verse in 1 John that is often repeated in the churches I have frequented, and it goes like this: "If we say that we have no sin, we deceive ourselves, and the truth is not in us" (1:8 NRSV).

The letter of 1 John pivots around the following paradox: John says that we are God's children now, children of God cannot sin, and we sin. This is clearly contradictory. Theologians have attempted to explain away this logical problem by talking about differences between human time and eternity. They've described things as both "true now" and "not yet true." This really doesn't solve the paradox; it just settles it into categories that separate the contradictory elements at a greater distance from one another, so that the tension is less.

There is a beauty in paradox when it comes to talking about things of ultimate concern. Paradox works against our tendency to stay superficial in our faith, or to rest on easy answers or categorical thinking. It breaks apart our categories by showing the inadequacy of them and by pointing to a reality larger than us, the reality of *gloria*, of light, of beyond-the-beyond. I like to call it *paradoxology*—the glory of paradox, paradox-doxology—which takes us somewhere we wouldn't be capable of going if we thought we had everything all wrapped up, if we thought we had attained full comprehension. The commitment to embracing the paradox and resisting the impulse to categorize people (ourselves included) is one of the ways we follow Jesus into that larger mysterious reality of light and love.

The Jesus Way: Walking the Love-Talk

It isn't always easy to love people. Misunderstandings, disagreements, and hurts rise up between us, just as they did in the community that John was addressing in his letter. Love is a spiritual practice that matures us as we try and try again to leave behind our isolation, expose our vulnerabilities, and make commitments to care truly for one another.

I've been striving to embody this spiritual practice in my current ministry in Wicker Park, a vibrant, art-filled urban community on the west side of Chicago. The Presbyterian Church (PC USA) sent me into this neighborhood as a pastor and said, "*Rethink church* for us. Drink a lot of coffee in neighborhood hangout places [literally, my first job description said, "drink 500 cups of chai latte . . ."]; get to know the people; take the church outside the building; start something new; and report back to us what you find."

After three years of building a small core group of neighborhood folks, we're actively exploring and sometimes struggling with what it means to be in community together. Many of our participants have had negative experiences of Christianity in the past and have found a spiritual home at Wicker Park Grace. There's a healing that needs to take place, and a lot of that healing takes place within community interaction. Healing happens when people receive and offer each other a grace-filled welcome, accepting each other in all our messy glory, with questions, insights, hurts, and new hope. This grace-filled welcome is an invitation to authenticity in human community.

In our faith community, which we do sometimes call *church* and other times just call *the grace community*, we affirm that we are centered in a generous and dynamic Christianity. There are three important words here: *centered, generous,* and *dynamic*. In being *centered* in Christianity, we are affirming that we are more concerned about where we find our center than our edges. Our permeable boundaries allow people to come in and also remind us to be continually engaged with the fullness of a world that is not primarily Christian. In all this, we are seeking to be centered in something specific, not just superficially perusing everything.

Being centered in a *generous* Christianity, we are committed to finding ways to love and serve the world as Jesus did. This is based on a belief that generosity will not only help the world, but it will deeply change us. Generosity is a direct challenge to the cultural forces that would isolate and make us fearful. Contemporary social/economic forces, for example, encourage us to hoard what we have or attend only to our own needs or our own family's needs. A *generous* Christianity is a more holistic Christianity, because it acknowledges how integrally interconnected we are with each other and with the world. We are striving to be with God and with our neighbors, as Jesus was and is with God and neighbor.

Dynamic Christianity is a spiritual way of being that is not afraid of change. In fact it affirms that Christianity has always been dynamic, that theologians have filled libraries with books recording their struggles with each other on the greatest metaphysical mysteries of all times. When we enter into this tradition of conversation, we enter in with our full voices, all our questions, and all our brilliant insights. We enter Christianity as full participants in discovering what the Spirit is speaking to us today and then articulating and enacting in the world what we hear.

So rather than using the first letter of John, or any other biblical text, to segregate people into the good/bad, children of God/children of the devil, saved/unsaved categories, we embrace the unknowability of a person's eternal status and instead strive to walk the love-talk and not just talk the talk. We want to invite everyone to the table and feed them, regardless of identity. If we can come together and eat and live and serve together, then *we* will be changed.

My Christmas concert experience of *gloria* was big, exuberant, joyful, and radiant. It was a mountaintop experience on a choir riser. That kind of experience can't be maintained all the time, but it does teach that God is bigger than we might imagine. There is a way to let God shine through us, and that's by providing a divine touch through our human hands, embracing the glory of paradox, extending a radical welcome, serving at the table and in the world, and treating everyone as though he or she is a beloved child of God, a brother or sister to each of us. I believe that is the Jesus Way.

4

THE POSTMODERN PARENT

Shifting Paradigms for the Ultimate Act of Re-Creation

CARLA BARNHILL

I've spent a decade studying Christian families, and in that time I've learned something interesting: most Christian families spend an inordinate amount of energy trying to become Christian families. They read books and attend seminars and listen to sermons and radio programs that are essentially built around the assumption that Christian parents don't know how to be Christian parents.

I suppose that could be true. If parenting is thought of as something we do, then yes, I guess there are right and wrong ways to do it. Certainly if Christianity is thought of as something we do, there are right and wrong ways to do it. Combining all of this right and wrong—and the attendant potential for failure—creates a special kind of fear in people who are in the midst of the one thing they really want to do well. The message is clear: failing as a Christian parent doesn't just mean your kid might end up in jail. It means he might end up in hell.

But it doesn't have to be that way. Just as it's possible to have a faith that is borne out of a desire to be part of God's work in the world and not out of a desire to avoid hell, it's possible to parent out of hope and not out of fear. Since the church has been one of the main perpetrators of parental fear-mongering, it's only fair we take up the cause of creating a culture of parenting that is less about what we *don't* want for our children and more about what we *do* want.

Carla Barnhill is the former editor of *Christian Parenting Today* magazine. She is also the author of *The Myth of the Perfect Mother* (Baker, 2004). Carla has edited several books for Emergent Village, including *Church Reimagined* (Zondervan, 2005) and *Preaching Reimagined* (Zondervan, 2005) by Doug Pagitt, *The Sacred Way* (Zondervan/Youth Specialties, 2005) by Tony Jones, and *The Out-of-Bounds Church* (Zondervan/Youth Specialties, 2005) by Steve Taylor. She has a master's degree in Literature from the University in Edinburgh, Scotland, and has taken almost a degree's worth of classes at Fuller Theological Seminary in Pasadena, California. Carla is the mother of three exceptional children and the wife of one extraordinary man. She and her family live in Minnesota and attend Solomon's Porch.

This kind of shift requires more than new messages. It requires a new understanding of what it means to be a parent. For so many Christian parents, church has become the one place they hate taking their children. It isn't because the kids are bored in Sunday school or that it's a pain to get everyone dressed and fed and out the door by nine on a weekend morning. It's because the church is the place where parents are reminded of all the ways they aren't measuring up. That message may come in subtle ways—the shaming looks that come when a child makes too much noise. Or it may come in more overt ways—the sermon that reminds parents they aren't doing nearly enough to protect their children from the world's dangers.

This message is underscored by the lack of support parents find in the church. Yes, there are moms' prayer groups and Wednesday night family jubilees, but there is little permission for a mom to talk about how desperately she wants to run away from home or for a dad to talk about how afraid he is of disappointing his kids. Little is said about the dramatic changes a child brings to a marriage. There is little help for parents who struggle with a difficult child.

There is little room for imperfect families.

Because of our peculiar demographic, emerging churches stand in a unique position to change all of that. As all of our twenty- and thirty-somethings hook up, get married, and have children, we are creating a new theology of the family, one that reflects the hopes and dreams we have for the world. For us, parenting isn't a job, a role, or even a category. It is fully integrated into who we are and how we see ourselves living out our faith.

Glimpses of a New Way to Be Mom and Dad

Here's what I mean: Javier and Sarah are the parents of two young children. Since the day he was born, their oldest child has been a communal child. On his first visit to our church—at the ripe old age of one week—he was passed around, cooed over, gazed at, nuzzled, and loved. When he began toddling, he toddled all over the place, wandering freely around our gathering space while we sang, listened, prayed, and discussed. He has shouted out the names of his friends from the balcony in the middle of a sermon. He has walked around the guy making announcements. He has been quite literally at the center of our worship on many a Sunday, walking around like he owns the place.

His parents haven't given him this kind of free reign because they're tired and ready for other people to take care of their kid for a couple of hours. Sarah says, "From the day Micah was born, I've made a conscious effort to let others be a part of his life. Not just to hold him for a moment, but to allow them to spend a significant amount of time with him so they can join me in watching his personality grow and develop and be amazed at life. People tell me he's a charismatic child, and I think it's because they have been allowed to be close enough to see his true character and he has been allowed to be comfortable sharing himself with people." In other words, Micah does indeed believe he owns the place. And isn't that how all parents want their children to feel about church? Like they belong there?

Javier adds, "We've been intentional about having our children engage with other age groups, not just with their peers. Micah is comfortable with lots of people, which is something we feel strongly about. We want him to grow up knowing that everyone has value, everyone is worth engaging."

The intentionality of emergent parents extends far beyond the walls of whatever kind of building we think of as church. Parents in our community are making conscious decisions about the food we feed our children, the clothes we buy, the neighborhoods we live in. Like our parents before us, we have made choices for our families that reflect our values. But those values have changed significantly.

We are parents who place humanity above homogeneity, sustainability over a false sense of safety. We make an effort to buy clothes produced by small, independent companies rather than running to Baby Gap. We trade advice on making our own baby food and finding the best wraps for our cloth diapers. We swap childcare and work collections of jobs so we can have the flexibility to be home with our children. The dads expect to be and usually are as involved in the children's daily lives as the moms.

Many of us choose to live in urban neighborhoods not only because they are often more affordable than suburban areas but because of a deep belief that the city offers the kind of life we want for our children. Sarah notes, "I live in a neighborhood many people consider to be less-than-desirable. There is some drug- and gang-related crime, and I have to admit that I don't always feel comfortable living here. The thing is, I find this to be a truer picture of life than the quarter-acre sprawling lot in a picturesque suburb. I want my children to see that life isn't always perfect and that God's blessing to humanity doesn't come in the form of money and prosperity. My son has a United Nations' worth of kids to play with at the playground instead of just one type. He gets to learn about life in a place where people don't always have it easy. Bad things can and have happened to us here, but bad things also happen to people in picturesque suburbs."

Another family at our church lives across the street from a crack house. But rather than shuttle their young family off to a place that appears safer, they are choosing to stay, with the belief that they can be agents of change in this neighborhood.

Still other families stay in the city because they like the idea of living in and restoring an old house rather than using more resources to build a new one. Others like that they can walk or take public transportation to the park or the playground or the school rather than gassing up the minivan.

These choices reflect a change in parental priorities. What I hear from and see in my fellow parents is a desire for their children to experience life, to know that God created and loves all kinds of people—clean people and grimy people, happy people and miserable people, people who drive nice cars and people who ride dirty buses.

Letting Our Children Be Present

Underlying these choices is a change in the way emergent parents think about children. When I speak to moms, I often ask them to think about a metaphor for their relationship with their kids. Do they see themselves as the teacher and the kids as students? Are they the expert and the kids the neophytes? Are they the drill sergeant breaking in a new class of plebes? I tell them that the trouble with these metaphors is that they assume the child is somehow in need of fixing and that the parent has all the answers. The church has long been guilty of treating children (and parents) the same way. Rather than taking them as they are—which is what we say we want for ourselves—we see children as lesser members of the community who have little to offer.

There is tremendous value in allowing children not only to be themselves but to *bring* themselves to the community. Rather than seeing children as somehow unfinished and unable to participate in the life of the church until they have learned something, we can encourage children to contribute to the community. When we treat them like full and essential members of the community, we allow their *Imago Dei* to shine through.

When I was a kid, there was no place I wanted to be less than church. Nothing about it was intended for me, and I knew it. Sunday school was no help; nothing sucks the life out of spiritual formation faster than treating it like a math class. I memorized all of *Luther's Small Catechism*, I knew all the Bible stories, I watched some great filmstrips. I learned a lot about Christian history, but I didn't learn much about Jesus or why his life should matter in mine.

My nine-year-old daughter, on the other hand, hasn't memorized a single Bible verse. She didn't know the words to "Awesome God" until she went to Bible camp with some friends last summer. But she has washed potatoes to help feed the poor. She has made blankets for children in a group home. She has washed her babysitter's feet during our Maundy Thursday gathering. And when she was in first grade, she came home from school and told me she'd started collecting shoes for kids in Guatemala. I asked her what she was talking about. She explained that she had asked her principal if she could set out a box in the office and ask kids to bring in shoes for her to send to Guatemala with some of our church friends. She made an announcement during lunch one day, and two weeks later had a huge box full of shoes. At seven years old, my daughter was living in the way of Jesus.

This isn't just good faith formation, it's good human formation. Javier says, "We want to be part of creating a community where our kids feel free to be who they are. We love that our church feels like a safe place for them to be themselves. They aren't expected to be adults, but they aren't looked down on for being kids, either. I know that as they grow up there will be all kinds of pressures to conform, to change who they are. If there's only one place they can be fully who they are, it should be church."

Valuing the image of God in our children extends to the particulars of parenting too. A look through the majority of Christian parenting literature makes it clear that the primary goal of Christian parenting is to raise well-behaved children. Nearly every parenting book for Christians—and frankly most of the ones for parents in general—deals with behavior and discipline. Even those that are about "character development" are essentially efforts to get children to act a certain way.

Of course, there's nothing wrong with well-behaved children. I certainly want my kids to be considerate, to be aware of other people, to adjust their behavior to match the situation. But too often the church has made appropriate behavior the mark of spiritual maturity. Every parent has faced the scornful looks of those who think our children are too loud, too busy, too rambunctious. But those behaviors have little to do with the true humanity of the child.

My friend Mimi says, "I grew up in a Christian environment where it was important to have obedient children. I don't remember hearing people commend creativity or uniqueness, but if there was an obedient child, parents would hear praise. Now as I talk with my childhood friends I hear a lot of the same stuff—the desire to have kids obey, to nip rebellion in the bud, to make them stop yelling, stop hitting, stop arguing. But I don't think that's always helpful for the child. I was an obedient child and received lots of praise for it. Yet as an adult I have struggled with knowing what I really think about something. I worked so hard to do what my parents wanted and to please others that I didn't take time to listen to my own thoughts. I didn't learn how to reason or figure out the natural consequences of my actions and decisions."

For Mimi and parents like her, parenting isn't about raising children who fit some external model of "good" children. Instead, parenting is, like faith itself, about the process of becoming—not only for the child but for the parent as well. Mimi says, "I want to deal with temper tantrums differently. I don't want to just quiet my son but acknowledge his frustration and help him learn why he is upset. I don't want my house to be spotless at the expense of my child discovering how things work—little Tupperware fits inside of bigger Tupperware, the blocks make a great noise when dumped out of the bin, and some day, how all the little parts of this DVD player fit together. I don't want him to learn to stand quietly, and never know what he is thinking, never understand what interests him, never consider his thoughts about the things around him. I want to teach him to be honest with me; to know that even if he disagrees, I want to know what he thinks and to have conversations about those differences. I want to have clear boundaries, but I don't want the appearance of perfection at the expense of individuality."

Where Parenting Leads

If all of this sounds like flaky parenting, consider the outcomes of the church's earlier efforts at helping parents: adults who have little connection with the faith of their childhood, levels of maternal depression that equal those of the general population, a generation of parents who wonder why their children are so attracted to the emerging church.

Parenting has never been exclusively about raising children. It has always been infused with ulterior, culturally driven motives. In tribal societies, parenting is about teaching children the ways of the tribe in order to perpetuate the tribe. In agrarian cultures, children are free labor as well as the future of the farm. In the early days of the United States, women were encouraged to instill in their children the values of the founders in order to people the new nation with like-minded citizens. Even now, some churches encourage their congregants to have children—and lots of them—in order to increase the number of Christians in a given city.

Indeed, parenting *is* about more than raising children. It is about investing in our hopes for the world. It is about joining in with our Creator in the ultimate act of re-creation. It is about pointing our children toward the work God has for them and giving them the resources to do it. It is about celebrating the goodness of life with God, a life that looks more like the kingdom with every generation.

5

THE ART OF EMERGENCE

Being God's Handiwork

TROY BRONSINK

Sometimes, like a song with a hook that I can't quite nail down or a scene from a movie that keeps haunting me, Emergent is that unfolding piece of artwork that puts me at odds with the world as I have assumed it to be. Emergence interrupts my line of vision, leaving me with new perspectives of that world. And so the interruption presses me to grasp for some sort of explanation.

These accidental habits toward "finding things out" remind me of my daughter, Eve.[1] The other day she saw a kite flying high above us at the beach and asked, "Why is it doing that?" It was a natural question. She was genuinely curious. And so I told her what I could, that the wind catches the plastic surface causing it to lift and the string provides resistance, making it float above us. But that was not enough of an answer. "Why?" And so I tried again. "You know how our jackets are blowing in the wind? Well, we each weigh enough that the wind can't pick us up, but did you notice how light the kite is?" Then she tried these explanations out on Mommy and one of the other kids in the house: "Kites fly because the wind can pick them up. They're not as heavy as we are. . . ."

But sometimes the answer to *why* doesn't make sense—when, for example, what you want to do and what can be done do not fit. Last week Eve was trying to put one of her oversized baby dolls in a small plastic stroller, and it wouldn't fit. She tried repeatedly, only to get angrier and angrier. It just wouldn't fit. Then she asked me to do it. I said I couldn't, but she insisted that I do it because she wanted it to fit, and experience has taught her that it should (when she has tried it with other babies,

---

Troy Bronsink is a singer-songwriter, a dad, a community organizer, and a minister in the Presbyterian Church (USA). For nearly a decade now he has enjoyed the poetry of making a life with his wife and daughter in and around downtown Atlanta, practicing theology in contexts as varied as intentional community, house church, suburban mainline congregation, and a small independent coffee shop. Contact Troy at www.churchasart.org.

they have fit). She kept asking why, and I kept grasping for more precise-yet-understandable explanations (because I have a lot of experience with things not fitting). This scene can repeat itself for hours until, eventually, she learns: some things fit, others do not.

Most of us adults have learned this lesson well. We have learned to live life with an appreciation of *tried-and-true* ideas. We sort out the lessons and experiences we've been handed into categories by which we live our lives. It's natural. We do this out of self-preservation, aiming to improve the efficiency of life by reducing the number of decisions to be made. We decide in real time what we will then believe is the best way to see things—until that unexpected moment, when our time-tested resolution is brought to a grinding halt and we realize, "Oh no, this may not be the best way to see things after all." Our experience teaches us an exception to the rule.

This is a bit of how Emergent came to be. A bunch of us had experience after experience that did not fit our views of the world. Something wasn't right. All sorts of Christian leaders discovered a *conversation* through negotiating the disorientations and new orientations that come with things not fitting—disorientations occurring between the way things used to be and the way things are today, as well as between the way things are today and how we once hoped they would be.[2] New orientations are brief acts of faith. They are usually just sketches, little attempts in a hopeful direction. They are deliberate choices to *make*. To use a metaphor from environmental design, Emergent's response to failing infrastructure has been *adaptive reuse* and *reconstruction* over and against disillusioned deconstruction or (awkward and ugly) "stabilization" tricks. To borrow from Jeremiah, new orientation is the choice to "build houses" and "plant gardens" and, as brief acts of faith, to make your best out of the constructs in which you find yourself—to locate your hope in what God will do, in the *here and now*.

Negotiating Practice and Story

Our *making* task is complicated and deeply entangled with our identity, the reason we believe we *are made*. The church, like Christ, has been commissioned to *incarnation*. Since the promise at the end of John's Gospel, "As the Father has sent me, so I send you" (20:21 NRSV), the church has relied on the breath of the Spirit to reconcile the story we have received with the story we have a share in making.[3] To differentiate between this *receiving* and *making*, let me take a few paragraphs to clarify two words: *story* and *practice*.

The *story* of the church is not hers; like a birthright, it becomes hers through the narrative unfolding of Scripture uniquely experienced through the person and work of Jesus Christ, the church's author. This story concerns the entire world and not the church alone. It is what Matthew quoted Jesus as calling the "kingdom of God" and Luke called the "way of Jesus" and Paul called the "new creation." This story, however, is not closed or finished, insofar as its author and finisher, Jesus Christ, is alive and the prophesied culmination of the story (the *eschaton*) has not yet come in fullness—"on earth as it is in heaven."[4]

Practice, then, is the deliberate and unconscious physical manifestation of our story. Practices are the sum total of what we do and, in their best moments, both the cause and fruit of our beliefs.[5] Two short examples might unpack the breadth of this term. On one hand, the liturgical practice of the Lord's Supper changes its participants' beliefs about themes in God's *story* such as "forgiveness" or "inclusion"; it repeats memories of stories including the Passover, the Last Supper, and the parable of the wedding feast, while narrating the next chapters of the *story* as well, "proclaiming the Lord's death until he comes." On the other hand, a supposedly less sacred practice, such as buying organic, locally grown produce, also changes our beliefs about God's story by changing our participation in that story. In the economics of food we then participate as "resident aliens" who are "not of this world" leveraging our buying power in capitalism to promote healthier farming practices in accordance to God's story being shown to the church. Consequently we find our beliefs about money, labor, and agriculture evolve contemporaneous with our understandings of God's story. Both practices of communion and buying produce can be done with intent or without awareness. Both are part of the good, true, and beautiful sacramental nature of life.[6] Whether intentional or unintentional practices participate in the story of God's action in the world, for better and worse.[7]

Learning from the incarnate way of Jesus Christ, the church expects that the Good News of the kingdom of God (the church's story) is most deeply made known by the Word becoming flesh—through material that is embodied in culturally specific ways (the church's practices). As

Christ's body, the church continues to regularly renegotiate *her* practicing of materials in her specific culture as colaborers with Christ. Let me explain this a bit more from the perspective of missiology.

Mission theologian Lesslie Newbigin says it this way:

> Jesus . . . did not write a book but formed a community. This community has as its heart the remembering and rehearsing of his words and deeds and the sacraments given by him through which it is enabled both to engraft new members into its life and to renew this life again and again through sharing in his risen life through the body broken and the lifeblood poured out. . . . In so far as it is true to its calling, [the church] becomes a place where men and women and children find that the gospel gives them the framework to understanding the "lenses" through which they are able to understand and cope with the world.[8]

Our practices themselves are lenses to the story, they require of the church a deep memory of God's commissioning work and regular attention to her contemporaneous embodiment. These practices of remembering, rehearsing, and renewing commissioned by Jesus (go make disciples of all nations . . . love God . . . your neighbor . . . as you forgive, I forgive . . . seek first the kingdom of God . . . pray, "Thy kingdom come . . . on earth as it is in heaven") are artistic tools and exercises available to the church through the Spirit of Jesus, the patron or benefactor of the church. In his commissioning of the disciples Jesus breathed the Spirit on the disciples saying, "As the Father sends me so I send you." The practices of the church are, then, gifts of the Holy Spirit and as such participation in God's embodied story. Not only that, but our very awareness of God's embodied story (even including the presence of Jesus Christ) is often in process, in motion between what is hidden and what is revealed. In such instances as Mary's encounter in the garden, the disciples' encounters with the stranger on the road to Emmaus, Philip's encounter with the Ethiopian eunuch, and Paul's encounter with the community of Cornelius the "God fearer," those in the Way of Jesus are regularly reminded that they see through a glass dimly. Jesus is not dead. The stories of Jesus's resurrection are true. The Prophecies are true. The practices of God's way are drawn up into the person and work of Jesus. In the same way the Holy Spirit of Jesus guides the church community to exchange old, tried-and-true assumptions of her story and practices to pick up new ones concurrent with her surroundings and the approaching kingdom of God.

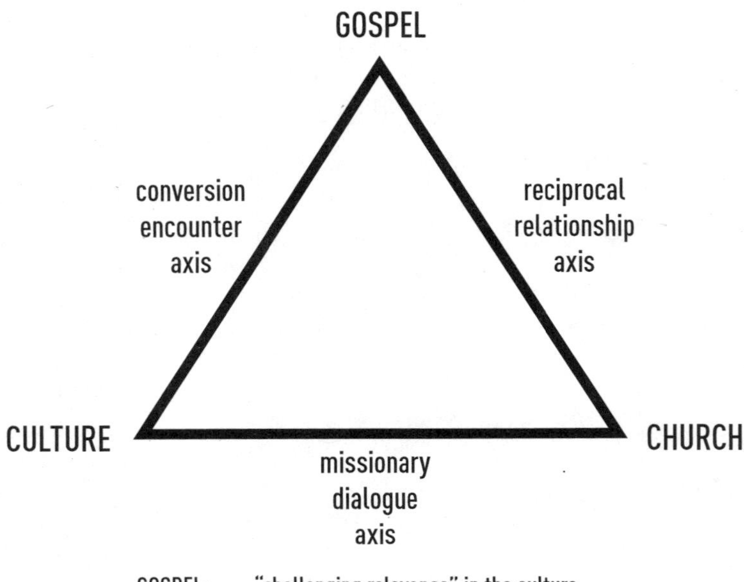

GOSPEL:	"challenging relevance" in the culture
	"hermeneutical circle" with the church
CULTURE:	radical discontinuity regarding the gospel
	radical independence regarding the church
CHURCH:	adherence to the given tradition
	dialogue with the varied cultures

The Gospel and Our Culture Network (GOCN) has illustrated this in the above triad.[9]

In a time of skepticism regarding Christendom's influence on the gospel and mixed with a deep conviction that the church become, again, yeast in late-Christendom culture, students of missions are thinking carefully about the *church* between *gospel* and *culture*. For the purposes of our discussion of story and practice, we should pay close attention to what George Hunsberger has called the "reciprocal relationship axis" found between gospel and church. Hunsberger of the GOCN writes:

> The gospel and its communication present to every culture a "challenging relevance." It is relevant insofar as it is embodied in terms by which people of the culture have learned to understand their world. It is challenging in that in every culture, Jesus is introduced as one who bursts open the

culture's models with power of a wholly new fact. . . . This encounter between gospel and culture . . . precipitates a fundamental paradigm shift that brings about a new ultimate commitment at the center. It entails in that sense, a "radical discontinuity," a break in new directions, for the one embracing the gospel . . . the gospel and a person's response to it of necessity remain embodied in a particular culture's way of seeing, feeling, and acting.[10]

This church story told as both challenge and relevance requires an approach to practices that can sustain and fund such "breaks in new directions." Emergent leaders out of their "renewed ultimate commitment" are finding themselves and their communities valuing little, short attempts at freeing up space for practicing the gospel with challenging relevance and radical discontinuity.

The Freedom of Sketching

I remember as a boy I'd look forward to Wednesday night church so I could sit with Tom Miller and draw. Tom was a young guy right out of graduate school who was an illustrator and engineer. He loved to tease out my imagination. We would do science experiments, visit our local amusement park, and make things out of old tools in his garage. On Wednesday nights we landed on this routine we called the "sketching game." After the church dinner we would keep our paper placemats and get out our pens. One of us would make a scribble with a single line, and the other's task was to make it into a convincing picture. The faces and buildings and birds and mountains that emerged from this free association practice exercised an often unexplored muscle—the freedom of guessing without huge consequences.

Karl Barth describes the community of Christ as those *freed* by God's "Yes" *for* the task of witnessing to God's "Yes" to the world. God's "Yes" frees us for service to God and the world. Like Christians of so many ages, Emergent also recognizes the charge and freedom rooted in this new reality of grace. In light of recent critiques of culture and our creative proclivities, our response has been to value open and divergent sketching in contrast to more disembodied laboratories of controlled tracing, measuring, and quantifying. Or as the apostle Paul put it in his correspondence with the Galatians: "It is for freedom that Christ has set us free. Stand firm, then, and do not let yourselves be burdened again by a yoke of slavery. . . . By faith we eagerly await through the Spirit the righteousness for which we hope. For in Christ Jesus . . . the only thing that counts is faith expressing itself through love" (Gal. 5:1, 5–6). And later to the Ephesians: "We are God's workmanship, created in Christ Jesus for good works, which God prepared in advance to be our way of life" (Eph. 2:10).

When we were children, many adults—perhaps well-intentioned—hedged in our creativity along with our imaginations for the purpose of preserving and protecting our lives to fit within a closed story of God. Those of us who succeeded in duplicating acceptable patterns were rewarded; those who had to figure life out for ourselves were seen as "strong willed" or "backslidden." More than time spent in church school, Christian school, or even with music and movies (limited as they were to conservative evangelical choices), my weekly half hour of free association with Tom Miller shaped in me a freedom to innovate.

Lack of freedom to innovate can retard the maturation of the church's story and practices. In the erosion of Christendom, the Western church institution threatened by freedom often appeals to its commitment to opening practice or story by restricting one or the other of practice or story. In my early evangelistic youth ministry experience, license was granted for innovation in church evangelism practices, but conservatism restrained any critical examination of our story. Sadly similar restricting took place in seminary. Due to the strengths of the academic institution, innovation was reserved for the church's understood story—the realm of theological ideas—while practices remained protected as "rituals of an exilic people." We were invited to see "life as sacramental," but the sacramental life of the church was separated from everyday life by high pulpits, liturgical robes, and magisterial prayer language awkwardly different from everyone's conversational voices.[11]

But what if God and God's commissioned people continue to sketch the practices and the story? What if the practices of the church and her story are continually being reshaped by the active work of God in our midst? Isn't this what we are thirsting for in our disorientation, in our dissatisfaction? Isn't this what Paul illustrates to the church in Rome as "the glory about to be revealed in us" (see Rom 8:18–23 NRSV)?

Recognizing the story of the gospel as planted within the very culture that it is destined to transform accounts for the story's own *transitory* nature. Our story in en route. As the gospel story is being finished in our midst, so are the practices of the gospel community. Jürgen Moltmann writes: "The *restless world* corresponds to the *restless hearts* of the children of Abraham. All transitory creatures are, along with Abraham's children, on the way to that future in which the restless God comes to rest and finds his home in the house of the completed creation."[12]

As the children of the restless God are, then, *en route* toward a promised future together with God's created world, so the church itself is a "transitory" and "restless" institution. The church is a community called together for "the meantime" to bear witness during this transitory passage.[13] Like an open sketch that others come along and add to, the church is under transformation. At the same time, the church is a community comprised of transformers adding its creative touches to both the restless world and the restless church. We are simultaneously living sketches and commissioned artists; *living sketches* prepared in advance by the Creator and *artists* commissioned to sketch the dreams and visions of Jesus who has commissioned us. This is what David Bosch has called "action in hope." The church is not a remnant of "otherworldly," disembodied, impersonal souls with no impact on this world. Neither are we prisoners of some exclusive ideology confined within the results of our actions. By the grace of God, we are artists freed like the romantics, gifted to sketch in participation with God, inspired by the breath of God to recognize and join the future of the story as it comes to us. "Instead of seeking to know God's future world plan, we ask about the Christian's involvement in the world. The world is no longer viewed as a hindrance but as a challenge."[14] Because of God's "Yes" to the world, the world is our canvas.

Like sketching and free-associating, emerging engenders divergent thinking. What if we saw the work of divergence as a generative act of fidelity instead of degenerate or disloyal? What if the church dared to embody its transitory nature, dared to say in her story and in her practice that more is to come and that we aren't the center of creation but called to love it, to give ourselves up for it? What if emerging churches were to sketch ways of being the story in ages yet to come instead of thinking of appealing to "cultural relevance" under the authorities of closed, feebly supported, tried-and-true rationales?

The Freedom in Fallible Love

Schools today are designing space and lesson plans to train students to provide the same answers as before, not to learn how to develop new answers. Music, dance, visual art, physical education, even playgrounds are disappearing to be replaced by "outcome oriented" practices to secure higher test scores. Former practices that equipped people to tell stories, to use their imaginations, and to explore learning physically are being bracketed out. Theory and practice are being judged by different criteria.

But the church has been equipped by Jesus's life and teaching to take an *integrated* approach to learning and to risk. We have been given the Holy Spirit for such a task. As the Son of God, both completely human and divine, two natures not confused, Jesus's own incarnation demonstrates the redemptive integrative creativity that Jesus's body, the church, is also called to risk. Theory and practice meet in the material reality of the incarnation.[15] Jesus taught that the kingdom of heaven arrives in real and surprising ways that change all of reality. In fact, the space of risking for the sake of faith is the very arena in which we are shaped to expect the reign of God.

Elizabeth O'Connor of the Church of the Savior put it this way:

> When we do not allow ourselves the possibility of failure, the Spirit cannot work in us. We are controlled by perfectionist strivings that inhibit the mysterious meshing of divergent lines within us. Spontaneity dies and the emergence of the unexpected ceases to be a possibility. . . . We cannot exercise our gifts and at the same time be defenders of the status quo. Our gifts put us in tension with things as they are.[16]

This is what I am beginning to discover Emergent to be. It is a gift given to all the church that is placing us in tension with things as they are. As the church orients her self-understanding to "sketches of God commissioned for the purpose of sketching the next pictures of the dreams of God," we will discover courage to let go of the old orientations, see creation expanding, and be drawn nearer to God's creative dreams.[17] Moltmann writes, "At issue is . . . an orientation of all the spheres of life towards the coming kingdom of God and toward an alteration of those spheres commensurate with that kingdom."[18] If the Emergent conversation is to have a "next chapter," it will need to learn from other sketches outside of Western Christendom as well as from within the depths of other traditions (denominations and communions) once dismissed on rational-political grounds, and it must continue, all the more, to seek ways of sketching that benefit the rest of creation. If the church is to persist, we must understand our creative place in the larger work of God.

System of Creativity: Relational Change

Emergent, and specifically the Emergent worship craze, has certainly been a *creative* contribution to the church. In this sense much of the discussion of openness has been around *practices*. Thus far I have tried to argue for a missional approach to practices that places a corresponding value on the *integration* of practice and theory. This, I hope, has at least given the reader a chance to consider how the church's *story* is also in an open posture. Nevertheless, Emergent worship has placed Emergent in the "artsy" or "creative" camp of church growth or renewal. There is a lot to be considered about this, the first point being that creative innovation is the result of a systematic relationship. Emergent practitioners are not doing anything creative from inside some objective churchless or acultural vacuum.

Recent systems theory studies are suggesting that creativity is less the work of one creative individual and more the result of the interrelationship of cultural factors. In his book *Creativity: Flow and the Psychology of Discovery and Invention,* Mihaly Csikszentmihalyi writes:

> Creativity cannot be understood by looking only at the people who appear to make it happen. Just as the sound of a tree crashing in the forest is unheard if nobody is there to hear it, so creative ideas vanish unless there is a receptive audience to record and implement them. And without the claims of outsiders there is no reliable way to decide whether the claims of a creative person are valid.[19]

For the sake of argument, then, I suggest we might view Emergent as a *group*, a creative agent in the midst of the church readapting prior symbols shared by postliberal and postevangelical Christians.[20] Emergent, in this sense, is a guild of prophets, so to speak, placed inside the church to pursue curiosity, to take little risks instead of staying in writer's block. Emergent's mission, then, is to orient the symbols of theological discourse so that existing practitioners of Christianity (church leaders, professionals, theologians, and laity) can put these patterns to use. This is very marketable, very compelling, and it sets Emergent up beautifully to address the current impasse in Christendom between ideologically bound preservationist and liberationist tendencies. This makes Emergent a sort of experimental "third way."

Csikszentmihalyi continues:

> Each of us is born with two contradictory sets of instructions; a conservative tendency, made up of instincts for self-preservation, self-aggrandizement, and saving energy, and an expansive tendency made up of instincts for exploring, for enjoying novelty and risk—the curiosity that leads to creativity belongs to this set. We need both of these programs. But whereas the first tendency requires little encouragement or support from the outside to motivate behavior, the second can wilt if it is not cultivated. If too few opportunities for curiosity are available, if too many obstacles are placed in the way of risk and exploration, the motivation to engage in creative behavior is easily extinguished.[21]

But a third way, alone, is easily co-opted by self-interests. This is especially true if Emergent were to find itself defined exclusively by any "spark" of knowledge about paradigms or a Darwinian theory of progress. Defining Emergent as a *group* of people committed to this program (those prophets exchanging symbols in relationship with the church) is then less significant than the *environment* that Emergent seeks to create—a studio for sketching, a place of freedom and divergence. Clearly the Emergent Village, in our events and communication, is more committed to equipping *any and all* for the process of emergence than being a movement of self-actualized Christian individuals in Western culture.

In this way Emergent and Emerging Theology are on the move. The better future for Emergent is a future where we are less preoccupied with differentiating ourselves from others and more concerned with creating space for communities to open their practices and story in light of God's dreams. I will use the rest of this chapter to discuss how I've stumbled into or been found by these insights in my own context.

Practicing: God and Creation versus God and Us

I discovered that in my little southwest Atlanta neighborhood the community did not want another church. My neighbors saw churches as clubs that put on programs for themselves. The Christian community of which I am a part found what missiologists predicted to be true, that as Christendom erodes in North America, the church can no longer lead from a position of authority in the city. So we set out in pursuit of a new set of patterns. It occurred to our community that plenty of God's story could be practiced in "neighborhood work" that we never before would have considered "church work." This came to a head in planning for Easter. Instead of planning an outdoor concert or dressing up and singing hymns or praise songs, we decided to fix up a local park. In a public demonstration of confession, we admitted that the park had been left for dead and so, like the women who went on that first Easter morning to visit the grave site and anoint the dead body of their Lord, we were to also keep an Easter vigil over the dead creation in our backyard. We met to hold a memorial service by picking up used condoms, broken malt liquor bottles, paper trash, empty plastic baggies, and vials used for weed and crack. Then in the hope of the resurrection we planted azaleas and water oaks and filled a sandbox with four tons of sand. At the end of the day, our Easter Sunday clothes were covered with dirt. We held hands and said to each other what the church has been saying for centuries: "He is risen. He is risen indeed!" For that brief moment, theory and practice were united. And we believed in the resurrection like never before because it was happening around us, blossoming before our very eyes.

Make Kingdom Living Sustainable

This event galvanized our group's (Christian community) identity. As we began to believe in our mission our resources and imagination poured more quickly back toward ourselves and our programs. In a very short amount of time we got into a rut of expecting ourselves to program more big events like the Easter one. Folks were bringing food, giving money, and chipping in to play with the kids during worship gatherings and, in exchange, expecting me, the pastor, to generate the next culture-transforming event. Meanwhile, I was growing tired, as was the rest of our little church, all of whom sincerely wanted to share the leadership load. We decided to pull the plug on weekly programs and simply find ways to sustain living in the city. Suddenly practices of meditation and contemplative Scripture reading were given new purpose. These practices were necessary if we were to be able to sustain our hope in the story and to engender even more beautiful practices of the kingdom work of social services and good neighboring beyond ourselves. Henri Nouwen's words took on fresh meaning: In the spiritual life, the word discipline means "the effort to create some space in which God can act." Discipline means to prevent everything in your life from being filled up. Discipline means that somewhere you're not occupied, and certainly not preoccupied. In the spiritual life, discipline means to create that space in which something can happen that you hadn't planned or counted on.[22]

Live Sustainably

These regular practices or disciplines gave us needed rest. We were being restored and our imaginations were being opened for the presence of God's coming in our neighborhood. It's almost as if our eyes rested enough to finally open wide.

In my case, living with eyes wide open meant I had time to step into a chairperson role in a neighborhood association committee fighting a bad development a few blocks from our house. I recognized the chance to offer needed leadership and could give it time because the "program load" of our church planting effort had been significantly reduced.

The opportunity came to organize residents and these Emergent thoughts of transitory stories and realism toward physical things sprang into action. It occurred to us that the residents were able to create positive change in their neighborhood, instead of becoming a group unified ideologically against change. Through the help of an inquiry facilitator, we were able to sketch some neighborhood dreams together and decide on steps to go in that direction. Suddenly a few members of our church community were able to join with other members of the neighborhood to recruit seventy residents for an event that has become the largest catalyst for healthy neighbor relationships in years. Now our other participating neighbors are discovering the same value of embodying the change we want to see in the world.

Conclusion

These experiences have led me to an evolving understanding of Emergent. On the one hand, Emergent is a new safe place for practitioners who are experimenting with story and practice. We are an incubator, of sorts, existing as a creative agent in relationship with the church system. But merely seeing ourselves as a creative agent *within the domain of the Christian church* will domesticate Emergent into what one critic has already claimed is an "asterisk on the landscape of American church growth."[23] On the other hand, seeing the integrated whole of the church (emerging and otherwise) as a creative agent *within creation*, Emergent can be a place where practitioners embody the church's creative agency for all of emerging society.[24]

Emergent's challenge continues to be practicing the change in the church that it hopes the church will practice in the world. But this is not out of some commitment to its own identity. Rather it is out of a commitment to the *whole church* as the body of our author Jesus Christ. *Emergent churches* within all traditions must take creative risks within an eroding Christendom because *the church* must take such creative risks within creation. This is resurrection, new creation, commission, and the power of the Holy Spirit. It is something that you and I and all of creation are being invited into day after day.

HOPE

PART 2

Communities of Hope

New Ways, Questions, and Outcomes for Churches of Our Day

Doug Pagitt

Emergence is a difficult thing for religion and for religious people. Emergence is about the new. It is about what is coming as well as what is and what has been. This is hard in part because as religious people we often have a strange relationship with the new. Often there is a greater level of mistrust of the new in religious circles than in many other disciplines. I have a theory on this. I think that for many people religion is meant to conserve, to keep, to protect. Religion is often at its finest when it serves to anchor people in the midst of turbulent change—to be a safe harbor in the midst of a storm of change. Many of us assume that our religion ought to provide certainty in uncertain times, safety when it is not clear where trust can be found. God is the only unchanging reality in a sea of change, so for religion to be engaged with the new can seem to undermine its very purpose.

While immovability may be a fine role for religion, it may not serve the story of God's action in the world very well. It seems to me that the story of God's agenda for the world has often found itself at odds with our desires for a religion of safety and stability.

It may be that the story of God's activity in the world is more like wind, fire, or water than an anchor or safe ground. I don't think it is possible to tell the story of faith from the posture of sameness and stability, for it is a story of involvement and activity. Think of the story of creation or the blessing of Abraham or Israel's entering Egypt and leaving it. There are stories of covenants made and stories lived and then told; there are stories of entering lands and being taken away, of the Promised One being sent to the unexpecting, of the Spirit coming on those who were clearly the outsiders, of death and resurrection, of healing and loving, of the calling of the select for the benefit of the whole and the calling of the whole for the benefit of the select.

Ours is a story of the expanding life of God generating new creation. This does not mean that we disparage the past or previous expressions of faith. The faithfulness of the past often serves as the soil for the faithful future. The well-worn may serve as the inspiration for the new.

For many of Emergence-faith, the way of honoring those of our past is doing in our day as they did in theirs. Many of us seek to understand faith and live it out by joining the opportunities of God wherever they are found.

So for those living the faith of Adam, Eve, Abraham, Sarah, Moses, Miriam, David, Jesus, Peter, Paul, and Mary, the new is not an attempt to make life more eventful. It is not seen as distraction from life with God. Rather it is an operative component of the Good News—it is new. It is the Good News of the kingdom of God, the story of the past now in our day, the invitation to join in the things God is doing now.

The following chapters describe the attempts of people today to live, structure, plan, and conceive new ways of collective faith. While the authors are active in their faith in varied contexts—Catholic, Protestant, and Pentecostal, as church leaders and prison counselors, and in their home communities—what they have in common is the desire for the hopeful life of God to be as evident in the years of their lives as it was in years gone by.

These are the stories of faithful people not only exhorting the faithful to new ways, for new outcomes, but doing it themselves. They have taken great risk. They are living in the space between the certain and the possible. They are seeking, knocking, and asking for the life of God to be theirs.

You may notice that some of the thinking is still being developed, and the few "answers" that are provided are not yet fully tested. But that is where the beauty lies.

I like to think of these and similar voices as the distant kin of the early church. The faithful of the first century of Christianity found themselves needing to recalibrate the way they lived, believed, interacted, and reconciled in light of God's activity in Jesus. Not only were they without answers, but the old questions were losing their meaning and the new questions seemed to be coming faster than they could manage. Still they moved forward in faith knowing that what they did would compel the faithful who followed them to keep living with God in the same way that a "cloud of witnesses" had compelled them to do.

The following contributions are hope-filled encouragement from a few of the twenty-first-century faithful.

6

AN EVER-RENEWED ADVENTURE OF FAITH

Notes from a Community

SHERRY AND GEOFF MADDOCK

It cannot be too often reiterated that the primary emphasis on the Church as an institution with creeds, sacraments and "orders," blocks at least at present the way to give first rank to the Church as an ever renewed adventure of faith, a response to God's great acts of salvation, redemption and reconciliation. The Church is not an end in itself, but a means to an end.

Hendrik Kraemer

We belong to a small missional community in Lexington, Kentucky. We call ourselves *Communality*, and our principle desire is to see God's kingdom come on earth as it is in heaven. We believe this happens when God's people are renewed around God's mission of love and justice in the world. We gather during the week in several fellowship and discipleship groups to reflect on our lives and to keep sending one another out into the world that God so loves. We began this journey as Communality in late 1998 and have been discovering that the church is born when applied missiology takes shape in the rituals and rhythms of a group of kingdom-oriented people. We are still learning to act as midwives to the church in our context as we move out into our city in the ways of Jesus. The following notes express some of the things we have been learning.

Sherry Maddock serves Communality (www.communality.us), a missional community in Lexington, Kentucky, while also working in local refugee resettlement. She is originally from Marietta, Georgia, and was raised in the United Methodist Church. She has a master of science in exercise physiology from Wake Forest University and a master of arts in mission studies from Asbury Theological Seminary. Sherry is the mother of three-year-old Isaac. She is a passionate gardener and cook and loves novels, exercise, and going to bed early.

Geoff Maddock also serves Communality in Lexington, and he works part-time at the downtown YMCA. He is originally from a small town in rural Australia called Yackandandah, where he grew up on a dairy farm. He has a bachelor's degree from the University of Melbourne and a master of arts in mission studies from Asbury Theological Seminary. Geoff loves travel, baking bread, eucalyptus trees, secondhand bookshops, and being Isaac's dad.

Salvation Reframed

Through God's leading we are compelled to look beyond the church's buildings and programs to see what God is up to in so-called secular places. Similarly, our ideas about salvation—what it means to be saved—break out of old paradigms as we move out in mission. Our weekly community gatherings provide the opportunity for reflecting on how we have met with God's salvation ways during the week. It is also a time for us to lament a lack of healing and faith while struggling to join in with God's initiatives. The following story recounts an experience Sherry shared in one of our fellowship gatherings about her work with refugee resettlement.

> It was a harrowing winter's day for an African refugee confined to the chaos of an emergency room in Lexington. Although she had a fractured ankle, of far greater concern was a pernicious infection in her leg. The physician's response was immediate as he rushed her to surgery. Hearing the doctor suggest that any delay would risk the loss of her leg triggered horrifying memories. In broken English she pleaded with me to stop them from cutting off her leg. With sobs of despair this woman recalled the brutal amputations she witnessed when she was on the run from rebels in Sierra Leone. I stayed with her, offering reassurance that she would not lose her leg. During the surgery, I wandered out of the hospital feeling despair and anger at a God who would allow such suffering. Listening to her brutal memories, I imagined the hacking of limbs from infants and children and questioned the existence of a God who is active and loving in this world. Bewildered and fully aware that in my empathy I had tasted just a hint of the gruesome reality known by so many West Africans, I felt unhinged from the saving work of God.

Many of us were raised with the understanding that salvation is the exact size and shape of a particular soul. This individualization of soteriology seems to fall short of the salvation imagery we find in the biblical drama. In his book *Salvation*, Joel Green proposes that across the whole story of Scripture God's saving work is best understood in terms of cosmic healing, holism, and liberation.[1] The Hebrew word *shalom* is one of the only words broad enough to gather up the fullness of this kind of dynamic, expansive, and restorative salvation.

As we confront the broader issues of systemic injustice, we expand our thinking about "getting saved." If we raise our sights to this cosmic horizon and walk with Jesus out into communities of despair, we are challenged to ask bigger questions about what it means to be saved from the things that ensnare and press down humanity—especially the poor. This, coupled with a careful reading of Scripture, leads us to see that the individual soul alone is too small a target for God's love and justice.

We discover that a community in mission to those on the cultural, political, and socio-economic margins generates an experience of salvation that is intimately attached. Our devotion to Jesus requires us to form interdependent relationships with people around us, and in so doing we more accurately reflect the mysterious image of the divine community—Father, Son, and Spirit. Paul reminds the church at Philippi that they must work out their salvation with fear and trembling (Phil. 2:12). The language he uses here is plural. In the South we might use the word "Y'all" to get the same effect—"work out y'all's salvation." It is our contention that salvation is more than personal renewal; it is at best a collective experience.

Salvation understood in this way—as communal and in motion (movemental)—leads us inevitably to take the risk of connecting our hope with the hope of the wider community around us. The living out of our faith is no longer just about "Jesus and me." When Sherry shared the story of this refugee with the fellowship group, more tears were shed and prayers were offered. No answers were given and her struggle did not end; however, she was spared from the hopelessness of walking alone in unfaith. At that moment it was enough to be present to the faith of others, and in their collective strength, her feeble faith could abide (see Luke 5:20).

This angle on salvation has reframed our experience of evangelism and mission. Through practices such as caring for AIDS sufferers, feeding the homeless, protesting the wanton destruction of the environment, or welcoming newly arrived refugees, we find salvation that is closer to the *shalom* of Scripture. These disciplines lead us deeper into the compelling and radical ways of Jesus. As educated, wealthy North Americans, the greatest saving might come to us as we are liberated from our unholy apathy and poisonous indifference to the majesty and misery of the world that God so loves.

In summary, we give the following statement of our understanding about the widening scope of salvation:

Not only *soul*, whole body!
Not only *whole body*, all of the faithful community!
Not only *all of the faithful community*, all of humanity!
Not only *all of humanity*, all of God's creation!

Redemption Expanded

A collective and movemental perspective of salvation nurtures an awareness that the ordinary things of life belong to the kingdom and become the sacramental elements of holy living. We believe that when we live in missional ways, we discover God most intimately where we encounter other kinds of intimacy. Jeremiah's message to the exiled people of God has provided us with a redemptive framework for this kind of missional life together, particularly Jeremiah 29:4–7. God instructs the Israelites in Babylon to build homes and live in them, plant gardens and eat the fruit of their labors, and to make families. This is a radical call—to love and live in such a way that their captivity and estrangement are redeemed. It is even more surprising that God's people are told to make plans for the long term, for their children to be given away in marriage. This is more than just pastoral advice to help God's people hunker down and hang in there while the going is rough. As Walter Brueggemann points out, it is "a large missional responsibility" that commands God's people to seek the welfare (shalom) of their (Babylonian) city.[2] Here are some of the ways we have translated this passage into our context.

Building and Living

Redemptive living situations are a significant component of our life together. We bought a home in Lexington with the expectation and commitment that it would be a central place of our mission work. We purchased our house in a downtown neighborhood as part of our commitment to grounded community. We hoped our presence in the neighborhood would add to the diversity and stability of a part of town known for drugs and violence. For the first two years in our home, we have shared it with another married couple with whom we experience a new form of family. Redeemed in accord with this passage, the homes in our community are more like staging grounds for hospitality and loving missionary work and less like fortresses to block out or escape from the world. We celebrate that buying a home is becoming another decision that has moved from "my business" to "kingdom business."

Family

By living closely with other families, in the same home or on neighboring streets, we are getting a fresh take on what it means to be family. Isaiah 56:3–5 declares that under the rule of God even eunuchs are given offspring. Family, then, is not just about genetics. Jesus further deconstructs the centrality of biological families when he declares that "whoever does the will of God" are his kin (see Mark 3:34–35). Often we talk about one another as family and, in an era when divorce and extreme dysfunction affect so many lives, we are discovering the healing power of extended households.

Planting

Gardening is a basic priority and pleasure of our community. Through this earthy practice, we discover new dimensions of theology and connect with our neighbors by sharing food. During the warmer months, not only do we support the local farmers' market, we continually hand vegetables over our fence to people passing by. Through learning the art of agriculture from a local farmer, we reconnect our created selves with the created order. Our own urban gardening and community-supported agriculture relationships foster a renewed appreciation for where food comes from and increased gratitude for the Creator, the farmers, and the field workers who partner to bring it to us each day.

Eating

God chose to wrap covenants like Passover and the Eucharist in food. It is no small thing that when Moses and the elders of Israel came face-to-face with God, their response was to eat and drink (Exod. 24:11). By recognizing that our salvation is a holistic gift, what we put into our bodies becomes a deeply spiritual matter. The family table has reclaimed a central place in our household and our community gatherings. Nowhere else are God's economy and intent for our lives more evident than at an open and inclusive meal. Often the most piercing truths and sought-after comforts come when we eat together. It is here we find that ordinary elements reveal sacred and significant meaning.

Work

The Jeremiah 29 passage teaches us to allow each component of our lives to come under the kingdom's influence. Our roommate Brad works at a local bike shop. He enjoys his job as much as the next bike salesman, but rather than isolate it from the other "spiritual" parts of his life, he has faithfully carried his kingdom imagination onto the shop floor. In recent years he and his colleagues have restored and donated dozens of bicycles to refugees. Through his occupation, he works to make our city more bike-friendly and therefore more environmentally friendly. His efforts include advocating for downtown riders, encouraging cycling through event sponsorship, partnering in the Yellow Bike program, and promoting the Rails-to-Trails initiative. An ordinary job becomes the basis for adventures in faithfulness that include justice work, charity, and civic action. Stories such as these are multiplied wherever followers of Jesus remember that they are kingdom people not (just) church people.

Reconciliation Lived

As Wendell Berry defines community, we are a "placed people."[3] We live on a particular patch of earth in a wider network of family, friends, neighbors, and strangers. This surrounding space is where we are in mission first. It is important to remember that our relationships are at once personal, spiritual, environmental, social, economic, and political. We find countless ways to move into mission by participating in all of the things that happen in the community around us. Our Aussie friend Alan Hirsch has taught us much about this kind of reconciled living. After an extended conversation with him concerning the vagaries of Christian mission and theology, his advice to us was to "embody your truth!"

The community of the faithful will be a place for peace and grace as we learn to close the gap between disembodied information and the flesh and blood of real life. As already mentioned, interdependence is beautifully captured in Jeremiah's advice to the exiles. By declaring that the shalom of the exiles is caught up with the shalom of Babylon, God's people are given a modus operandi for kingdom living. Isaiah 58:6–9 resonates with the same astonishing link between how we practice our devotion and our ability to properly encounter God's love.

From this passage in Isaiah, it is immediately clear that if and when God's people start following these kinds of ethics en masse, we will soon find ourselves engaged with the broader social, economic, environmental, and political issues of the day. In sharing our bread, we will ask questions about where our food comes from and why some people have so little sustenance. In opening our homes, we will ask why there is so little affordable housing. As we clothe the naked, we will recognize them as family left by the wayside and ask why the social fabric is threadbare. When we start to wrestle with these questions and work with God to bring *shalom*, then we are assured of healing and we will experience the fullness of God's salvation. In the words of Isaiah, we will "make the community livable again" (58:12 Message).

Some of the ways we have sought this reconciled living are:

- joining our neighborhood associations
- buying fairly traded and locally grown food
- sponsoring ONE (Make Poverty History) campaign gatherings in our city
- joining with local environmental groups to protest Mountain Top Removal (www.ilovemountains.org)
- delivering meals to AIDS sufferers
- volunteering at homeless shelters, drug and alcohol recovery programs, and soup kitchens

The End (and the Means)

No doubt the life of a group of people attempting to follow God's lead in mission is messy. We learn that "journeying out" in venturesome love, as Ann Morisy puts it, leads to ambiguity, conflict, and unanswered questions.[4] After several years of work in Lexington, Kentucky, we are certain of less and humbled by our failures. As vehicles of grace, mistakes have redirected us and shaped our lives together. We find that success, after all, is best measured by faithfulness not by outcomes.

Many of us had to weed out the desire to wear exhaustion and busyness as badges of honor; somehow we imagined that these proved our commitment. At present we are no less eager to see change in our world nor are we any less committed to working for kingdom purposes. But we are more likely to celebrate slowness, meekness, and the tender art of contentment as part of the treasured kingdom coming. We are slowly learning to live in the tension of this gentle urgency.

From David Bosch we get the ambiguous phrase "transforming mission" as the title for his influential book on missiology and mission history. Captured in this phrase is the belief that as we move out in humble mission, we are agents for change in the world (salvation, redemption, and reconciliation), *and* our very lives are profoundly transformed. We realize that it is one thing to systematically categorize the world around you and subsequently strategize to engage the world with the gospel, and quite another to find yourself in varying degrees of anguish and disappointment at how things turn out when you are trying to be faithful.

In the midst of such liminality we have learned that sustainable missional living requires a spirituality that takes on board the following disciplines:

- opting to be vulnerable
- being taken advantage of
- absorbing pain and suffering
- receiving the gift of inconvenience
- taking risks and being overwhelmed
- seeking to ask creative questions more than giving clever answers
- growing in relationships of interdependence, accountability, and mutual submission

We are now convinced that these disciplines are not obstacles to avoid but occasions for discipleship. We immerse ourselves in such experiences with the faith that God's Spirit and God's people around us will safeguard us from exhaustion. With the same faith, we allow the unpredictable, offensive, disruptive nature of mission to make us more Christlike and carry us deeper into communion with one another. This is the twin heartbeat of missional spirituality: being agents for change while being continually transformed.

One last story to share how our missional living has taught us to expect God to be present and active outside the church. Our community initiated a relationship with an environmental group situated in the Sequatchie Valley of eastern Tennessee. We were motivated to learn about environmentally sustainable lifestyle practices. They were equally interested in finding out why we were concerned about such matters—most of the Christians they had met were fiercely antienvironmentalist. During one of our discussions, we began to lose hope under the burdensome awareness of rampant environmental destruction worldwide. Someone in the group wondered out loud how we might continue with the energy needed to educate people and inspire change. In response, john johnson, an environmental educator and activist, exclaimed, "We need to live like we have already won!" Those of us in the room with Christian worldviews immediately recognized this as a powerful way to encapsulate hope in action.

To live like we have already won is to live with the assumption that God's kingdom is in the present tense. It is recognizing the essential nature of the church as a means to an end—the cosmic fullness of God's influence. To live under the canopy of the grace and healing that the kingdom of God offers is to embrace a spirituality with skin and breath. It is a celebration of the holiness of humanity in which the fullness of God was pleased to dwell. Finally, it is our holy fleshiness as the body of Jesus Christ that is at its most compelling and life-giving when we step outside the church building as agents of and witnesses to God's already-coming kingdom.

7

JAILHOUSE FAITH

A Community of Jesus in an Unlikely Place

THOMAS MALCOLM OLSON

It's helpful for me to think of the gospel as the overthrow of human expectations. Like the shell game played at the carnival, you try to predict where the gospel is hiding and usually end up getting it wrong. You think it's under that one there; but see, it's actually under this one. Try to keep your eye on it. Where did it go? Oh, look, it's right here behind your ear. The gospel feels like that to me.

The inverted values of this upside-down kingdom play out in surprising ways. Leaders and servants swap places. The people at the end of the line get to go in first. And—at least where I work—convicted murderers, drug dealers, and sex offenders can become vehicles of grace and redemption.

For the past few years I've worked as an addictions counselor with a voluntary, faith-based prerelease program for inmates operating inside a medium-security prison north of Minneapolis. I'm in charge of the ninety-day substance abuse component, and my feelings about my job can best be summed up by relating two scenes from *Waiting for Guffman* and *Fight Club*.

In *Waiting for Guffman* there's a scene where Dr. Allan Pearl (a mild-mannered dentist played by Eugene Levy) reveals how he developed his distinctive approach to comedy: "People often say to me, 'You must have been the class clown,' and I say, 'No, I wasn't—but I sat beside the class clown . . . and I studied him, and I learned how he made people laugh.'" When people find out I'm a substance abuse counselor, they sometimes ask if I've struggled with chemical dependency issues in my own life and I say, "No, I haven't, but I spend a lot of time with addicts . . . and I study them." They teach me about redemption. I can safely say

---

Thomas Malcolm Olson is an addictions counselor and theater director. He holds the MDiv from Princeton Theological Seminary and resides in Minneapolis with his wife, Colleen, and daughter, Charlotte. He can be reached at ThomOlson@mac.com.

prison inmates—especially the chemically addicted ones—are the major forces shaping my theology, allowing me to experience God's character up close and showing me what it means to be a faithful witness to this upside-down gospel.

The second scene is from *Fight Club,* when Ed Norton's character begins attending support and recovery group meetings and promptly develops an addiction to attending support and recovery group meetings. He gets hooked on what support groups provide—unconditional acceptance and the feeling of being understood. The initial attraction turns obsessive, and he goes on a binge and pretends he is dying from a wide variety of terminal illnesses. His unshakable craving for just one more meeting grew out of control. But I understand his motives; support groups hold undeniable appeal for me. Fortunately, there's no need to go to the extremes that this character did, since I have a built-in excuse to attend recovery meetings. It's my job!

Each time I attend, I'm struck by the posture of humility and vulnerability people willingly adopt with one another. It's contagious. There's an attitude of "I don't have it all figured out and I need your help," which seems like good theology to me. Recovery groups are the easiest, most natural way people can "bear one another's burdens, and thereby fulfill the law of Christ" (Gal. 6:2 NASB). The dynamic of the group becomes the catalyst for living faithful lives.

In these meetings there is an expectation that we are going to talk straight with each other. When someone asks, "So how was your week?" they (*warning*: revolutionary concept ahead) genuinely want to know, of all things, how your week went. In recovery groups, people can share their life without the pressure to minimize, embellish, or otherwise spiritually airbrush the warts and blemishes. But a transparent community like this takes practice, and so groups meet together at least once a week to get better at it. The group knows things about you and loves you anyway, which is the upside-down kingdom at work.

God's Favored People: Inmates

I believe there are certain groups of people who are in the privileged position of grasping something of God's character that the rest of us miss. Off the top of my head, it would be farmers, musicians, and prisoners.

The agricultural metaphors spread throughout the Bible are best appreciated by farmers, while the rest of us have to take their word for it. Musicians pick up subtleties and nuance, especially in the Psalms, that elude the rest of us. The same is true for prisoners. Whenever the Bible talks about freedom, it registers on a deeper and more direct level for them, a level that may be closer to the original intent.

Inmates are drawn to the program where I work because it functions like a spiritual boot camp. The emphasis is on training disciplined servant-leaders. The idea is if Christianity can work here, it can work anywhere. But for me it also functions as a theological laboratory; if Christianity doesn't work here, then it doesn't work at all.

One of the luxuries of working inside a prison is not having to waste time convincing inmates that their lives have become unmanageable. Our program is voluntary and inmates must apply to get in. The prisoners arrive motivated and eager to make changes. They agree to commit themselves to learning and practicing the habits of "a new creation": honesty, humility, accountability, community, and restoration. The only way to attain these habits is to practice them. It's simple—all they have to do is change their whole life.

For a criminal, this is no easy task. Honesty requires giving up a survival tactic. Humility is showing weakness. Accountability is allowing other people to meddle in your business. Community is admitting you aren't strong enough on your own. Restoration means you did something wrong. The new-creation values collide head-on with the prison code of conduct (which is, no snitching; do your own time; trust no one). And that's the whole point.

Encouraging prisoners to take on the habits of a new creation presupposes an "old creation" way of doing things. Setting aside theological nuance for the sake of simplicity, the old creation is filled with unhealthy core beliefs about ourselves and the way we see the world. Core beliefs are the unquestioned assumptions governing our thoughts, feelings, and behavior. For prisoners, it is imperative to replace destructive core beliefs and learn to challenge criminal and addictive thought patterns. The process is arduous, time-consuming, and not very glamorous. But without this emphasis, long-lasting change is only wishful thinking, and our program becomes a bunch of spiritual criminals sitting around quoting Bible verses.

Jesus loves convicted sex offenders. I've thought about putting that slogan on a T-shirt, but it probably wouldn't go over the way I intend.

They are modern-day hybrids of the tax collector and leper. (Here's an experiment: try substituting "sex offender" whenever you read "tax collector" and "leper" in your Bible, and you will be closer to the original scandal people felt when Jesus associated with them.) Before applying to our program, sex offenders must first graduate from sex offender treatment, where they learn to take complete responsibility for their crime and the hurt they caused others. Once accepted to our program, it takes about ten months before they reach my class. I can hardly wait. They're usually the ones who teach me the most about God's grace. Invariably, even as they remain tragically broken individuals, they model to the rest of the class how to talk vulnerably and openly about their life without minimizing or making excuses for behavior. Sex offenders keep the class more honest, and their presence in class is a constant unspoken reminder of the extent of God's love and forgiveness.

Sometimes when we have prayer time in class, I invite inmates to adopt a posture of inconvenience that moves beyond a bowed head and folded hands. I want them to get down on their knees and make it hurt a little bit, to lean into the pain and allow it to inform the prayer. It feels awkward and uncomfortable. The soreness and discomfort they experience parallel the suffering they are seeking to have God alleviate, and the relief they feel when they stand up anticipates the hope of God's healing. That's how I teach the importance of prayer to prisoners.

The Drama of Redemption

Before working as an addictions counselor, I made my living as a stage director in theater. I haven't so much changed careers as I have switched venues (the skill sets of a stage director and an addictions counselor are remarkably transferable). The amount of drama is the same, but now I deal in the personal kind. I still spend a majority of my time facilitating change and witnessing transformation. The prisoners I encounter are in the midst of living out a story, and part of my job as their counselor is to help them make sense of it. I still get to sit in the front row and watch.

Like all of us, inmates cast themselves as the main character in their story. Their narrative arc takes on a familiar rhythm and bares an uncanny resemblance to the story of the prodigal son found in Luke 15. It's like watching a modern-day reenactment verse by verse. They haven't finished living out their story, and it appears they are stuck. On further inspection I can see the action is getting bogged down somewhere between exiting verse 16 ("feeding the pigs") and entering verse 17 ("When he came to his senses"). In AA vernacular, that's somewhere between "hitting rock bottom" and experiencing "a moment of clarity." It's a fun place to work, and the best is yet to come. The homecoming scene hasn't been staged yet.

For the story to move forward, the inmates must make a decision to move beyond verse 16. If prisoners do not experience a moment of clarity, they are left feeding the pigs and thinking, *This is all my life is going to amount to.* But the prodigal son story didn't end there. Our program exists to remind prisoners: "You were not meant to live like this." The new-creation values of honesty, humility, accountability, community, and restoration reinforce the conviction that there is a better way to live.

But the prisoners have to want it, which leads to my "Three Irrefutable Laws of Substance Abuse Counseling." The first day of class I draw a triangle on the dry erase board and explain how each side of the triangle represents an absolute law that cannot be ignored. Whatever good we do this quarter, I tell them, it's going to stay inside the three boundaries. Along one side I write, "You are ready to hear what you are ready to hear." Along the opposite side I write, "You are ready to talk about what you are ready to talk about." Along the bottom I write, "You are going to do what you want to do." I draw several more triangles, ranging from tiny dots to ones taking up the entire board. Then I ask them to look at the board and choose a triangle representing the amount of change they are willing to make. I remind them that long-term change (as opposed to a short-term fix) boils down to hearing things they haven't been willing to hear before, talking about things they haven't been willing to talk about before, and doing things they haven't been willing to do before. It's rare for inmates to choose the smallest triangle, which indicates they want to stay in their comfort zone, but when they do, I give them my standard reply: "See you in three to five years."

Most opt for the big triangles. I want them to imagine how their life will look when it's fully connected to God and connected to others, but they're not able to see it yet. But I can. It's the lens I look through when I teach them about recovery. I don't judge them based on the worst thing they've ever done. My reading of the prodigal son story convinces me there are many more verses in their life waiting to be lived out.

I ask inmates to write out a detailed description of the life they've always wanted and the type of person they want to become. I encourage them to look beyond material possessions and focus on character traits. We enjoy a lively discussion as each inmate shares the vision he has for his life. At the end of class I say that the rules of behavior in the classroom have changed. From then on I expect each one to begin practicing the life he has always wanted.

This is when things get interesting and when my front row seats come in handy. I've seen inmates from rival street gangs practice on each other the act of forgiveness. I've listened to inmates pray with their foreheads pressed to the ground: "Lord Jesus Christ, Son of God, have mercy on me, a sinner." I've baptized Level 3 sex offenders. These events can't help but leave permanent marks on your theology. Prison ministry is a type of spiritual formation that works both ways—it changes everyone involved.

Church as Penitentiary

It would be good for Christianity if churches imitated penitentiaries and encouraged their parishioners to act more like prisoners. (It took me three decades of being a Christian to come up with that one, which explains why I make my living as an addictions counselor instead of a church growth consultant.) But I think I'm on to something. Every person needs one safe place where he or she is able to stop pretending, a place of ruthless honesty and unconditional love where no one is allowed to fly underneath the radar. It's the type of setting we strive to create in prison—a culture where inmates regularly hear from each other: "I can't con you; you can't con me. I love you and I think you're full of crap and we're going to get through this together."

The stakes are admittedly higher here. Normally, if people experience a relapse in their recovery, they're able to pick themselves up, face the consequences, and then return to their group. It's different with prisoners. When they relapse, really bad things can happen, so we encourage inmates to practice and participate in high-accountability support groups while they are still incarcerated. The lone ranger act isn't going to cut it anymore. Sometimes an inmate will try to convince me he doesn't need weekly recovery meetings to stay sober and that joining a church and attending Bible studies will suffice. I give my standard reply: "See you in three to five years."

God loves prisoners. It's the reason Jesus reminds us to look after "the least of these"—specifically mentioning prisoners in Matthew

25:43—as proof we are members of this upside-down kingdom. Inmates can't learn Christianity through a correspondence course; it requires day-to-day, life-on-life interaction. Caring for prisoners is a natural outgrowth of a desire to be a blessing in the world by living out God's agenda. And if Christian community can work here, it will work anywhere.

8

THE EXISTING CHURCH/ EMERGING CHURCH MATRIX

Collision, Credibility, Missional Collaboration, and Generative Friendship

TIM CONDER

I am one of many who have witnessed and experienced the accelerating momentum of the emerging church from both the inside and outside. I have often been the lost son of Luke's narrative, finding a redemptive space and a warm home in the embrace of the Emergent community, but at times I have been forced by vocation to stand on the outside of the party like the older brother.

I have been privileged—no, downright blessed—to be a leader in Emergent Village and its organizational forbears for now approaching a decade. Like many in this community, though, my passion and enthusiasm for its values had greatly predated some of the first national gatherings on "Generation X ministries" and "the postmodern church" that served as public unveilings for what would become the emerging church movement. I have watched this community experience so many metamorphoses—from being virtually unnoticed to struggling to manage the interest generated; from predominantly deconstructing traditional Christianity to having a seat at the table in many institutional expressions of Christianity; from being defined by its ideological differences and eccentricities to being identified by the creativity and impact of its communities; from being a harmless curiosity to a target of harsh criticism and a focal point of fear; from a posture of prophetic critic of the Enlightenment and modernity to poetic creativity and apostolic temerity in the burgeoning postmodern world.

Tim Conder is the pastor of Emmaus Way, an emergent community in Durham, North Carolina, and remains a standing elder and friend of the Chapel Hill Bible Church, a fellowship he copastored for fifteen years. Tim is a member of the coordinating team for Emergent Village, a member of the board of directors of the Mars Hill Graduate School, and the author of *The Journey of Existing Churches into the Emerging Culture* (Zondervan, 2006). He is married to Mimi and they have two children, Keenan and Kendall.

I have also experienced these same metamorphoses from the outside. Most of my tenure as a leader within Emergent has occurred while serving as a pastor of a mainstream evangelical church that has both confluences with and some significantly divergent philosophical/theological sensitivities from those of the emergent community. In this environment I have heard many of the fears and critiques of Emergent; I have been sensitized to occasions when the emerging church has caricatured the existing church; and I have seen some of the contemporary norms of Christian community that demand a movement such as this.

My dual citizenship has come with a few costs. There have been times when I've felt a bit displaced in the Emergent community. At one of my first Emergent leadership meetings, the spouse of an emerging church planter, on hearing a brief description of my church, asked pointedly, "Why are you here?" The question was not intended to be unkind. The gulf of interest and trust between the emerging church and the landscape of existing churches of all traditions seemed immense and insurmountable. At home there were times when my ideas were met with mistrust or blank confusion. The church I served was often simultaneously fascinated by and fearful of the emerging culture. Despite these costs, my leadership journey in the existing church and the emerging church has given me a vision for the future matrix of relationships between existing churches and the emergent community and the missional possibilities for this potential friendship.

Collisions and Conflict

These missional possibilities have not always been apparent. The early relationship of the existing church and the church emerging in postmodernity can be characterized by a series of dramatic collisions. Just a partial list of these ecclesiological struggles would include sharp collisions in ethics, epistemologies (the nature and understanding of truth), theology, gospel, mission, biblical interpretation, leadership, spiritual formation, and the nature of Christian community. I've used the following chart of generalizations to facilitate conversation in our existing church about the heart and passions of the emergent community.

	Existing/Modern	Emergent/Postmodern
Ethics	personal/absolute	corporate/contextual
Epistemology	abstract/absolute/ transcendent	experiential/perceptual/ local
Theology	systematic/propositional	narrative/missional
Gospel	eternal salvation	present reign of God in this world
Mission	defined by personal, spiritual needs	defined by God's redemptive agenda
Biblical Interpretation	propositional/dependent on theological systems	contextual/narrative
Leadership	positional/hierarchical	relational/egalitarian
Spiritual Formation	linear/cognitive/ personal	nonlinear/holistic/communal
Basis of Community Formation	boundaries formed by doctrine/confession	boundaries shaped by ethical and missional commitments

Don't get overwhelmed if these terms are unfamiliar. There are many resources to help anyone unpack the nuances between modernity and postmodernity and then the corollary differences between emergent and existing church communities.[1] The primary point here is to accentuate the potential magnitude of differences between the church formed in modernity and the church emerging in postmodernity.[2]

Given these differences, as you can imagine, at times the demarcation between these two churches has been so presuppositional or foundational and the tone of dialogue so sharp that no meaningful conversation seemed possible. I'll offer a single disagreement between a former colleague and me that expresses some of these differences.

Some years ago as a youth pastor, I had an extremely gifted volunteer whose spiritual journey caused him to question some of the church's presuppositions. He struggled with the amount of sermon material that focused on personal moral decisions as compared to the near silence on corporate, social ethics. Our teaching seemed to center on eternal salvation and the lifestyle of those who embraced this salvation. He became frustrated that social issues like the environment, racism, poverty, and other systemic injustices did not often appear on our radar. Our hopes seemed to be pinned entirely on the eternity God promised rather than collaboration with God's redemptive work in the present. An ardent student of the Bible, he felt that our mode of biblical interpretation was a constant reduction of texts to cognitive propositions that supported evangelical theological systems. From his vantage point, this method often ignored the narrative of the Scriptures, glossed over significant tensions within the text, and minimized experiential interaction with the text. Despite these concerns, he remained deeply loyal to our fellowship and his relationships with our teens reflected great integrity and sensitivity to our values.

With his permission I shared some of his frustrations with a colleague who had kids in our youth ministry that had been cared for wonderfully by this volunteer. Having vocalized similar concerns in staff meetings, I was shocked by the intensity of my colleague's reaction and the ultimate severity of his opinion. His immediate judgment was that this friend should be promptly asked to leave our youth team. A few years later in the context of another disagreement, this same colleague confessed that he could no longer fully trust my integrity or ministry judgment as a result of my unwillingness to follow his advice regarding this volunteer years earlier. Our disagreement over this volunteer clearly had created far-reaching consequences in our staff community.

After long reflection on this dispute, I eventually realized that this incident was neither the overreaction of a protective father nor an act of harsh judgment. My colleague constantly insisted, as we debriefed this event, that he intended no malice or critique of my personal integrity, which he saw as separate from my leadership capacity. He had a far greater and less personal issue in mind. The real issue involved the collision of two rival conceptions of Christian community and two polarized paradigms for ministry. For my colleague, Christian community is defined by doctrinal boundaries and a shared confession of primary beliefs. In his mind the study and affirmation of doctrine catalyzes spiritual formation. Theological systems guide our theological inquiries and biblical interpretation. Our doctrinal foundation shapes personal ethics and absolute propositions about truth. Put more bluntly, when this youth leader stepped off our fellowship's "doctrinal bus," by his own decision he stepped outside the boundaries of our fellowship and left the community. My colleague's strong expectation that I "fire" this friend was only a formal acknowledgment of a departure that had already taken place, and my failure to do as my colleague suggested implied that I no longer fit on the bus either. I was either questioning or disregarding the foundational principle of our community as he perceived it.

My perspective was entirely different. Having a philosophy rooted in emergent ways of thinking, and working with many persons in our community who shared this viewpoint, I defined the boundaries of our community by the impetus of persons and groups to share our missional commitments and their willingness to accept and follow personal and corporate ethical commitments that were appropriate to this mission. I thought doctrinal exploration and affirmations were certainly important in our ministry, but they were not our primary criteria of inclusion or exclusion. In evaluating our leaders, I started with a different set of questions. My core evaluative question was something like, "Does this person share in and contribute to our mission in an appropriate and authentic manner?" I was far more wary of leaders who may have joined our community with relational skills that demeaned students or any number of inappropriate motives. Again I didn't dismiss doctrine as a component of community, but I viewed both leaders and students who came to our community with honest and respectful doctrinal inquiries as essential catalysts to the kind of spiritual authenticity that we wanted to guide our community.

This dispute was framed within the potentially explosive category of "integrity." In reality it was a collision of ideologies about mission and community formation. Serving as an elder and teaching pastor in an existing church in the evangelical tradition with an Emergent worldview for fifteen years, I have a staggering number of stories about such collisions. Friends and family members who lead and pastor mainline Protestant and Catholic fellowships report different versions of the very same collisions.

In the current landscape there is great demand for fellowships driven by an Emergent philosophy, connected to the historical church, and not embroiled in the conflict formed by these colliding paradigms. That church has not fully arrived. As a board member of Mars Hill Graduate School, I have had many interactions with gifted and mature spiritual leaders who graduate with excellent training but with few places to land except in forming new missional communities. Even as I was typing this paragraph in a local café, a fellow citizen of the roving laptop community who had heard me speak on this subject the previous weekend interrupted me. Completing his professional degree and moving this spring, he asked if I knew of fellowships in his destination that were within his familiar tradition but with emerging culture passions.

Moving beyond the Matrix of Collision

Moving beyond the existing church/emerging church matrix is an absolutely essential ecclesiological shift for Christian community in the present. The existing church must find its way into the emerging culture to retain its missiological credibility or perhaps even to survive. The emerging church's formation is delayed, despite significant demand for its presence and passions, by the opposition of the established, existing church.

Now I am a dual citizen in an entirely different posture. I am leading an emergent missional community (Emmaus Way in Durham, North Carolina) in intimate friendship with an existing church community. This new, third vantage point has taught me some seminal lessons. First, emerging culture passions and perspectives have become deeply embedded in the existing church. In our initial discussions for our mission, there was great interest and curiosity across every demographic line. Second, the line of demarcation between the existing church and emerging church need not be a Gaza Strip of inflexibility, fear, or mistrust. This line has a potential future that can be less a border crossing and more a gentle erasure.

At the beginning, collisions and deconstruction defined the existing church/emerging church matrix, but connectivity, collaboration, and a new language of Christian community can characterize its future. How do we move from collision to collaboration?

If collision is the natural antecedent of mistrust, accusation, and separation, then mutual credibility can be the precursor to respect, missional collaboration, and generative friendship. Three paths of inquiry and practice will accelerate this journey to credibility and beyond: a critical analysis of culture, a less selective appropriation of history, and a relocation of theological dialogue from the border of initiation to the creative embrace of mission.

Critical Analysis of Culture

A critical analysis of culture is a pathway toward credibility on both sides of the existing church/emerging church matrix. Brian Walsh and

Sylvia Keesmaat's recent publication *Colossians Remixed: Subverting the Empire*[3] describes an exegetical trajectory that can be extremely fruitful for both the existing church and emerging church. Their reading of Colossians as an anti-imperial treatise against the mythology, oppression, and ritual of the Roman Empire has influenced my reading of the whole New Testament. Walsh and Keesmaat also offer a confronting hermeneutic, that the church finds itself in the midst of another suffocating empire, an empire of nationalism, consumerism, individualism, materialism, and misguided hope.

The existing church has a lot to gain from applying this cultural analysis inwardly. In its recent history the existing church has seen itself as a sanctuary, unadulterated by external cultural threats, without realizing that many of these cultural threats have often been incorporated and "baptized" within the communal life of the fellowship. When I hear of churches raffling away cars and motorcycles as a part of worship services to attract "outsiders," it seems obvious that our cultural myths of personal accumulation and entitlement have found a comfortable home within the church. So strong is the notion of a pure church and a pure gospel in some existing churches that members of these fellowships have asked me to literally name just one way that culture has influenced their understanding of the gospel. The notion of a pure gospel unaffected by culture blinds us to circumstances where consumerism or competition with other fellowships have driven ministry decisions, occasions when wealth or physical beauty have been unspoken criteria for leadership positions, or even the tragic situations when institutional forms of prejudice or racism have gone undetected. We're all guilty on some level! A critical cultural analysis applied inwardly to the ministries and messages of the existing church can yield a much greater sensitivity and credibility to the reactive posture of the emergent movement.

Many self-proclaimed emerging churches could stand to apply this cultural analysis externally. We can become so enamored with our engagement of culture that essential distinctives and practices of the Christian community vanish or become indiscernible. An emerging church pastor made this very point to me during their worship gathering after we heard a long announcement about a group viewing of a newly released film and then a quick word about an upcoming baptism. This was a simple case of poor prioritization that an observant pastor quickly corrected, but more critical analysis of surrounding culture can infuse emerging churches with some of the natural protectiveness and gradated cultural disengagement of the existing church.

Critical examination of the empire that is both external and internal to the church can offer a sense of cultural mutuality to existing and emerging churches. They both share an orientation toward the same imperial presence.

Less Selective Appropriation of History

Greater mutual credibility can also be furthered by a less selective appropriation of history. Particularly the Protestant church often finds its heritage solely in the Reformation and in portions of the first-century church. A sense of continuity with pre-Christian Judaism (and the scriptural narrative of God's redemptive work in Israel) and pre-Reformation Christianity is often absent. So many of the passions of emergent Christianity, such as mysticism, mystery, experiential faith practices, community, appreciation for the narrative of Scriptures, and monasticism, find stronger historical precedents in these "blacked-out" eras of God's redemptive history.

The same point could be applied to the emerging church in regard to the Reformation. As we rapidly move into post-Reformation Christianity, there is a natural tendency to reserve our harshest reactions to the most recent era in the Christian community's historical narrative; this reflects what I believe is inappropriate disrespect for the existing church. Though many of the presuppositions of the Enlightenment-shaped Reformation are waning or being challenged in postmodernity, the church emerging stands squarely on the narrative shoulders of the Reformation church. We need to rediscover and study the genius of the Reformation (recognizing that we will certainly need to continue reforming). In some cases, we need to find our heritage less in Foucault and postmodern critics and more in formative thoughts of Reformation theologians whose battle with modernity carved our path into postmodernity.

This warning to avoid disregarding the contributions of the recent past can be zoomed in radically to the very recent past. Many emerging churches have found their missional voice in the wake of the Jesus movement, the seeker-church movement, and other contemporary expressions of Christianity. Even when this missional voice utters correction to these movements, they deserve our gratitude and respect. I learned this lesson in my long season of dual citizenship. I remember returning home from Emergent gatherings visibly proud of creative innovations, which I found had already been *discovered* and more substantively *developed* in my existing church, which had retained many of its radical, missional values from its genesis in the early 1970s. The servings of crow and resulting humility were good for me!

Relocation of Theological Dialogue

A final path to mutual credibility involves not only greater theological dialogue but also a movement of this dialogue from the community borders of initiation to the inner spaces of missional imagination. As my earlier story illustrated, so much of our theological dialogue is in the potentially punitive, high-consequence categories of inclusion and exclusion. So many communities form and function on the insistence (and often the myth!) of doctrinal consensus. Ordinations and the selection of lay leaders are often preceded by theological hazings. The consent for church membership, marriage, and promotion of professional staff are predicated on making doctrinal affirmations in familiar language. In addition, our theologies can be predominantly presented by monologue in the pulpit and classroom settings. These phenomena, when present, silence theological dialogue because of the potential consequence of exclusion.

Encouraging theological dialogue in safe places would reveal the magnitude of theological and lifestyle diversity in our fellowships. Questions, doubts, and concerns would be transformed from painful secrets to catalysts for community spiritual formation. In a climate of theological openness, emergent passions would certainly have greater credibility because of the sheer volume of persons who share them. Existing church concerns can also be allayed as emergent passions lose their secret revolutionary flavor and become open to authentic scrutiny.

When theological dialogue moves from fearful, punitive places to spaces of missional imagination, diversity becomes a huge asset. When conversations turn to the imagination of an embodiment of God's gracious character and redemptive intentions, differences become possibilities, opportunities, and components of a wider vision.

Emergent Village has been in the business of theological dialogue throughout its short existence. One thing we have done well has been to create safe places for theological inquiry and exploration. Even in our brief history, we have seen respect, friendship, and creative initiatives grow like kudzu across many of the deepest chasms of Christian tradition. This final path of dialogue may be the most sacred. On its heels, one can see far beyond the first steps of credibility and respect to the sacred places of missional collaboration and generative friendship.

The existing church/emerging church matrix can dissolve into missional collaboration and generative friendship. Obviously there is much work to do before this can occur. The paths of cultural analysis, historical exploration, and relocated theological dialogue are arduous trails that demand persistence and firm resolve. Fortunately, mission and friendship are worth it.

9

THE AMERICAN CATHOLIC MERGER-CHURCH

A Too Small Answer

BRIAN MITCHELL

Take a shortage of priests, a shortage of dollars, and a hint of megachurch envy, and what have you got? You've got the contributing factors to what is dramatically changing the face of Roman Catholicism in the United States. The process can be complicated, hard-fought, and lengthy, but the end result is often the same: consolidation. If not an easy response at which a community might arrive, consolidation is perhaps the simplest. Many believe that the pooling of priests and financial resources will result in economies of a scale that will sustain the community into the future. This larger expression of parish life is creating an entirely new experience of church for Catholics entering the third millennium, the merger-church.

Roman Catholicism began its existence in the United States with close ties to the European immigrant communities that brought it from the Old World. Initially Catholic parishes appeared as missions on the frontier. As towns and cities grew, they became centers where Catholics could retain an intertwined experience of the Mother Church and the motherland. Families settled in neighborhoods defined by faith and ethnicity. Parishes became social and cultural hubs for Catholics. Early generations of immigrants could find jobs, friends, and even spouses among the blend of social gatherings and religious services. Catholic culture was set up in the midst of and alongside the broader American culture.

In rural areas longer distances exaggerated the importance of parishes as social and cultural centers. In cities modest means of transportation and cultural homogeneity limited the geography of parishes to neigh-

---

Brian Mitchell is a lifelong Catholic. He is the president of interGen, a staffing development and multimedia consulting company in Oshkosh, Wisconsin. Brian has provided leadership and consulted for a number of large Catholic parish consolidations in the upper Midwest.

borhoods. Without question, parishes were the base unit of the early immigrant model of church.

This model of church served Catholics well as the United States transitioned from a rural agricultural to an urban industrial nation. Roman Catholicism flourished throughout the twentieth century in the United States. Growing from not quite 11 million (14 percent of the overall US population) in 1900 to 60 million (22 percent of the population) in 2000, Roman Catholicism is the single largest denomination in the country.[1] Catholic presence grew out of the immigrant neighborhoods and into the very center of American consciousness. This phenomenon was perhaps best symbolized in 1961 when John F. Kennedy was elected as the first Roman Catholic president.

The Current Leadership Paradigm

At the dawn of the third millennium, a number of factors created tension for centuries-old church structures, yet the struggle to maintain parishes continues. As the number of Catholics continues to increase as a percentage of overall Americans, the number of priests available to serve parishes is in decline and has been for some time. This phenomenon has been masked by simply demanding more of fewer and fewer priests.

Additionally, the number of religious women and men who filled so many parish and leadership roles in the immigrant model of parish life has declined significantly. Now they maintain at best a residual presence in parish leadership. The retirement of religious nuns and brothers and the overall decline of new religious vocations have left a huge void in parish services and leadership.

Previously, neighborhood parishes had a rectory with the pastor, several associate pastors, and a housekeeper. Ordained and religious personnel offered the overwhelming majority of services. Priests or other religious handled administration, teaching at the parish and Catholic schools, counseling and hospital visits, and of course the worship and sacramental needs of the community.[2] Today more and more of these tasks have been handed over to lay staff members, and the retirement age of priests has been extended. Also, whereas in the past a newly ordained priest would spend the first two-thirds of his career as an associate pastor of a modest neighborhood parish, these days the newly ordained frequently serve as associates for about two years before being assigned to groups of rural parishes or large urban parishes.

All of these adjustments have allowed the Catholic Church in the United States to maintain the parish as the base unit of church life. Even so, cracks in the facade are beginning to show. Current structures operate on the assumption that every priest who comes out of seminary has strong administrative and leadership skills, yet practical experience indicates priests have a wide range of gifts and talents, sometimes administrative, sometimes not.

Much of the impetus for consolidation is the megachurch model. There are churches in the United States made up of more than five thousand people with just one senior pastor, and these churches seem to hum along just fine. Seeing this, some in the Catholic Church believe that it's no problem for priests to oversee multiple parishes and large numbers of people. Yet the megachurch model presumes that every priest is not only gifted but exceptionally gifted in the areas of organizational development, change management, staff administration, and leadership. This presumption is simply not realistic.

The reality is that almost always it is dynamic, charismatic, and highly skilled leadership *teams* that start successful Protestant megachurches. If these churches are not currently led by the original team, at some point a succession process replaced the original leadership with new, qualified, and proven candidates. The large size of these churches is driven in significant part by the pastoral team's ability to lead and manage the organization. Leadership and church grow organically, side by side.

The increasing size of individual Catholic churches is following a different path. In most cases either new parishes are being established to serve larger suburban communities, or groups of neighborhood parishes are being consolidated to serve geographically tight areas that are less divided along ethnic lines than they once were.

When a local parish needs a new priest, it does not conduct a national, regional, or even statewide search for the best candidate. Instead, the bishop of the diocese appoints a pastor out of a diminishing pool of priests from within the relatively limited geographical region of the diocese. Exacerbating the problem is an uneven distribution of Catholic priests among different dioceses in the United States. Add to this the fact that most dioceses have a set compensation for all priests regardless of placement. This creates a built-in disincentive for taking on the immense responsibility of pastoring a large parish. The increasingly difficult position in which we place our pastors makes it less likely they will interact with young men who might have an interest in the priesthood. When they do interact, it can be difficult for priests to communicate a sense of joy amid the demands of the lifestyle. This thwarts vocational initiatives and carries the possibility of shortages well into the future.

As each community struggles to resolve economic and priest shortages, people assume that the community cannot jettison existing models of church. The community must somehow retrofit new realities to these old structures. But what if the discussion began with the needs of the community and moved to how churches should be structured to best meet those needs? Frequently the missional purpose in the church gets lost in the practical questions that grow from an assumption that the church must be as it is: Which parishes will close and which will consolidate? In what order will our active priests retire? How can we reconfigure existing resources to function without them? If the parish is the base unit, the drive to consolidation is perhaps the only truly viable response. It is simply the most efficient way to share resources.

But what if we set the parish assumption aside? This idea might at first seem scandalous to Catholics. Having already acknowledged the primacy of the parish model in the American Catholic experience, a change this dramatic might be more disruptive than the reconfiguration and consolidation of the current paradigm. On the other hand, we must remember that the concept and experience of parishes as we know them today are relatively recent developments. House churches, guilds, monasteries, and religious orders have all served as the primary organizing structures of the church in centuries past. Historically, the "local church" referred more to the diocese than the parish. However, few lay Catholics think first of the regional structure of the diocese as their primary frame of reference for belonging to the "local church."

I'm not suggesting an abolition of the parish. I'm suggesting a rethinking of its role in the overall structure of the church, a reinterpretation of what the word *parish* means. The neighborhood parish as the dominant unit within which American Catholicism was experienced in the last two centuries has clearly run its course. What is its best successor? If parish is not the atomic unit, what is? The best answer is the historical one. It is the diocese.

For centuries the structure of Catholicism was best understood as a communion of local churches defined as a diocese rather than as a multi-tiered hierarchy centered in an organizational structure of leaders. Each diocese has always been led by a bishop overseeing the presbyters (eventually priests) who were ordained to preach, preside at liturgy, and ultimately represent the bishop as head of the local church in the bishop's absence. In the United States a diocese is generally smaller than a state but larger than a city (excepting large metropolitan areas). As an example, Wisconsin has five dioceses centered in Milwaukee, Madison, Green Bay, La Crosse, and Superior, which covers a large, less densely populated area in the northwest part of the state.

Many will argue that the diocese is already the official structure of the local church. Technically (canonically) they are right. Practically speaking, the average Catholic in the pew thinks about this building, my priest, and this group of friends and neighbors when he or she hears the word *church*. Clearly the technical understanding and the lived reality are in tension.

If the merger-church lacks personal connection, one objection goes, the move to diocese as prime organizational unit necessarily institutes a complete breakdown of personal connection between the church and the individuals that make up its membership. The diocese is too large to provide truly relational ministry. However, it does free local expressions of the church to organize in ways that both are relational and best serve the needs of the community. It is a move away from the parochialism of this parish, with this priest, for this ethnic group, in this neighborhood that will provide opportunities for "church" to organize in the various sizes and ways necessary to provide for the needs of the local community. Ministry can be as intimate, personal, and local as appropriate to the needs being met. It can also be as universal as Catholic Relief Services.

The diocese provides a freer framework within which the local church can then organize ministry and resources to best meet needs. The organizational process can draw on the rich tradition of monasticism, guilds, house churches, neighborhood parishes, and other types of ministry as inspiration for what the church might become. It is unlikely that it will return purely or exclusively to any of these models. They simply provide a beginning for the conversation and the encouragement that Catholicism has a long and varied history of molding its form to effectively meet the needs of ever-changing global cultures.

The Role of the Priesthood

As individual parishes grow larger with a smaller number of priests serving, parish communities tend to reflect the personal pastoral style of their priests. This is especially true as priests' length of time with a particular parish and strength of leadership increase. When retirement or the reassignment of a priest becomes necessary, this personal affiliation can make the changes especially difficult. With the diocese being the center, the role of bishop becomes more prominent at the local level. There is a heightened awareness of ministry driven from the diocese and less investment of communities into the idiosyncrasies of their individual priests.

This scenario would allow for a number of substantial benefits. It would remove the intensity of administrative pressure from priests who are not well suited to run large organizations, allowing these holy men to live out the vocation to which they were called, namely that of Sacramental and Eucharistic ministers. This structure would not remove the opportunity for priests who are great organizational leaders to use those gifts in service to the church. It would merely create the possibility, for those who may not have strong talents in the area of administration, of responding to a priestly vocation.

Every priest should be blessed with the opportunity to answer two simple questions in response to God's call: What am I able to provide as a priest that a lay leader cannot? How might I use my own unique interests, gifts, and talents to live out joyously my call to the priesthood? The answer to the first question is simple and universal. The only areas of ministry that require priestly ordination are celebration of the Sacraments and Eucharist. The answer to the second question is too often crushed under the administrative demands made by the present model of church.

There is a metaphor that presents another way to look at the problem. We have assumed that priests must be the shaman and the chieftain of our parish village. Might it be possible to let them simply be the shaman? Lest there be concern about governance and canon law, there is no confusion in the village that the individual that can trump the chieftain is the shaman. However, the holy man spends the bulk of his time tending to the spiritual needs of the community and leaves overall care of the community to others under his guidance.

This refocus of Catholic life from parish to diocese also creates greater flexibility in how individual priests realize their ministry. It creates greater flexibility for the diocese when relocating priests, as changes are less disruptive to local churches (the church loses only its "shaman," not its "chieftain" too). The support structures for priests move from the rectory (many of which have been experiences of solitude for some time) to fraternal connection within the diocese. This in turn reinforces an understanding of church that extends beyond the neighborhood or even city of residence. Issues of need and poverty become the collective concern of all Catholics within the diocese, not simply of the individual parishes where the problems are most manifest.

An additional benefit of this rethinking of the role of priest within the diocese is that it returns hierarchy to its original form. Every layer in hierarchical structure exists to serve the layer beneath, not the other way around. This is what separates true hierarchy from feudalism. The priest is no longer ruler over his fiefdom, but rather servant to the spiritual needs of the community.

Lay Leadership in a New Paradigm

As church structures are envisioned anew in local communities, increased leadership possibilities for laity begin to surface. There is at least one major concern that needs to be addressed for greater implementation of lay leadership. From where will this leadership come? Just as younger priests are receiving less experience before taking on a large parish, lay leaders also lack the opportunity to develop professionally before they take on the responsibility of ministering to communities with thousands of families.

What is the incubator for this new type of lay leader? Creating a competitive market from the best leaders of the church and business world seems a good first step. The greatest concern here is that while many business practices can greatly improve the efficiency of an organization, fundamental differences exist between churches and businesses. An overemphasis on the business acumen of lay leaders runs the risk of deemphasizing a caring, pastoral sensibility in leadership.

It is easy to assume the church is a service organization that exists to provide for the religious needs of its members. That is a neat, tidy, businesslike model. It is also folly and not at all connected to the gospel. It is folly because any church following this path puts itself in direct competition with every other business seeking to provide better service. It plays into the "cafeteria Catholicism" that is so bemoaned among church leadership. The mantra of this model is "Join our church and we will take care of you." Customer service rules the day. Eventually this devolves into ever more frequent requests for resources to maintain the appropriate level of customer service. As giving is on the honor system, members now evaluate the value of their experience to determine the investment they are willing to make. This is completely counter to giving out of a spirit of gratitude for our blessings and for the benefit of others. Ironically, stewardship campaigns frequently refer to the importance of providing value for membership.

It must be remembered that parish staff exist and are hired for only one reason: to empower the church to more fully live out the transformative gospel call to be the presence of Christ for the world. Whether they are hired for education, administration, youth ministry, or leadership, every staff position in a church exists to empower the community of faith to live out their baptismal call to serve. The best leaders serve the servants. Any church that hires people to serve itself is a dying church. It is dying because nobody joins a church to maintain a building. People join churches because they believe they can walk the journey of faith more fully within a community that is making a difference.

How can leadership better empower the community of faith to live out the gospel? Any church leadership that can effectively answer that question has found the answer for church growth—growth that is not only quantified by people in the pews but also qualified by a spirit of Christian charity in the streets of the community.

Current lay leaders often have great pastoral sensibility and a deep understanding of how to invite a community to live out its mission. However, the danger of drawing from lay leadership within the church is that current channels of training and development within the church don't always provide the organizational acumen and skills to direct ever-larger Catholic parishes.

An additional pool of potential to draw from is that of academia. But while academics are knowledgeable in the history and theology that provide the underpinnings for our communities of faith, frequently they lack the savvy of the business world and the pastoral sensibility of the church world.

What is needed most is a combination of the skills discussed above. Where is this unique combination to be found? What are the long-term incentives for individuals to plan for this type of personal and professional development? The upfront costs are high. The long-term outlook is uncertain when one prepares for leadership within a church in which organizing principles are in flux.

Beyond the Merger Model

There is an irony in the merger-church transformation that seems lost on many who are participating in it. In fighting to preserve the parish as base unit, we are losing the relational intimacy that makes parishes so appealing as social and cultural centers in the first place.

American Catholicism is undergoing a dramatic transformation. There is a conversation that appears absent in the midst of the rush to merger-size American Catholicism. What are the implications for how the average lay Catholic will live out a life of faith in the merger-community? Is it possible for a community to become larger and more relational at the same time? How does the church prevent the needs of individuals from falling through the cracks? From where will the new form of leadership required to lead the larger organizations come? What are the roles of priests, laity, and religious in the new structure?

There is a rich tradition of diverse organizational possibilities from which the American Catholic Church can draw as it discerns how best to empower nearly a quarter of all Americans to respond to their baptismal call. Exploring these options will require the church to rethink how leadership is identified and formed. It will require creativity and courage to rethink the most basic assumptions that are conjured when using words like *church*, *pastor*, and *parish*. It will take the insight to look beyond the poverty of the shortages that are initiating the move to merger-size the church into a mere facsimile of the megachurch up the street. A truly "universal" church should embrace all of these possibilities, for then Catholics will live up to the definition of their name.

10

PRESBYMERGENT

The Story of One Mainliner's Quest to Be a Loyal Radical

ADAM WALKER CLEAVELAND

We sat on the front steps of her house in Hagerman, Idaho, and I shared my plans to attend Princeton Theological Seminary in the fall. I had visited the school, enjoyed the community, and decided Princeton was where I would further my theological education. I explained the various perceived benefits of attending Princeton, but she was not convinced. Finally, my friend looked at me and said, "Why on earth are you going to Princeton? Isn't that the most *un*-Emergent school there is?" And there it was. I had just recently become an avid blogger and involved in this new movement, conversation, or whatever it was, and apparently I had chosen the school that was "the man" and would indoctrinate me into "the system," and I would lose all chances of ever *becoming* Emergent. At best, I was *submerging*.

Becoming Presbyterian

Before I begin to explain how I became involved with Emergent, it's important to understand one thing about my denominational heritage: it's a mixed bag. In his early twenties my father became a Christian through a Plymouth Brethren gathering in Kentucky, and my mother grew up in a large Mennonite family on an Illinois farm. I was dedicated (not baptized) as an infant in a Presbyterian Church (PC USA), and I went to a Nazarene church youth group in junior high, an Assemblies of God youth group in high school, and a variety of mainline, evangelical, and

---

Adam Walker Cleaveland is a husband (married to Sarah Walker Cleaveland), a blogger (pomomusings.com), a freelance designer (cleavedesign.com) and an MDiv/MA (youth ministry) student at Princeton Theological Seminary. Adam has been actively involved in two Presbyterian (PC USA) camping ministries and served as Director of Youth Ministries for Living Waters Presbyterian Church in Wendell, Idaho, for two years. Adam is a part of the Emergent Coordinating Group and on the ordination track with the Presbyterian Church (USA). He can be contacted at cleave@gmail.com.

nondenominational churches in college. To say I'm a denominational mutt is probably an understatement.

When someone asks how I chose to become Presbyterian, I usually shrug my shoulders and say something to the effect of "It seems to be the place that I've ended up—God must have something to do with that." Throughout my life, I've had a connection to PC (USA)–affiliated churches, colleges, and summer camps. After college graduation, I eventually found myself serving as director of youth ministries for a PC (USA) church in Wendell, Idaho. It's been an interesting journey, to say the least. As a freshman religion major, one of the most vexing theological crises I encountered was the question of God's will: what *was* God's will for my life? Through the counsel of a professor, I was able to see that the will of God was not one of life's ultimate secrets or a hidden treasure that needed to be carefully sought after. Rather, the will of God was in fact a way of life, a way of looking at the world, a way of relating to God and to the others in my life. Once I realized this, the questions that had been so debilitating for me, such as which Christian summer camp I would work at for the summer, became superfluous. While I still sought counsel and advice from close friends and family on major life decisions, I didn't let those decisions cause me much frustration. It was this new way of looking at the world that led me to the edge of a riverbank at Thousand Springs in Wendell, where I was about to be immersed into icy cold waters on Palm Sunday, my twenty-third birthday. I would arise a new creation, a baptized believer, a Presbyterian.

Remaining Presbyterian

I write this now as a member of the Presbyterian Church (USA), a seminarian at the largest PC (USA) seminary, and someone who is currently a candidate of the Presbyterian ordination process. I'm also an active blogger and I often receive emails from people who find my blog while searching for information related to Emergent, the PC (USA), or Princeton Seminary. The emails generally read something like this: "I grew up Presbyterian and am now a youth worker at a Presbyterian church. Yet I really resonate with a lot of this Emergent stuff I'm reading. So I'm not really sure what to do. I see you're both into Emergent stuff and also a Presbyterian. I'm writing to find out why you want to stay Presbyterian."

One recent email came from someone who was struggling to be, in his words, a faithful "Presbymergent."

In drafting my responses to these inquiries, I've needed to think seriously about what draws me to the Presbyterian Church. One of the questions on my application to become a candidate for ordination asked, "What does it mean to be Presbyterian?" When I think about how to answer this question, part of the answer stems from the fact that I have just sort of "ended up" here in this season of my life through my education, jobs, and friendships. In fact this is the answer I gave to my session (the governing board of a Presbyterian congregation) as I began the ordination process. When an Orthodox priest friend reflected on it with me, he sat silent for a moment and then said, "Well, that's okay, Adam. That tells me how you got here. But it tells me nothing about what's going to keep you here."

What is going to keep me in the Presbyterian Church? Honestly, there are some days I find myself asking that question more often than others. While I see the benefits of a process of ordination and the strict prerequisites (exams, psychological assessments, years of meeting with committees), it often feels more like a painful process of jumping through the right hoops than a helpful or Spirit-led process. Also many say the PC (USA) is dying; we lost around forty-one thousand members in 2004 alone. So why stay?

The first thing that comes to mind is the friendships that have developed during my time in the Presbyterian Church. Through intimate small groups during college and seminary, close mentors who were both professors and pastors, and fellow staff members at the camps where I spent summers, I have consistently been with people who have encouraged, challenged, and spoken truth into my life. Along the same lines, it's important to mention how significant the role of community is to the Presbyterian Church. A former pastor I worked with once said, "It's impossible to be a Presbyterian lone ranger." And really, it's true. The importance of community is ingrained in the Presbyterian system and reflected throughout our committees, polity, and potlucks. When I decided to begin the ordination process, my church's session recommended that I become an Inquirer (one who is "inquiring" about becoming a Presbyterian minister), and then the Committee on Preparation for Ministry recommended me to the Presbytery (the regional governing body). Both times, after interviewing me, they laid hands on me and prayed for me. The experience of having people lay hands on me and pray for my discernment and for God and God's Spirit to lead me was a beautiful picture of a community joining together to help guide someone through the process of discerning his call and future vocation.

Ecclesia reformata, semper reformanda: The church reformed and always reforming (or always being reformed). This is the Presbyterian and Reformed rallying cry. It reminds Presbyterians of the church's history and tradition, as well as the necessity to continue to be open to new waves of the Spirit. I appreciate that the Presbyterian Church is rooted in history. Presbyterians have a rich theological history and played a significant role in the sixteenth-century Protestant Reformation. Being part of a denomination that has significant historical roots gives one the sense of belonging to something bigger than oneself. When people realize their faith in God is much more than just a personal, individual decision, that they belong to a great "cloud of witnesses" of those who have gone before them, their vision of the church is both deepened and enlarged.

The church, as she finds herself in new and uncharted waters, needs to be able to adapt to different contexts, to continually reform. The motto above is sometimes clarified by adding *secundum verbi Dei*, so it means "the church reformed and always being reformed, according to the Word of God." Again, because of the communal nature of Presbyterians, change does not come about solely through an individual. Change and continual reformation come about through communities being guided by Word and Spirit, seeking to bring about the kingdom of God in a changing world. And there is plenty of room in Reformed theology to allow for an open and organic vision of church; I know of a few PC (USA) churches that are striving to meet the changing needs in their contexts and are becoming very creative in the ways they are seeking to minister. (The Portico in Charlotte, North Carolina, and Wicker Park Grace, in Chicago, are two examples.) Presbyterian ministers are now beginning to see new ways by which we can continue reforming the church. As with so many aspects of the Christian life, the ongoing reformation of the church is a journey and a process—a process that I, and many others, hope to join.

Becoming Emergent

Early in the morning on the last day of the National Youth Workers Convention, I slowly walked through a prayer labyrinth, a large maze-like path that was drawn out on a canvas that blanketed the floor of a dimly lit room. The accompanying audio CD instructed me to be still, to begin a journey inward, to become self-aware, to commune with the Divine, and then to journey outward. I looked in a mirror, dropped a stone in a bucket, and stepped in a sandbox. Each act had meaning. Each of the everyday objects took on new significance. I was not just dropping a rock into a bucket; I was relinquishing my fears, my doubts, and my concerns to God and receiving God's grace and peace. As I left the labyrinth that morning, I felt refreshed, still, and peaceful; I had encountered God in a new way.

I'll be the first to admit it: I am a convention junkie. I love the name tags, the freebies, the schedules, the networking. I attended the first Emergent convention in San Diego and found a group of people who were struggling with issues I struggled with, who were working hard to think of creative and new ways to worship, to think theologically, and to be the church in the world today. I was intrigued first by ideas of how worship could be done differently; I fell into awe of all things *alt.worship*. The alt.worship (alternative worship) movement began in Europe and was a way to create ways of connecting liturgy and worship experiences with new media. While alt.worship was certainly my gateway drug into Emergent, it became clear to me that Emergent was about much more than just this. Some in the emergent community seek authentic and creative ways of worshiping God today. Others seek an alternative vision for how to be a politically and socially conscious Christian. Still others continue looking at our theologies and ways of thinking and ask questions about what a new theology might look like in our changing world today. These projects excited me and continue to give me hope that Emergent and the church emerging are working to share the Good News of God's kingdom and to open that vision up for those who may not have been open to it before. That is something worth investing in.

Remaining Emergent

When it comes to thinking about the future, being involved with the emerging church seems to be a pretty natural step for me. For many reasons, the emerging church atmosphere, ethos, and trajectory just make sense to me. One of the joys of becoming more involved with the Emergent conversation has been the friendships I've been able to establish through emails, blogs, conventions, smaller gatherings, and regional cohorts. These friends helped and encouraged me as I was going through many changes in my thoughts on faith and church while being fairly isolated in southern Idaho.

One of the things I appreciate most about these friendships is the unspoken understanding that it is acceptable to question, critique, and deconstruct much of what we think and believe. Many today have more questions than answers, and the church has not always done a good job of creating safe places for people to ask questions and share concerns. Whether one is part of a more conservative evangelical congregation that is not open to questioning certain doctrines or a mainline Protestant church that is not open to questioning certain traditions or the way things have always been done, churches today often do not present themselves as being open to critique and deconstruction. I am grateful for the space Emergent has given to those like me who have been desperate to find a safe place for this process.

Those involved in the emerging church movement are not black-or-white thinkers. We strive to seek alternative visions and third ways beyond the polarities that have so dramatically seeped into our culture and our faith. This involves a true openness to the Spirit and a desire to avoid squelching anything that might be from and of the Spirit. This openness leads to safe places where friendship thrives, where people can come and be involved in the process of deconstructing ideas and practices, all while remaining open to the movements and new waves of the Spirit that can bring about renewal and reformation within the church today.

Some have criticized Emergent for focusing too much on deconstruction, implying that somehow Emergent will prove itself to be nothing more than one more fatalistic nihilism. It is clear to me, though, that Emergent's deconstruction is simply a necessary means to an end, and that end is clearly reconstruction, revitalization, and reform—the emergence of a new way of being Christian and a new way of being the church.

Identity and Creativity

So where does this leave those of us who find ourselves sitting on the fence between mainline denominations and those churches and groups within the church emerging? Is it necessary to choose between the two, or is there a way to integrate these two streams of the faith?

That integration may be found in a phrase used by Bob Hopkins, who copioneered the Anglican Church Planting Initiatives with his wife, Mary, in the United Kingdom. When asked about how those in mainline theological education could be interacting with those students interested in Emergent expressions of faith, Hopkins said mainline churches need to be encouraging and supporting "loyal radicals," those who stay on the *inside* to bring about creative, emergent expressions of historic faith.

In our North American context, it could be tempting for those who have grown up in mainline churches to leave their denominations so they can pursue more creative ways of being the church. However, if all leaders who felt frustrated by aspects of the PC (USA) were to leave, there would be an even greater denominational crisis. The PC (USA) knows it cannot afford to lose new leaders, so some mainline Presbyterians are finding renewed interest in church planting through the New Church Development Office of the PC (USA) and granting more freedom to those who want to create new expressions of the Presbyterian faith. Hopkins hopes that mainline and traditional denominations will create the freedom and permission-giving space for more nontraditional leaders to be able to stay within their denomination and bring about fresh expressions of a faith that is rooted in tradition.

One of the joys (for some) and frustrations (for others) of Emergent is that it is very hard to say, "This is what Emergent believes about X." There is great diversity of theological and methodological beliefs within Emergent. Some within Emergent do, in fact, have problems with the institutional aspect of mainline churches. They see them as standing in the way of vision, reform, and creative emergence within the church today. However, that is not the official Emergent stance by any means. There are many within the emerging church conversation who are deeply connected to mainline denominations. They believe mainline denominations have much to offer the emerging church movement, just as the emerging church has much to offer in return. Future pastors are yearning to be given the permission to be loyal radicals within their respective denominations. Each person has different reasons for remaining loyal to his or her tradition, while still being open to new movements within the broader Christian culture. Whatever the reason, it is important that these people be given the room to follow their calling to discover creative and new ways of being the mainline church in the twenty-first century.

I believe the PC (USA) has room for loyal radicals. It is not necessarily easy to be a grassroots or subversive voice in this context, but I doubt it would be easier in a different context. The problems of another environment (in a nondenominational church plant, for example) may be different from those in this environment, but they would still be problems. And I'm encouraged to hear of (and from) many in the PC (USA) who realize how much they stand to benefit from loyal radicals.

I am committed to the Presbyterian Church (USA). I choose to stay, as do many other Emergent thinkers in mainline denominations. Yet our staying may well lead to expressions of mainline faith that look far different from more familiar expressions. I trust and hope that mainline leaders will see these emerging expressions as reassuring signs of the Holy Spirit still at work in our midst. *Ecclesia reformata, semper reformanda.*

HOPE

PART 3

A Hopeful Faith

Christianity and the "God of Good Hope"

Tony Jones

The Cape of Good Hope is at the southern tip of the African continent. It was named such—*Cabo da Boa Esperança*—by John II of Portugal because of the great hope for sailors when they made it around the treacherous passage. But before John II, the same stretch of sea and land was called *Cabo das Tormentas*, the Cape of Storms. It's amazing what the shift of a word or phrase can do. It can shift our sensibilities, shift our perspective. It can open our imaginations to new vistas. Surely that slight shift in phrasing has had a momentous impact on myriad sailors over the past five centuries.

I'm asked a lot, "What is it that folks in the emerging church have in common?" People ask that because it's become clear that there's no statement of faith, no common set of practices, no denominational boundaries that quite capture the breadth of the movement. This, of course, is deeply frustrating for some. For others, however, it's the best news they've had in a long time.

So I've poked around, trying to figure out exactly what's going on in the emerging church, and in Emergent Village in particular. And if there's one core conviction that I can put my finger on, it's an *eschatology of hope*. What I mean is that the folks who hang around the emerging church tend to see goodness and light in God's future, not darkness and gnashing of teeth. While that may seem obvious to some followers of God, pop theology today is facing the other way. The evangelical psyche has been shaped by Frank Peretti, Tim LaHaye, and Jerry Jenkins into thinking that it's not getting better and better, it's getting worse and worse (and, if my acquaintances are any indication, that has rippled out to the mainline Protestant and Roman Catholic psyches too). Those novelists and the theologians who provide them their material take the view that we're in a downward spiral, and when things "down here" become bad enough, Jesus will return in glory.

But those of us represented in this book take the contrary view. God's promised future is *good*, and it awaits us, beckoning us forward. We're caught in the tractor beam of redemption and re-creation, and there's no sense fighting it, so we might as well cooperate.

Of course, there's a whole lot of conversation to be had about *how* we live into that good, *who* is being included and who's being left out, and *what* the future really should look like. The essays that follow are a few forays into those very questions. I hope that they may similarly shift your perspective, not unlike the sailor who thinks of the Cape of Good Hope rather than the Cape of Storms. Maybe it's not a 180-degree turnaround for you—maybe these essays provoke a shift of just a couple of points on the compass. The important thing is that when you start to look to the future with hope instead of dread, it really makes a bigger difference than you could ever imagine.

11

FOLLOWING JESUS INTO CULTURE

Emerging Church as Social Movement

RYAN BOLGER

God created cultures to order the world, and ultimately it is Christ who holds these cultures together. Cultures are fallen—they were meant to serve and liberate but instead they became oppressive. These cultural practices led humanity to practice idolatry through domination and fear. However, because these cultures are God's creation, they are not without hope.

Jesus did not reject culture; it is where he started with people. He engaged them and spoke their language. Jesus was not countercultural as much as he was nonconformed within culture. As a cultural insider, he embodied a message of life in those places where the culture advocated death. Jesus lived in two realms simultaneously—both within human culture and submitted to the reign of God.

Cultures influence the practice of religion in a given society. It is often very difficult for people to know the tendencies of their own culture, both in terms of its place in history (for example, modernity or post-modernity) and its relationship to the world powers (for example, as an empire or a colony). As difficult as it might be, it is especially helpful for Christ-followers to know the toxic aspects of their culture so that they might propose alternatives where appropriate.

Throughout history the church has taken on the forms and structures of its surrounding culture. This is not to be lamented—churches must culturally represent the very people that form their community. However, each and every culture is fallen, and so, if a local church desires to embody the reign of God, it must listen and allow for that same kingdom to offer critique.

Ryan Bolger (PhD) is assistant professor of church in contemporary culture in the School of Intercultural Studies, Fuller Theological Seminary. He teaches classes on contemporary culture, on Jesus, and on new forms of church. Ryan is the coauthor (with Eddie Gibbs) of *Emerging Churches: Creating Christian Community in Postmodern Cultures* (Baker, 2005).

Besides kingdom feedback, the church must listen to the culture as well. The church often creates its own subculture, apart from kingdom and apart from the surrounding culture. For the church to really serve as a "city on a hill" to those outside, it must dynamically interact with the surrounding culture in ways that make sense to those outside. In sum, the local church must listen to both kingdom and culture if it is to take Jesus's model of mission seriously.

The Church in Western Culture Today

Many subcultures in the West today are holistic. They see connections between art, spirituality, economics, and politics. They construct their world in webs and networks—not simply in linear fashion. They create their way of life around images rather than the printed word. As with all cultures, these changes represent both life-giving and destructive dynamics.

The church, if it is to be heard, must speak politically, spiritually, and artistically, using images and activities as its primary communication media. The church must not be naive—the medium truly is the message. While communicating through these forms, the church must offer embrace and critique to both the medium itself and the messages contained within. Although God created the cultures to order creation, because they are fallen, they must be transformed.

God's Mission

Prior to Jesus's preaching of the kingdom and the existence of the church is the mission of God. God demonstrated his mission in ancient Israel, in Jesus, in the early church, and in the various movements in church history. These were not alternative missions but various instances of God's single mission—restoring creation. The church today is a recipient of mission before it ever is an agent of mission. God's mission is open to all who desire to participate with God. Today churches do not need to discover their particular mission; rather, they must find God's mission, get behind it, and run with it. The church need not wrestle over what God's mission is in the world—to this day, God's mission resembles the work Jesus performed within Palestinian culture.

In Jesus we see the mission of God made flesh. At Pentecost the Holy Spirit empowered the church to continue the work of Jesus in the world. Just as Jesus was sent to Israel, so the church is sent to all other cultures. The Holy Spirit leads and sustains the church to embody the gospel in all contexts, until the end of time.

A kingdomlike church follows God's mission into the world because that is where God's mission is located. Such a church does not seek to create a "come-to-us" structure and convince others to become members—God's reign is much bigger than the membership rolls of local churches.

Those who follow God's reign embody Good News among those they know—whether in their workplace, their kids' clubs, their neighborhoods, even their faith community. They live with the understanding that primarily the gospel addresses how to live life—not solely one's eternal destination. The church has the opportunity to participate with God in the world's redemption. It is through the very lives of people that the gospel is made real.

Movements of the Reign of God

Jesus created a counter-temple movement infused with alternative perspectives on Torah. He challenged those activities from the outside, offered critique, and modeled a different way. While remaining within the macroculture of Judaism in his day, Jesus created kingdomlike alternatives to the temple practices that opposed God's reign, such as the priesthood, the temple, and the monarchy.

Renewal movements occur away from centers of institutional power, often in organic expressions on the periphery. Jesus and John baptized their followers into a movement, into an alternative way of being the people of God. The Israelites who came to the river Jordan repented of the way they understood their faith and prepared themselves for another way. They heard the message that God's reign was near, were baptized, and joined a movement within the religious structures of the day.

Kingdomlike movements provide a contrast to all other powers, even religious ones. They are not focused on a single issue; rather, they provide a contrast to all aspects of life—in the culture, in the economy, and within the social and political structures. When Christians live an alternative logic within these powers, they begin to transform those same powers.

Kingdomlike movements unmask the powers by naming them and living a different way within them. They demonstrate that the powers are not the ultimate authority. Because of the reign of God, these powers can no longer dominate.

Below I explore five aspects of these godlike movements.

A Communal Movement

Every activity Jesus performed he did in a sociopolitical context. Jesus could have simply sought to transform society at the macrolevel, but instead he created a microsociety to transform the culture. This 24/7 community addressed all of life. As a new type of family, they practiced alternative politics, economics, and social structure. The Sermon on the Mount served as their founding charter.

The main task of kingdomlike churches is to equip those within the community to serve under the reign of God. To embody this kingdom, community formation must be central and involves a practical training in the gospel: how to serve, how to forgive, how to love, and how to open up your home. More important than any programs, community formation provides an avenue for a person to enact an entirely different way of life.

Today those seeking to begin new churches must always ask kingdom questions. A local church is just another social institution—there is no guarantee that it reflects the kingdom of God. Only when the local community follows God's reign, both in its life as a microsociety and in its witness in the culture at large, does it serve to reflect God's kingdom.

A Movement of Reconciliation

Jesus transforms the notion of revolutionary. Although he could have been called a revolutionary, he advocated love instead of war. His followers would have followed him in a violent uprising, but Jesus chose not to perpetuate the aggression of the culture as a whole. He encouraged his communities to have no enemies but Satan and to forego all national loyalties. His movement was much different from the revolutionary movements that had gone before. He did not advocate hatred of the "out groups." Instead, he gathered the outsiders together.

The church, in kind, must involve all peoples who submit to God's rule, creating a new kind of people. They are to model a different way of human interaction between unlike parties. The church's new order is one of reconciliation, with different races, ages, ethnicities, genders, and classes coming together.

Church members must bring "outsiders" into the community or they will not learn the skills of reconciliation. The church's community life helps its people overcome their racism and their suspicion of those who are different and teaches them how to forgive. Within the faith community, people overcome their hatred so that loving becomes a real possibility in their witness.

Kingdomlike communities help heal divisions in the culture as well. These practitioners serve as advocates and guides. They demonstrate a life of inclusion, forgiveness, reconciliation, and nonviolence, and they invite the world to come into the church to learn these skills as well.

A Movement of Hospitality

Jesus announced that the poor would be liberated, that they would have enough, and that they would be included at the banquet table. Jesus announced Jubilee, a time where sharing would lead to overflowing, and he declared that the time of hunger was over.

Proclaiming the remission of debts, Jesus calls his followers to be agents of generosity. Today the church finds itself in the context of consumer capitalism, a culture where self-interested exchange feeds an insatiable desire. The church's challenge is to transform these exchanges into the Jubilee-type relationships of a gift economy. Perhaps now "release to the captive" might speak to the one in bondage to the never-ending cycle of consumer desire. A church that rebukes the powers of consumption might respond by consuming less—for example, by minimizing commuting, careerism, busyness, eating fast food, or buying clothing made in sweatshops.

The church faces the challenge of how to live in a consumer economy while turning the rules upside down—so that the poor win. The church must create practices that set free those oppressed by consumer capitalism, while endorsing and supporting those practices within a capitalist economy that offer relief to the poor, the outcast, and the environment. Living in this way provides a contrast to unmitigated desire.

As part of the witness of the kingdomlike church, the people will extend their family life to those outside, sharing what they have with others. Their actions in the workplace or neighborhood will model the gift rather than the exchange.

A Movement of Freedom

Jesus created a patriarchal-free community where rich and poor, men and women, insiders and outsiders were given equal space. Jesus addressed those without status as equal partners. Although the culture valued patriarchal relationships, Jesus created an alternative to this system. In his community there is no father—only mothers, brothers, and sisters.

If the church today is to follow Jesus in relation to power, the church must create a space for the governing of a domination-free movement—a community of true freedom. It must ascertain how to operate while refusing to exercise certain types of power, even for legitimate ends, and refusing to practice coercion of any kind, either physical or psychological.

Even those with the gift of leadership submit themselves to the kingdom of God—a sphere free of domination, finding ways to lead that exclude coercion of any kind. The same holds for managers, entrepreneurs, or missionary leaders, as well as counselors, managers, and technicians. If they create systems of control, they are not working in the kingdom of God and their practices must be transformed. In a domination-free system, the only viable mode of leadership is persuasion through servanthood.

Kingdomlike leaders create contexts where the reign of God is embraced and where the church is empowered to follow Jesus into the world. Facilitating these times of discernment, church leaders help develop the gifts of the less trained. There is no difference, in terms of power, between clergy and laity, as all are invited to make the important decisions and all have equal power to fulfill their calling in the community.

Jesus spoke to abuses of power in the religious-political establishment. He proclaimed an order of peace as opposed to an order of domination. Like Jesus, the church must speak to every sphere of society to cease dominating—to hear the outcast, the lowly, and the voiceless. We can serve as a model to those outside the church of what it is like for all to speak and to listen. In its witness, the church will prophetically denounce all efforts to silence or exclude people from conversation.

The church dispersed refuses to participate in controlling others. The people refuse to coerce others through position, influence, or physical force. If the church finds itself at the bottom of the social ladder, the people will pursue transformation through their willing subordination, never seeking to seize power. If the church is at the top of that same ladder, the people will still refuse to dominate.

A Movement of Spirituality

Jesus taught the early church community to bind and to loose, to confront and to forgive. Thus the community is formed in the ways of God. Kingdomlike churches pray together, confess their sins to one another, watch over each other, and encourage one another. At times, they suffer together—sometime as a result of one another. A kingdomlike church must be skilled in the disciplines of confession, confrontation, and forgiveness. It is these practices that mark these communities as unique in the world.

Within the culture the church shares in the prophetic critique concerning the dearth of spiritual practices. Spirituality discussions decry secularization, the fragmentation of life spheres, and the destruction of the environment. Centuries ago the church gave up on a secular critique and accepted its minimal role in the private sphere, but the kingdomlike church embraces these moves by the culture. However, these churches must exercise discernment—the practice of spirituality varies greatly from culture to culture, especially in regard to internalized religion.

As a movement, kingdomlike churches see themselves as a contrast to the assumptions in Christendom of what religion looks like. They observe that the fading powers of Christendom determined the form of their faithfulness. Kingdomlike churches must now establish that their primary allegiance is to the reign of God—not to American congregational forms of religion.

Resulting Worship

How do the alternative practices of this movement, this microsociety of reconciliation, generosity, and freedom within a postmodern culture, transform the practice of worship? There are certain worship practices that might undergo change as a consequence of the reign of God.

Overcoming many of the dualisms of modernity, liturgy becomes holistic, bringing the body back into worship as it welcomes mystery. Liturgy connects all of life with spirituality, overcoming the sacred/secular split. It is the language of the people, so it will speak in the common idiom of spirituality, frequently through images. Worship becomes a place where members gain skills in forgiving and receiving forgiveness.

Worship becomes a place where class divisions are overcome, and every group plays a role in its expression. There is no preferential treatment of one cultural practice over another. Worship demonstrates this new order, this new social reality of all peoples coming together to worship God. Through this experience, the congregation becomes a new kind of people. They rehearse how they are different from the world through acts of reconciling love. Worship makes two kinds of people one.

Worship might be marked by a common meal or by economic sharing. The Eucharist creates a context of abundance, and economic help is given to those who need it. The church service itself serves as the foretaste of the coming banquet.

Worship expresses the giftedness of every member, without one gift taking priority over others. Worship comprises a rich offering filled with many gifts, all equally respected. Each one comes to worship to create, participate, share, and to be heard in significant ways, and each one is needed to discern where the Holy Spirit is going. Liturgy demonstrates how the powers have been held back and demonstrates a different way to participate in power, and it shows that history is not determined by the powerful but by the Lamb.

To resemble Jesus in Palestine and Paul in the Roman Empire, a movement under God's reign must serve both as a contrast and as a transforming agent to the world's dominant political powers. If Christ-followers seek a kingdomlike life both in their church community and within the surrounding culture, they must operate as a movement that follows God's mission to the world. In this chapter we explored a few practices that communities in any context would practice if they are to embody the kingdom of God in their midst. It is hoped that this informal discussion might inspire others to take such a step. How to become a social movement that serves as a sign of the kingdom of God within culture remains the challenge of our time.

12

CHURCH EMERGING

Or Why I Still Use the Word *Postmodern* but with Mixed Feelings

BRIAN D. MCLAREN

A few years ago I wrote an article explaining why I still used the term *postmodern* to describe the issues many of us grapple with in the emerging church.[1] In spite of the controversy around the term, and in spite of its wildly varying usages, I felt it still served a good purpose. I still feel that way, even though many of my religious friends persist in using the word as a synonym for absolute nihilism, mindless relativism, moral anarchy, and other rotten things. The word has become the latest in a series of religious epithets (remember *secular humanist*?) used to discredit ideas or people or organizations that fail to conform to certain theological or ideological standards. Like its predecessors, *postmodern*-as-epithet will probably have a limited shelf life as a useful way to arouse fear, raise money, maintain boundaries, rush people to judgment, and inhibit careful thinking. Then some new term will appear and the tradition will continue.

A Slippery Slope

Meanwhile, some well-intentioned folk have reduced the whole conversation about modernity and postmodernity to an oversimplified and unnuanced argument about epistemology—the philosophical discipline that examines knowledge, doubt, and certainty. For these sincere people,

---

Brian D. McLaren is a pastor, author, speaker, and networker among innovative Christian leaders, thinkers, and activists. A frequent guest on television, radio, and news media programs, he has appeared on *Larry King Live*, *Religion & Ethics Newsweekly*, and *Nightline*. His work has also been covered in *Time* (where he was listed as one of America's twenty-five most influential evangelicals), *Christianity Today*, *Christian Century*, and many other print media. He is the author of several books, the most recent being *The Secret Message of Jesus* (W Publishing, 2006). He serves as a board member for Sojourners/Call to Renewal and Emergent Village and is on the international steering team for Emergent.

truth is an open-and-shut, black-and-white case. I get the feeling that either I hold their simple, commonsense view of epistemology (with its attendant understandings of such things as foundationalism, the correspondence theory of truth, and so on) or I have abandoned the truth entirely. Or short of that, I'm sliding blindly down a slippery slope that leads to hot places.

I don't want to argue with these good people about these matters. Partly, I'm too busy with other endeavors. Partly, I am not too concerned whether or not a person is a philosophical foundationalist, whether or not he or she agrees with (or understands) the correspondence theory of truth, or how enlightened he or she is about the Enlightenment, Descartes, Derrida, Reid, or Rorty. (Instead, I'm more concerned whether the person is doing justice, loving mercy, and walking humbly with God.) Partly, I'm aware that those who see postmodernism as truth decay are against something worth being against. Rather than unsettle or antagonize them and push them into new territories of questioning they don't want to explore, I'm happy to agree with them that yes, there are dangers and risks in postmodernism, and not push the matter any further. Secretly, I suppose, I hope that my agreement with them on the dangers of postmodernism might invite them to also take more seriously some of the corresponding dangers of modernity and the ways in which we have already slipped far down the slope in our accommodation to modernity—philosophically, socially, and politically, for example. In any case, I appreciate the fact that they are sounding a warning about the dangers of postmodernity because those dangers are—I acknowledge once again—very real.[2]

More important, though, I've become convinced that the conversation about modernity and postmodernity is the "tails" side of the coin, and the "heads" side is a related but different conversation. So I am hereby giving notice that I'm not interested in arguing with anyone about modernity and postmodernity, but I would very much like to engage in honest conversation about colonialism and postcolonialism.

By *colonialism*, I mean "the extension of a nation's sovereignty over territory and people outside its own boundaries, often to facilitate economic domination over their resources, labor, and usually markets. The term also refers to a set of beliefs used to legitimize or promote this system, especially the belief that the mores of the colonizer are superior to those of the colonized."[3]

I, a descendant of colonizers, cannot explore this subject without realizing that I am personally linked to the story of colonialism. Likewise, my nonwhite friends are part of the same story—my African American friends who are descendants of slaves who were bought and sold to work colonial plantations, my African and Latin American and Asian friends who are descendants of the colonized, my First Nations friends whose lands were stolen and whose ancestors endured attempted genocide. My ancestors profited from colonialism, and I am the heir of inescapable privileges that came at the expense of the colonized, while my friends are the heirs of colonialism's inescapable and irretrievable losses and disadvantages.[4]

Dark Side

It's not that postmodern thought is irrelevant to postcolonialism; the two are in fact more deeply related than many of my religious colleagues seem to realize. I see the postmodern conversation as a profoundly moral project in intention at least, a kind of corporate repentance among European intellectuals in the decades after the Holocaust. They began assessing the causes of the Holocaust, which led them to see a dark side in Western history, including colonialism. Coincidentally (or maybe not), at that very postwar moment, one colonized nation after another sought an end to colonial occupation and exploitation. Each colonial nation had to decide how brutal it would become in seeking to maintain its control; one by one, the colonial powers divested themselves of their colonial-era holdings.

As I see it, these European intellectuals diagnosed intuitively the disease that caused a range of related symptoms—including the Holocaust and colonialism—as an *excessive confidence* among Western Christians and the civilization they created. These Western Christians never seemed to question whether, for example, they had received the God-given right to take the lands and resources of people in the rest of the world. Nor did they seem capable of doubting that their own European culture was superior and advanced and civilized, which gave them the right to despise as "savage" all other cultures, annihilating and replacing them with white European culture. Nor did they seem capable of seeing the atrocities of their history as anything but anomalies, unrelated to anything inherent in their own cultures, corporate character, or beliefs.

Having made this diagnosis, these European intellectuals treated the cancer of excessive Western confidence with the chemotherapy of pluralism and then, when that didn't work, they mixed in the stronger chemotherapy of relativism. In this way, the postmodern project is an attempt to weaken Western overconfidence.

My religious friends seem quick to understand the weaknesses and dangers of the pluralist/relativist chemo cocktail (which is usually what they mean by the term *postmodernism*). One of my sons is a cancer survivor, so I too know something about the dangers of chemotherapy. But few of my religious friends seem able to acknowledge the existence, much less the dangers, of malignant, modern Western overconfidence—whether in the distant past or in the present. Again I cannot force them to ponder things they don't wish to ponder. But neither can they keep the rest of us from facing these facets of our history and taking them seriously and talking about them in light of our faith in Jesus Christ. Nowhere do the problems of excessive Western confidence become more clear than in the story of colonialism—and in the denial of its downsides in most of the so-called Christian West.

Two Protests

Whenever I bring the subject up, I hear two predictable responses. First comes the protest that all cultures have violence, injustice, and atrocities in their closets. To that, I respond, "Yes, but not all cultures claim to be based on the tradition that is rooted in the law and prophets of Judaism and in the life and teachings of Jesus. From those to whom much has been given, more is expected." Besides, one would be hard-pressed to excuse the magnitude of Western atrocities in the colonial era by saying, "They weren't so bad. Just think of what X did to Y."

Then comes the protest that the West has made great contributions to humanity. To that I respond, "Yes, that is true and cannot be overlooked. The West's contributions are as impressive as are her injustices. But the man who beats his wife can't excuse his violence by saying that he also supports her on a good salary and buys her nice clothes that cover up her bruises." The old Jewish proverb speaks truth to civilizations as well as to individuals: "Those who conceal their sins do not prosper, but those who confess and renounce them find mercy" (Prov. 28:13 TNIV). Without confession and truth telling, there can be no true reconciliation.

Recently Dr. Mabiala Kenzo wrote a powerful introduction to this subject. Kenzo is a Twa theologian from the Congo, so he is well positioned to see the ugly underbelly of colonialism: "One cannot underestimate the extent to which the global South has been impacted by the colonial experience. The gap that stands between the present and the pre-colonial past is unbridgeable." What was lost during colonialism can never be regained, Kenzo says. Those who gained so much from colonialism may prefer to leave the past behind and not face its dark side, but that is not so easy for those who lost so much. He continues to explain why postmodernism is seen as an ally of postcolonialism:

> Most non-Westerners seem to prefer to use the term *postcolonialism* to describe the struggle for identity in the non-Western cultural context today. Those non-Western thinkers who have embraced the notion of postcolonialism join hands with all those who, wherever they may be found, are seeking to come to terms with the experience of colonization and its aftermath. Postmodernism turns out to be an ally of postcolonialism in that those who are seeking to come to terms with the experience of colonization and its long-term effects see in postmodernism not only the possibility of an alternative discourse that affirms and celebrates otherness, but also a strategy for the "deconstruction of the concept, the authority, and assumed primacy of the category of 'the West.'"[5]

Proper Confidence?

That "assumed primacy . . . of the West" is Kenzo's description of what I'm calling the West's excessive confidence. Where postmodernism is failing to cure the disease, or where it has produced side effects that are potentially lethal, I wonder if a radical and progressive Christian faith can do a better job.[6] Will a vigorous Christian faith promote recognition and repentance of the West's colonial history? Or will it aid and abet ongoing denial, continuing to fuel Western—or, perhaps better said, American—excessive confidence by assuring it that its primacy is valid, perhaps even God-ordained? Will a postcolonial Christian faith challenge excessive confidence wherever it appears, without veering into the opposite danger of insufficient confidence, so that a proper confidence can emerge?

Many of the people who are most critical of Emergent conversations about postmodernity and postcolonialism, I have noticed, seem to package Christian faith and Western Civilization (or American Manifest Destiny) in a single box, so that the two are inseparable. But our brothers and sisters from the global South cannot follow that path so easily. They love Christ and have bonded with the Christian message, but they have long known the ugly colonial face of Western civilization. They are seeking to unbundle the package so they can keep Christianity, without Western civilization and its colonial discontents thrown in. Kenzo further explains:

> Theology in a postcolonial context is a highly political affair. Postcolonial theologies will not settle for a position at the margins of their Western counterparts. Rather, they surreptitiously seek to turn the margin into the centre, thereby disrupting the serenity grounded on the assumption that Western formulations are self-evident. In so doing they display a great deal of creativity. . . . One catches a glimpse of this creativity in theological projects that have recently come out of Africa, in which classical Christological categories inherited from Chalcedon are reopened to make room for African ones. The result is hybridized Christology where Christ is worshipped as "Chief" (Kabasele), "Ancestor" (Pobee, Bujo, Bediako, and Nyamiti), "Master of initiation" (Sanon), "Healer" (Kolié), or "Elder Brother" (Kabasele).[7]

Many of us (by no means all) in the United States and Europe who have been talking in recent years about postmodernity and postcolonialism are white Western Christians who have begun to wake up to Western Christianity's dark side. We realize that we are latecomers to a conversation that has been going on for a long, long time.

For example, African and African American Christians (Black theology) and Latin American Christians (liberation theology, integral missiology) have been hitting these themes with intelligence and passion for decades, but few of us listened to their spokespeople, whether it was Dr. King or Desmond Tutu, Gustavo Gutierrez or Rene Padilla. Eco-feminist theology—articulated by authors like Sallie McFague and Mary Grey—has explored the ways in which the Western approach to knowledge was also very much about Western males seizing and maintaining power.

As well, missionaries and missiologists from E. Stanley Jones to Lesslie Newbigin have seen colonialism from "both sides now" and have tried to speak the truth to the Western Christian community. Most recently, Native Christians like Richard Twiss, Terry LaBlanc, Randy Woodley, Ray Aldred, and others have been articulating a postcolonial critique of Western Christian colonialism. In many ways all of these voices echo what earlier Christian leaders (from Charles Finney to William Seymour to Walter Rauschenbusch to Clarence Jordan) had been saying: the modern Western understanding of the gospel was too often truncated, shallow, thin, bland, anemic, privatized, personalized, polarized, and compromised.

So, although participants in the Emergent conversation are arriving late to a conversation already in progress, we are here and eager to learn and contribute all we can.[8] Here in the United States we see large sectors of the Christian community associated with American hyperconfidence, white privilege, institutional racism, civil religion, neocolonialism, and nationalistic militarism—often fortified by a privatized faith in a privatized nationalistic/tribal god. We sense in many of the arguments about epistemology an unacknowledged power play in which we do not wish to participate. We find ourselves awakening to a pervasive mindset that feels incapable of self-doubt and is quick to judge "the other," slow to admit its own faults, eager to point out splinters in the eyes of others, but oblivious to the planks in its own.

That hyperconfident tone makes us all the more grateful to people like Kenzo, who help us Western Christians not only see ourselves and our culture through the perspective of another but also see new dimensions of the gospel of Jesus Christ. In the native idioms of nonwhite and nonwestern Christians, we are getting beyond what Kenzo calls the monotonous sameness of Western Christianity. Through them we are hearing new melodies and harmonies, new rhythms and overtones in the rich world music of the gospel that we had never before heard, and that music makes us want to dance. The Good News is richer, fuller, better, more radical than we had ever realized!

Kenzo writes:

> Evangelical faith encounters in postcolonial theology what it always wanted: a contextual theology for the so-called Third World. Indeed, for many years, evangelicals have championed the cause of a self-theologizing Church,

> which they argued is the fourth woefully needed addition to the classical three-selves of the indigenous Church (self-governing, self-supporting, and self-propagating). In postcolonial theologies, their dream has finally come true. The (subaltern) latecomer has finally spoken in her own native idiom. Evangelical faith, which has hitherto been articulated and formulated in the stable idiom of Western rationalism that guaranteed its sameness, suddenly finds itself confronted with other idioms that disturb both the stability of classical formulations and the appeal of sameness. Will evangelical faith break or stretch? Therein lies the question.[9]

The other day I was conversing with some friends about Kenzo's insights and his final haunting question when a new realization struck me. It was something I suppose I had known but had never articulated, and I felt electrified. *What are we in the so-called emerging churches seeking to emerge from?* I asked myself. *We are seeking to emerge from modern Western Christianity, from colonial Christianity, from Christianity as a "white man's religion."* (Perhaps this is why so many young white people across Europe and North America and elsewhere are distancing themselves from Christianity. As white people, they do not want to be part of a white man's religion either; that feels like a step backward or a malingering in a world that should be left behind.)

Not a Slice but a Growing Edge

In this way, we do not see ourselves as *the emerging church*—meaning a slice, sector, or division of the church that is roughly analogous to "the charismatic church" or "the seeker church." Instead, we see ourselves as the *church emerging*, meaning a growing edge of the church at large in all its forms, stretching from the margins into new territory beyond modern, Western Christianity.

That means we are emerging into a postcolonial faith, a post-Western faith—not a faith that wants to forget and deny the many blessings of Christian faith in Western idioms, but a faith that no longer wants to be in denial about the dark sides of our history. We are emerging into a new era of Christian faith as a "living color" global community, from a religion of conquest and control to a faith of collaborative mission and humble service. We are emerging from a version of faith that is wedded to various nationalisms, rationalisms, and political and economic ideologies into a new vision of prophetic faith that seeks God's kingdom and God's justice for all. We are emerging from a "two-party system" or "cold war" Christianity that is polarized and paralyzed by left/liberal and right/conservative cleavages, and we are emerging into an integral, holistic, creative, and transforming vision of the *missio Dei* in which we all participate as colaborers with God.[10]

It is immediately clear that this kind of emergence must lead to a convergence—in the West, across denominations and across current polarizations, a convergence of postconservatives and postliberals into what Hans Frei and Stanley Grenz termed a new "generous orthodoxy."[11] But no less important: we must forge a historic convergence of Christians from the West with our sisters and brothers from the global South and the East too—the descendants of the colonized who are beginning to articulate the gospel in their own idioms, not just echo the conventional Western translations of faith. Where we go from here, we must go together, not as colonizers and colonized, but as reconciled brothers and sisters in Christ, with a new humility, a new dignity, and a proper confidence.[12]

In this way we must go beyond simply condemning colonialism, which, once recognized, is an easy target. Instead, we have to embrace with regret the story of colonialism as our story, and then in some way we must seek to bring whatever good we can out of the situation. Those of us from the West, descendants of the colonizers, have a unique challenge in this regard. We are rich in resources gained at the expense of the colonized (money, technology, time, freedom) that can be used to serve them and to foster a more equitable and collaborative future. But we also have a bad habit of self-centeredness and domination, so we will have to invest our energy and resources generously while taking the "lower place," listening not lecturing, serving not rushing, earning but not demanding trust, learning and telling the truth about our own history, asking forgiveness, showing respect and honor, and receiving the gifts and treasures from other cultures that in the past we spurned or abused or exploited. We have to build a new relationship of mutual respect and creative collaboration—a kind of relationship that has never before existed.

These sentiments sound grandiose, you may be saying, and perhaps naive as well. I know. I felt the same way as I first thought them, and even now as I just wrote them. But once I articulated them, I found I couldn't shrink back to hoping for less.

The grandeur of this vision is what makes me want to avoid getting stuck in intramural debates about epistemology and the word *postmodern*. Those are Western debates from beginning to end, and to the degree we stay stuck in them we aren't emerging at all but are arguing about emerging. (That's not to say there is no place for such debates, but only to say that they themselves can be a kind of slippery slope—sliding back into Westerners talking to Westerners about Western preoccupations that ultimately reinforce Western domination. If, however, they prepare the way for new conversations, they have served their purpose well.) By advancing the conversation from postmodern to postcolonial, we build from theoretical matters of knowledge, language, truth, and certainty to intensely practical and ethical matters of violence, domination, justice, and power (remembering that injustice is, at heart, an abuse of God-given power). This seems to me to be the path of hope.

Center to Margins

Kenzo's question "Will evangelical faith break or stretch?" also applies to traditional (or mainline) Protestant faith, Roman Catholic faith, and Eastern Orthodox faith. I know that many of my traditional Protestant friends think they have this whole problem solved. They have had diversity training, after all. Now I'm all for diversity training, but I can't help but think that many of the struggles my traditional Protestant friends face are rooted in the fact that their structures are essentially colonial structures—designed not for empowerment at the margins but for control from the center, and the center is nearly always a place of white or Western privilege.

We must be realistic and acknowledge that many groups will neither break nor stretch; they will simply ignore this emergence and convergence and carry on with business as usual as long as they can. And many will react and oppose this emergence, seeking to maintain the hegemony of the West (and especially the United States) and the privileged position of Western (American) Christianity, perhaps even seeking a revival of crusading Christendom. But I hope that many of us will stretch and listen and learn. That will bring blessing to the church, and through the church, to the world. May this be the dream of the church emerging, our common prayer, and our shared mission for the adventure ahead. And may lesser conversations not distract us.

13

THE END OF REINVENTION

Mission Beyond Market Adoption Cycles

WILL SAMSON

Living out the mission of God has always required wrestling with three questions: Who is God? What is God doing in this context? and How can I be a part of this work of God? These concerns live in iterative tension with each other. However, because the contemporary Western church has assumed the answers to the first two questions, it spends most of its time wrestling with the third. The end result of this wrestling means a cycle of new marketing models that never ask more core missional questions. This chapter will show how our answers to the first two questions are often predicated on faulty assumptions, which has implications for our responses to the third question. It will end with a snapshot of how we might be formed to live missionally.

Who Is God?

Several years ago my wife and I were involved in a multivehicle accident on Interstate 95. The news coverage of the collision and the eyewitness accounts from nearby cars revealed the deep problems we humans have with pure objectivity, as each participant offered a slightly different account of the events. This should come as no surprise. Social theorists from Durkheim to Festinger have described the difficulty a person has in discussing an objective reality. Even when explaining a very real event, such as a car crash, each person interprets the phenomenon through

---

Will Samson is presently pursuing graduate studies in theology and sociology. He holds a BA from Liberty University and an MS in information systems from The George Washington University. Will and his wife, novelist Lisa Samson, and their family are participants in the life of Communality, a missional Christian community in the city of Lexington, Kentucky. Will serves on the Coordinating Group of Emergent Village and is on the Board of Advisors at Relational Tithe.

his or her own lens. How much more do we interpret God, a deeply metaphysical entity, through our own lenses?

Something shifted fundamentally in the theology of the church during the historical period known as the Enlightenment. Confronted with vast amounts of newly gathered scientific data, the church sought to create equally scientific arguments for God. Pascal, Descartes, and other thinkers during this period formulated a series of evidences for the existence of God. Contemporary Western theology is the philosophical heir of this reasoning.

Peruse the aisles of any Christian bookstore and you will see this scientific method at work. Books that purport to provide evidentiary proof of God fill the shelves. In Western culture the need for proof of God's existence dominates current theological thought. Of course this search for proof presumes that knowledge of God can be objectively demonstrated, the way a scientist would detail the laws of gravity or physics.

Prior to the Enlightenment there was greater understanding that the answer to the question Who is God? was not an objective fact, which could be separated from the subject asking the question. Even Aquinas, with his famous declarations regarding the rationality of Christian faith, argued that we cannot understand God *a priori*, or separate from verification. To Aquinas, God is not to be understood the way we understand natural laws. He argued instead that we need an *a posteriori* understanding of God, an understanding that follows our interaction with God. In light of this, it seems valid to ask whether God changed during the Enlightenment, or whether the change was in the church. Perhaps we have ceded a more authentic understanding of God to our cultural need for certainty.

The need for certainty in the sphere of theological inquiry is evident in contemporary conservative biblical scholarship, which is dominated by an objective, scientific approach to Scripture. Seminarians and lay educators in this tradition are trained to dissect the Bible in an effort to find the definitive truth about God. This is what George Lindbeck referred to as a cognitive, or propositional, approach to theological inquiry.[1]

A rallying cry of the Protestant Reformation was *sola scriptura*, or Scripture alone. And while this doctrine may have arisen as a necessary corrective to abuses of church leadership in the Reformation period, it is in full effect today. Preachers speak of the Bible as an instruction book or as the only data necessary for spiritual living. But this diminishes some critical elements of theological knowledge. *Sola scriptura* does not account for the history of the church in shaping our theological understanding, even though, ironically, it was the church itself that shaped and determined what we now know as Scripture. *Sola scriptura* also tends to downplay the role of God's Spirit in shaping the direction of the church. Of greatest importance to this discussion is the fact that often people subscribing to *sola scriptura* do not take into account the subjectivity of human interpreters.

To illustrate this point, three hundred participants from thirty different faith traditions attended a recent worship gathering. Each attendee came with a certain assumption about his or her faithfulness to both God and Scripture, and there was significant diversity of theological perspective represented in the group. But these three hundred people had gathered in one place for a similar purpose. Imagine the heterogeneity among more than one billion Christian adherents worldwide.

This is not to say we cannot discover God through Scripture. The Bible remains the one holy text that all the various streams of the Christian church have in common. Rather, it is to illustrate the lack of objectivity we have in our understanding of God when we use Scripture alone. To quote N. T. Wright on this matter: "We believe the Bible, so we had better understand all of the things in it to which our traditions . . . have made us blind."[2] Conservative, cognitive/propositional approaches to understanding God exclusively through the text often do not take fully into account the lack of objectivity of human readers, nor do they fully appreciate the biases we bring as subjective readers.

More liberal approaches to understanding God have focused on experience rather than Scripture. Lindbeck labeled an approach to theological inquiry "experiential-expressivist."[3] Adherents to this methodology seek aesthetic evidence for the nature and person of God. Even those who are not bound to scriptural evidence for all statements about the nature and character of God seek validation from their own experience. We are, it seems, people in need of proof.

But unmediated experience is as problematic as seeking an objective reading of the text. We are bound by culture, history, and language, generally and perhaps especially when we describe our spiritual experience. Therefore it seems presumptuous to believe that we can describe God apart from these factors.

So, as we seek to join the mission of God, we must admit our own failings to understand God fully. We must confess our inability to answer objectively and definitively the question Who is God? But we do not exist without hope. We belong to a long line of people who believe that God was revealed in the person and work of Christ. And while our inability to achieve objectivity may prevent a clear understanding of God, we can at least confess that the hope of Christ and the possibility of living in the story that he initiated give us a starting point for the mission of God in our time.

What Is God Doing in This Context?

Our lack of objectivity causes no less a struggle when we try to answer the question What is God doing in this context? Context refers to the location of our missional work. For some of us, that may be the inner city; for others, it may be the American suburbs; for still others, an African village. Each of us lives in a particular setting, a unique local culture with its own values, mores, and interpretive framework.

Contextual theology is rooted in the notion that God's kingdom is vast and diverse, and it is our task as followers of Jesus to understand the diversity of God's work in the world and join that effort. But this is not a simple task.

The Cultural Challenge

The first challenge to seeing what God is doing in our context is cultural in nature. We are immersed in, and active contributors to, our culture. Often theologians and pastors have asked about the relationship the church wishes to have with the culture.[4] Suffice it to say, the church is both affected by and affects culture.

As illustrated by the parable of the weeds in Matthew 13:24–30, God's kingdom is broad and may sometimes be difficult to distinguish from that which is not of God. This makes us uneasy. As Westerners we have an inbred fear of the untested or the unknown. To ask what God is doing in our context implies that we may not know the answer to the question, at least not fully. For many, this is like that bad dream we have where we show up to a big exam and have not studied. Any individual who is a product of a Western educational system thinks through the lens of the scientific method, and being open to new understandings of God's work in our time is not the kind of posture we have been trained to assume.

In the West we tend to learn about God's activity the way we learn other subjects. Consider, for example, the rather soft science of grammar. It begins with a simple song: "a, b, c, d, e, f, g . . ." This familiar pattern, the alphabet, is so ingrained that, if you learned English in a Western system, the tune we all learned likely floated through your mind as you read those letters. After learning the basic alphabet, we begin to learn words. Words soon come to be identified in particular ways—nouns, verbs, adjectives, and so on—and eventually we progress to learning how these different parts of speech interact with each other to form sentences. In school educators test students' knowledge of the rules of communication until they are sure of their facility with the language.

So, in a Western context, even something as basic as the rules of communication conform to a testable methodology. Compare this with more precise disciplines like chemistry and geometry, disciplines generally required of Western students, and you begin to see the level to which each of us has been trained to think within a particular cultural framework. Suggesting that God is doing something that may not conform to our previous understandings requires us to think more broadly. Assuming that God may be doing a "new thing" is not exactly testable.

Historical Bias

A second concern surfaces when seeking to understand God's work in the world, and that is one of historical bias. We may think it just a contemporary concern that Christ-followers care about doctrine more than Christian practice. And while this move toward certitude may have been shaped and strengthened by the Enlightenment, the church has struggled with this bias throughout her history. For example, the Council of Nicea, an ecumenical synod, met in 325 CE to affirm the divinity of Jesus and create a creedal statement that, although modified, has stood for more than sixteen hundred years as one of the most concise statements of Christian belief. It is helpful to have a common understanding of belief to which all who claim to be Christians can subscribe. But it also may be true that councils like that of Nicea set a precedent for the notion that people can be a part of the story of God through their belief in Jesus, regardless of how they act.

This notion of being able to join the work of God simply through belief statements has had a negative impact on the health of the church.

Consider that the insertion of three words—"and the Son"—into later iterations of the Nicene statement was one of the major factors in the split of 1054 CE into Western Catholicism and Eastern Orthodoxy. At another major delta in the church, the Protestant Reformation, the belief in justification by faith alone caused large parts of the church to split off from what was the global unified church.

Some would argue that these splits were necessary to correct false understandings of what it means to be the people of God. But this would raise a deeper question about the role of the church in interpreting the character and work of God in our culture. Lesslie Newbigin described the church as a "hermeneutic of the gospel."[5] So if by our actions we say that being right is more important than being together, what does that say about the God who formed our communities or how that God wishes to interact with contemporary humanity?

Fast forward five hundred years from the Reformation, and one can see the problem of belief without practice in multiple ways. The church has become captive to marketing metrics to verify her health. We don't often ask if people are being converted into "those who are being saved" (one well-known Christian organization can actually provide you with a "cost per conversion" rate of forty-one cents per soul for the evangelism work they are doing on the Web) or if more people are being shaped into the imitation of Christ or if the movement of God in a local context is causing people to "do justice, and to love kindness, and to walk humbly with [their] God" (Mic. 6:8 NRSV). Instead, we tend to ask about the number of individuals making salvation decisions, the number of people in our small groups, and the number of people who put their rear ends in the pew during our regular weekly gathering.

Individual conversion is vital and small-group involvement and church attendance are good things, but perhaps these metrics tend to be emphasized as measurements of the health of the church because they are easier to evaluate than the hard work of asking if the people who are following God in the way of Jesus are, in fact, becoming more and more conformed to the way of Jesus.

When asking, "What is God doing in this context?" we would like to assume that God is working through the organized public institution known as the church and that the sign of God's work is greater numbers. We have very little missional imagination that would allow us to see God at work in a multitude of places, both inside and outside of the institutional church and in both large and small congregations.

We should all work for more disciples to the way of Christ. This is our task as people who live in light of the Great Commission. But numbers alone do not answer the question of whether people are joining in the work of God in their context. Consider the work of evangelists such as Charles Finney and John Wesley. While both were deeply concerned that more and more people follow Jesus, they also recognized that conversion of the heart meant conversion of life. They cared deeply about what we today might call *social justice*. In today's society that phrase has become infused with all kinds of political meaning, but until recently, acting justly in our public political forums was an integral part of being a follower of Jesus.

Finney claimed to have helped more than five hundred thousand people convert to Jesus. Arguably he had more influence on contemporary forms of evangelism than anyone else in history. However, Finney was an abolitionist who regularly spoke against slavery. He even went so far as to deny the Eucharist to slaveholders.

Similarly, Wesley was an abolitionist and encouraged his Methodists to organize and help end slavery. He was also actively involved in prison reform. One wonders how he would respond to the conditions of the American prison system today.

Rather than ask what would cause people to act in ways that mark them as disciples of Christ, Christians have tended to ask what would compel people to act within their particular moral code, and what would cause people to elect others who conform to this view. This is true for the politically liberal as well as the politically conservative.

So then, as we ask, What is God doing in this context? we must analyze and confess our cultural and historical biases. We must acknowledge that, while God does not change, we must always seek to understand better the work of God in our time and in our context.

How Can I Be a Part of This?

Knowledge of God and God's work cannot be determined in a disinterested, scientific manner. But if this is true, what hope do we have for joining the work of God? Questions of God's activity simply cannot exist apart from a given community. And so as we seek to join the mission of God, a good first step is to see this mission as existing outside the individual.

Apart from a community-mediated sense of mission, our only hope is a detached model of corporate development. This was the story of the Western church in the twentieth century, and that century saw massive reinvention of the church. The move to a market-driven, megachurch style of ecclesiology is the most easily identified of these reinventions.

Ironically this reinvention has been detrimental to the growth of the church. According to the American Religious Identification Survey (ARIS), self-identification with the Christian faith in America diminished nearly 10 percent between 1990 and 2001. As we have focused on better product marketing and increasing our numbers, fewer people have "bought" the product.

One idea that is worth exploring in light of the issues this chapter has raised is that of a *social Christology*. What if we formed communities and social systems not only to interpret Christ for the larger culture but also to provide "communally authoritative rules of discourse, attitude, and action"?[6] This may be the best antidote to our lack of objectivity.

14

CONVERTING CHRISTIANITY

The End and Beginning of Faith

BARRY TAYLOR

God is nowhere. God is now here." In his book *Hey Nostradamus!* Douglas Coupland tells the story of Cheryl Anway, a Christian teen, pregnant and secretly married, who scribbles this epigram on her school binder before a rampaging trio of misfit classmates gun her down in a Columbine-style high school shooting.[1]

Since I read those words in Coupland's book a couple of years ago, I have been turning them over and over in my mind. For me, this linguistic trick sums up much of how I feel about the present condition of faith in the twenty-first century. The spacing of the letters transforms God from absent to present, and this is surely indicative of the current situation. God may have always been Immanuel ("God with us") to the church, but the same cannot be said of the wider culture.

Much has been said and written about the collapse of the secular project and the subsequent reenchantment of Western culture that is characterized by a rising interest in issues of faith and the "return of God" to the public realm. God, it seems, is a topic of interest once again, and in our postsecular world it is possible and permissible to speak of God and find a willing conversation partner in our culture.

But before we get too excited about the return of God to our cultural landscape, I think we should be aware that God's return is not a return to business as usual for religion, nor is it a wholesale embrace of traditional

---

Barry Taylor lives and works in Los Angeles, California. He has a master's degree in cross-cultural studies and a PhD in intercultural studies with an emphasis on the relationship between faith and contemporary culture. Barry teaches at Fuller Theological Seminary in California, where he has developed a number of courses focusing on the intersections between theology and popular culture. He also teaches advertising at the Art Center College of Design in Pasadena. Along with teaching, Barry is a songwriter and composer, recently working on film scores as well as with his own recordings. He travels widely as a lecturer and speaker at international events exploring emerging global culture. As a Brit living in "exile," he is constantly searching for the perfect cup of tea!

faiths by the broader culture. In fact the literary device Coupland uses resonates so much because it represents the ongoing tension that exists in the arena of faith today; God is both present *and* absent in that the return to God is not a return to traditional concepts and ideas of God. "Throughout history people have discarded a conception of God when it no longer works for them," wrote Karen Armstrong in her book *A History of God*.[2] Faith in the twenty-first century is not exclusively centered on concepts of God.

Postmod God

We live in a post-Nietzschean world of faith and spirituality. Nietzsche's declaration that God is dead still holds true, since interest in all things spiritual does not necessarily translate to a belief in a metaphysical God or the tenets and dogmas of a particular faith. The return to God we are experiencing today is not a resurrection of the premodern God as much as it is a new iteration of concepts of the divine, based not on medieval scholasticism or metaphysics but rather on the daring and often precarious notions of postmodern culture.

The challenges for Christian faith in times like these are immense. The vapor trails of Christianity remain on the cultural landscape, but the once dominant religion of the West no longer has the last word on matters of faith.[3] Whether "Christianity" has any future at all as a vibrant expression of faith in the Man from Galilee is a matter of debate as far as I am concerned. Perhaps the times call for something else, something other, not merely the repackaging of old metaphors (playing the "relevant" game), but a new incarnation of what it means to follow Jesus.

Traditional faiths of every kind are experiencing challenges to their hegemony, to their claims on the truth, and to their self-proclaimed right to speak authoritatively on behalf of God. The rise of fundamentalism seems to be a constant reminder that religion can be a source of chaos and confusion as well as a provider of comfort and consolation. For many, the former seems to outweigh the latter. This dynamic, which has only gathered more steam post–9/11, is just a small part of the erosion of confidence in traditional religion in our time.

The cultural perception of an immense difference between those who consider themselves "spiritual" and those who consider themselves "religious" is another example of the shift in our understanding of the divine.

What it means exactly when a person declares himself or herself to be "spiritual but not religious" is a matter of some debate. Some people find the word *spiritual* irritating, because it means nothing of any real substance, a marker for a sort of "wishy-washy" sentimentalism that passes itself off as real faith. Others have embraced it wholeheartedly, and the rise of "spiritual language" in sermons and discussions, as well as a growing interest in "spiritual directors" in many churches, point to an embrace of the term on some levels even among the "religious."

I don't think there is one definition for the term or for its usage. *Spirituality* is an umbrella word, a catchall concept used to characterize a commitment to the sacred elements of life. It defies a singular definition, lending to its fluidity, and its meaning is evolving.

One thing that it *does* signify, almost universally, is the rejection of traditional faiths as a primary source of connection to the divine. I would argue that traditional faiths are no longer the first resource that people go to for developing and nurturing their spiritual lives. Instead, traditional faiths function more as secondary archives from which new spiritual permutations are created. Those who do choose to explore their spiritual quests within traditional faith environments do so with very different eyes and intentions than previous generations of seekers have. It seems safe to say that spirituality *is* the religion of the twenty-first century. This is a dramatic shift, and one that some might contest, but the momentum seems to be toward this perspective.

It should come as no surprise to us that our understanding of religion is undergoing a transformation. In times of significant cultural change, all the ways in which we order ourselves socially are usually affected. For instance, religion as it was experienced in the post-Reformation period was quite unlike its pre-Reformation incarnation.[4] That faith in the postmodern world is showing itself to be markedly different from the faith in modernity only serves to underscore the significance of the cultural changes we are presently experiencing. *God is nowhere. God is now here.*

If then we truly find ourselves in a new situation, one in which the old ways simply no longer suffice, what then of the future for Christian faith? I have already raised the notion that there may not be a future for "Christianity," the religion of Christian faith. I mean no disrespect to historic Christianity when I make this comment, nor do I seek to simply dismiss centuries of faithful service, worship, and theology.

I think that the Christian faith has been held captive to a "pseudo-orthodoxy" for much of the late twentieth century. Christianity's love affair with modernity and its universalizing tendencies created a climate in which the general assumption has been that what constitutes Christian faith has been "settled," and therefore any challenge to the status quo is often rejected as unbiblical or unorthodox. The assumption is a singular understanding of the faith.[5] The easiest way to undermine different perspectives on issues like faith and practice during my lifetime has been to call someone's commitment to orthodoxy into question. But Christian faith is open to discussion. Historically it always has been. It can be questioned and reinterpreted. In fact I would argue that it is meant to be questioned and reinterpreted.

Religion is always a cultural production, and the role of sociocultural issues cannot be discounted from the ways in which we envision and understand faith.[6] Issues and questions raised by our particular cultural situation not only inform but shape the various ways in which we interpret the gospel. If there ever was a time to question the status quo, it is now.

Converting the Converted

For the rest of this chapter, I simply want to explore what the future might look like if we consider the past two thousand years as an evolution of faith and not as something that has been static and fixed, something that a few disgruntled people are trying to unravel and undermine.

What I offer is not complete by any stretch of the imagination. I realize that a short essay cannot do justice to most of the issues that I have raised thus far, and that I will have probably raised more questions than answers, but it is intended to generate conversation and ongoing reflection as much as anything else.

God is nowhere. God is now here.

The times in which we live are intense on any number of levels. The threat of terror haunts the world like a specter; issues of global poverty and disease are constant reminders of economic disparity and human despair. Our world has also recently been rocked by a series of natural disasters, the sheer force of which has raised renewed concerns about environmental issues and the ramifications of our commitment to fossil fuels, chemicals, and other resources on the planet. The impact of globalization and its many discontents in various parts of the world continue to be part of our daily lives. Along with this we in the West find ourselves drowning in choices, trying to balance our rampant materialism with a renewed desire for meaning and purpose.

A major focus for much of the church today appears to be geared toward self-preservation or maybe just toward maintaining the institution "as is." Everywhere we turn we see books, conferences, workshops, and a host of other resources that focus on what can be done to preserve the church, and we are willing, it seems, to employ any marketing device to make it happen. Trend watchers and marketing strategists offer ways in which churches can connect with the culture. Attempting to make Christianity viable again, we resort to branding and marketing it.

But what if we let go of our need for a branded and marketable entity and turn instead toward a new way of living and being in the world? This is not an entirely new idea. Dietrich Bonhoeffer posited a "religionless Christianity" in the 1940s. Perhaps it is an idea whose time has finally come. What if "religion"—and by this I mean the institutional and organizational form around faith—is no longer necessary for the future of faith?

Religions exist in certainty and sanctity; faith lives in inquiry and fluidity. The reason traditional faiths are having a hard time is that the present situation is one in which certainty is suspect and sanctity is being redefined. We should consider letting go of our obsession with certainty; we do, after all, "see through a glass darkly," as the apostle Paul reminds us. It is hard to claim clarity when shadows linger over what is revealed. The future of faith does not lie in the declaration of certainties, but in the living out of uncertainty. "Believing that one believes" is how philosopher Gianni Vattimo puts it: "To believe means having faith, conviction, or certainty in something, but also to opine—that is, to think with a certain degree of uncertainty."[7] Our declarations about matters of faith are always fragmentary and provisional.

This idea challenges religion's commitment to sanctity. Sanctity implies security and inviolability—the territory is delineated, the lines clearly drawn. Contemporary society is reluctant to draw such lines of division; sometimes it is difficult to tell where one idea ends and another begins.

One of the most interesting dynamics of the present time is the collapse of distinction between the sacred and the profane. Contemporary society allows for the "holy" to be found in the most unexpected places. As Christopher Partridge writes: "The new spiritual awakening makes use of thought-forms, ideas and practices, which are not at all alien to the majority of Westerners. They emerge from an essentially non-Christian religio-cultural milieu, a milieu that both resources and is resourced by popular culture."[8] The future of Christian faith lies in its ability to inhabit this gray world, not attempting to "sort it out" as much as to be available to help others navigate and negotiate the complexities that such a dynamic raises. To "go with the flow" might seem a trite way of describing theological engagement, but a commitment to fluidity and a willingness to swim in the cultural waters rather than insisting on one's own paddling pool is a necessary perspective.

All of these thoughts can be summarized as a commitment to weakness rather than strength. "Muscular Christianity" and "robust faith" are views that worked well in modernity's concrete world, but the viability of Christian faith in the twenty-first century is not guaranteed by claims to power and declarations of strengths and doctrinal postures. This is not a slide into relativism but a commitment to nondogmatic specificity. We can tell the gospel story without resorting to competition, exclusivism, or elitism.

God is nowhere. God is now here.

When discussing the conversion of African slaves to Christianity, W. E. B. Du Bois argued that Africans did not convert to Christianity but rather converted Christianity to the basic themes, rhythms, and interests of African religion.[9] In considering the future of Christian faith in the twenty-first century, I find this idea of reverse conversion to be really helpful.

The concerns of religion are different from those of faith. Religion is concerned with right belief, faith with believing in the right way. This was something that Jesus confronted continually in his encounters with the Pharisees. Their commitment to right belief actually led them to wrongful living, to exclusion, judgment, and prejudice. I believe our commitment to the religion of Christianity has led us into a cul-de-sac of ineffectuality and redundancy. Our concerns with converting the world to our way of looking at things are completely out of sync with the dynamics of faith in our time. We need a conversion of sorts, a reverse conversion, to the themes, rhythms, and interests of postsecular Western culture, not so that we become just like the culture, but so that our countercultural way of living can be seen from within the culture. I have heard a lot of sermons in my time about not being "of the world," but that is only part of the admonition from Jesus. For too long Christianity has attempted to exist outside of cultural situations, seeing itself as acultural, as if such a thing were truly possible. Perhaps this had some resonance in modernity, with its commitment to objective rationalism, but in today's world such a view seems hopelessly remote and out of touch.

I firmly believe that Jesus did his theology and lived out his life in the marketplace of the culture. His ministry was conducted outside the sacred spaces of his own faith tradition. His forays into sacred space and time were usually to deliver pronouncements and challenges to the religious establishment.

For the Christian faith to remain viable, we are going to have to let go of the attractional model—inviting people to come to us—and instead go to where they live, and to there live out our faith. A Chinese proverb says we should "Go to the people. Live among them, learn from them, love them, start with what they know, build on what they have."[10] The rhythm and content of this proverb offer some clues as to the actions we might take.

To learn from others requires that we listen to understand. Another chapter could be written on the positive influence silence might have on the Christian faith in postsecular times. "Start with what they know, build on what they have"—this shifts the ground of discourse from the abstract to the actual. Our theological engagement and concerns ought to be developed from the questions and needs of the world around us. For too long we have gone out into the world to tell people what we think they ought to know rather than seeking to discover what they are interested in and where they are looking for answers. This is reminiscent of Paul's encounter in Athens, a city devoted to questions of ultimate meaning, a place so intent on religious propriety that it erected an altar to an unknown god, just in case. Paul began with what they had and built from there. His declaration that God is not far from any one of us (see Acts 17:27) is a profound missional lesson for us all; we don't have to take God anywhere; we just have to discover where he is already at work.

God is nowhere. God is now here. God is present; God is absent. The future of faith rests in the tension between these words, and it is from this place of discomfort and complexity that new life emerges.

HOPE

PART 4

A Hopeful Way Forward

Theology of Practice, Practice of Theology

Doug Pagitt

The dance between theology and practice has been performed for all of humanity. The way we believe shapes what we do and what we do forms our belief. However, in recent times the integration of these partners has been threatened. Faith that focuses on one approach or the other—theology first or "What would Jesus do?"—is increasingly common.

But the integrated way makes more sense to many of us. We have seen this integration in the history of the Christian faith—the Scriptures come from and inform the church—in the interaction of people with one another (act kind and it makes you kind), even in the development of the brain, e.g., live under stress and the endorphins released reshape the brain. The integration of faith and practice is increasingly important to those living in our highly informed age.

It is into this dance that the hopeful Christian enters with excitement. In the following chapters you will find calls for a theology-shaped practice and a practice-shaped theology. Embedded in these writings is the assumption that gone are the days of believing that only after we have made cognitive assent to theological concepts can we turn to right living, or the opposite—when right life is formed, right belief will follow. And no longer are benefits promised for a system where practices trump understanding, intention, and meaning. Ahead are the days of a "new" way of understanding and living Christianity where there is no distinction in faith and practice. Many will rightly say to themselves on reading such words: *This is nothing new. This is just what the Christian faith has always called for—from Jesus to James—faith and works living in harmony.* To which I would say, "Amen." This pursuit is not something new to the faith, but far too often it is something new in our experience.

The world of physics has a history that may be instructive for the church in this integration. For hundreds of years physicists struggled with the concept of gravity. How was it that gravitational pull worked? Did an object send out a beam, which grabbed another object to exert its force? If so, how did this work, and which beam came first? How did one object affect the other? Finally Einstein answered the dilemma by suggesting another way of thinking of the entire system. Gravity was not a force applied by one object on the other, but rather the bending effect of space-time on all objects. His breakthrough was in understanding that space and time are not two things in the gravitational world but are better thought of as one thing: space-time. This is something that does not take brilliance to comprehend, but it takes an integrated way of understanding. Einstein was not making up new realities; he found what was always there, and he gave us a means by which we could understand reality.

This same rethinking is needed in the area of practice and theology. We need "theology-practice," where theology is not understood as the ivory tower activity of the elite and lived faith is not left to uninformed dilettantes. Ahead are the days when "multiple intelligences," as coined by Howard Gardner and popularized by Thomas Armstrong, are in play with all of the practices—those with long histories and those that are yet to be perfected.[1] What would Christian faith look like if all the intelligences we experience intersected with all the practices?

Armstrong and Gardner suggest that everyone has at least one of the following intelligences:

linguistic intelligence (word smart)
logical-mathematical intelligence (number-reasoning smart)
spatial intelligence (picture smart)
bodily-kinesthetic intelligence (body smart)
musical intelligence (music smart)
interpersonal intelligence (people smart)
intrapersonal intelligence (self smart)
naturalist intelligence (nature smart)[2]

This kind of integrated faith, where all that we know impacts all we do and what we do opens options for our knowing, will not only be a hallmark of a hopeful Christianity, but it will be a requirement for its emergence.

So as you read, you may realize that no one leader, no matter how competent, can develop this kind of integrated faith. For we all, regardless of pedigree, are intelligent and ignorant in different things. And in this world we need multiple intelligences and multiple practices combined in new ways for new opportunities that will result in new outcomes.

No one will be able to completely integrate his or her faith. Rather, we move into a world of interrelationship, where we are connecting theology and practice as well as connecting person to person and community to community. Our thoughts on how to begin such connections follow.

15

SALLY MORGENTHALER

LEADERSHIP IN A FLATTENED WORLD

Grassroots Culture and the Demise of the CEO Model

What is leadership in an age of unprecedented connectedness? When information is as accessible as the Blackberry in your back pocket? When the world no longer needs data brokers, when the word *authority* inspires only suspicion and revolt, and when business, political, and religious icons are deconstructed at the click of a mouse button? What does it really mean to be in charge of anything?

Nothing. Because, in the new and increasingly flattened world, being in charge is an illusion. Being in charge worked (and marginally so) only in a world of slow change, in a predictable universe where information (and thus, power) is ensconced in the hands of a few. But that world is gone. With the rise of the individual (the power of one) and the rise of the tribe (the power of one connected), all bets are off. From Al-Qaeda to the post-Katrina revolt to fragmenting retail markets to the small-enterprise explosion in India and China, we see the old world of "big and powerful" unraveling.

Still, we hang on to our illusions. We retreat into the old story: leadership as domination and control. Margaret Wheatley describes our desperate attempts to hang on to what is gone:

> Ever since uncertainty became our insistent twenty-first-century companion, leadership strategies have taken a great leap backward to the familiar

---

Sally Morgenthaler is recognized as an innovator in Christian practices worldwide. Her prophetic role among church leaders and local congregations continues to increase in denominational scope and impact, as her work now broadens into the arena of new forms of leadership and the untapped potential of women. Known best for her book, *Worship Evangelism* (Zondervan, 1998), Morgenthaler became a trusted interpreter of postmodern culture and a guide to the crucial shifts the North American church must make if it is to become a transforming presence within pre-Christian communities. In 2005, Morgenthaler launched a unique retreat model for women (entitled "Conversations," www.trueconversations.com) where discussions center around the female advantage in a flattened-culture relationship.

> territory of command and control. . . . How is it that we failed to learn that whenever we try to impose control on people and situations, we only serve to make them more uncontrollable? All of life resists control. All of life reacts to any process that inhibits its freedom to create itself. When we deny life's need to create, life pushes back. We label it resistance and invent strategies to overcome it. But we would do far better if we changed the story and learned how to invoke the resident creativity of those in our organizations. We need to work with these insistent creative forces or they will be provoked to work against us.[1]

Perhaps what Wheatley describes has always been a reality: human beings are simply wired to push back. Maybe the real shift is that now we have an unprecedented ability to do so. Now eighty-year-old Uncle Harold can post his very own book review on Amazon.com. Aunt Sarah can finally sell her Hummel collection, not at the neighborhood garage sale but on eBay. Now we have Google in our hip pockets, and our cell phones double as personal computers, televisions, cameras, video recorders, and stereo systems. Do we really get the significance of those sideways, post-terrorist clips from the bowels of a London subway system? Suddenly it actually matters that we exist, that we live in a certain place and time. No matter what our income or educational level, we can join the posse of several thousand bloggers and send CBS's Dan Rather a group message. A big and terrifyingly audible message: "Dan, we smell a rat. We know too much. Get the story right or get out."

To Know and Be Known

Having found our long-lost voices, not only are we finding ways to push back, we are moving out of anonymity to a fledgling, halting culture of communities. Yes, we may still crave cocoon time, but the Starbucks "third-place" concept—whether real or virtual—has literally revived what it is to have a public life.[2] From village-concept malls to Internet cafés, Listservs, chat rooms, match sites, video-gaming events, Texas Holdem parties, martini bars, and neighborhood 12-step groups, we're trying to figure out how to be in conversation with each other.

We may not be at the level of mature exchange in all of these venues, but even our attempts at community say something. At our deepest levels, we want to know and be known; we want to put a stamp on life.

And now that we've tasted what it is like to be noticed—to be connected and together, to make a difference—our expectation of influence is at an all-time high. Whether at work, in school, online, on our iPods, or at the Home Depot do-it-yourself design center, we want our stories, passions, preferences, and opinions to matter. And the most successful companies and innovations of the past fifteen years—eBay, Google, Amazon, Comcast On Demand, Match.com, Blizzard (multiplayer online video gaming), Starbucks, Netflix, Myspace.com, Apple's iPod Nano and iTunes, Blackberry, and others—have figured this out. Creating interactive, personalized experiences for their customers is primary. But these companies don't stop there. The value they have for significance—for participation and personal engagement—permeates their organizational structures as well. And the reason is as simple as the dollar sign. When their companies are interactive and self-organizing at their core, profits increase.

Leadership theorist Margaret Wheatley agrees: "We have known for nearly a half century that self-managed teams are far more productive than any other form of organizing. There is a clear correlation between participation and productivity. In fact, productivity gains in truly self-managed work environments are at minimum 35 percent higher than in traditionally managed organizations."[3]

Why are self-managed teams more productive? If personalized participation is such a high value in our culture, it is going to be indispensable in the place where people spend most of their time: work. People want to have their opinions heard. They want to push back on company practices without having to fear that their job is at stake. And they want to belong—to know their cohorts care what is going on in their lives as well as their minds. Self-managed teams make for a better, more connective work environment, and in turn, more productive workers.

Collective Intelligence

But there is another theory surrounding the success of self-managed teams that goes beyond mere social dynamics: people seem to make better decisions together than apart. They are collectively "more intelligent." James Surowiecki, in his book *The Wisdom of Crowds,* uses Google's wildly successful search engine technology as an example. Google pushed ahead of Yahoo! and every other search engine in the early 2000s. At the core of the Google system is a calculating method called "PageRank"—an algorithm that allows the collected human wisdom of the web to cull for essential information and rate the results for relevance. Surowiecki explains: "In that 0.12 seconds, what Google is doing is asking the entire Web to decide which page contains the most useful information, and the page that gets the most votes goes first on the list. And that page, or the one immediately beneath it, more often than not is in fact the one with the most useful information."[4]

Collective intelligence isn't just about the aggregate human brain on the Internet, however. It is increasingly how the best business, scientific, and creative work gets done. In its internal operations, Google applies the same principle of groupthink that it does to its technology. Employees are encouraged to post ideas for new products on an internal website. Then colleagues vote for their favorite idea. Those ideas with the most votes get pushed to the top for strategic attention.[5] In 2005 Google sponsored a contest that drew 14,500 eager programmers. The contest resulted in an entire library of competitive new products.

In *The Wisdom of Crowds* Surowiecki contrasts traditional, top-down decision making with collective intelligence:

> [The wisdom of crowds] . . . helps explain why, for the past fifteen years, a few hundred amateur traders in the middle of Iowa have done a better job of predicting election results than Gallup polls have. The wisdom of crowds has something to tell us about why the stock market works (and about why, every so often, it stops working). . . . It's essential to good science, and it has the potential to make a profound difference in the way companies do business. . . . We feel the need to "chase the expert." [But] the argument of this book is that chasing the expert is a mistake, and a costly one at that. We should stop hunting and ask the crowd (which, of course, includes the geniuses as well as everyone else) instead. Chances are, it knows.[6]

Surowiecki's summary of the scientific collaboration involved in the discovery of the SARS virus is riveting. On March 17, 2003, after China had announced the spread of an unknown and deadly virus, the World Health Organization embarked on an unprecedented effort termed the "collaborative multi-center research project." By April 16 they announced their findings: the Corona virus was the one that had caused SARS. By isolating it so quickly, they were able to save the lives of potentially millions of people. The most incredible aspect of this project, however, was that no one was actually "in charge." Surowiecki explains:

> Although WHO orchestrated the creation of the network of labs, there was no one at the top dictating what different labs would do, what viruses or samples they would work on, or how information would be exchanged. The labs agreed that they would share all the relevant data they had, and they agreed to talk every morning, but other than that it was really up to them to make the collaboration work. . . . In the absence of top-down direction, the laboratories did a remarkably good job of organizing themselves. The collaborative nature of the project gave each lab the freedom to focus on what it believed to be the most promising lines of investigation. . . . And the result was that this cobbled-together multinational alliance found an answer to its problem as quickly and efficiently as any top-down organization could have.[7]

Missing the Memo

Significance, influence, interaction, collective intelligence—all of these values describe an essential shift from passivity to reflexivity. We are no longer content to travel in lockstep fashion through life like faceless, isolated units performing our one little job on an assembly line. This attitudinal shift is nothing short of revolutionary. True to form, Western Christendom seems oblivious to its implications. But it is the entrepreneurial church (congregations of roughly one thousand and above) that seems particularly clueless about the shift from the passive to the reflexive. And this, despite all its posturing about cultural relevance.

This disconnect shouldn't really surprise us. Large-church leaders have been trained in the modern, command-and-control paradigm for thirty years. Here, organizations aren't seen so much as gatherings of people with a common purpose but as machines. There is no irony here. Machine parts don't have minds or muscles to flex. They don't contribute to a process or innovate improvements. Machine parts simply do their job, which is, of course, to keep the machine functioning.

The mechanical paradigm or organization largely explains why modern church leaders are trained as CEOs, not shepherds. Sheep have their own ideas of what, where, and when they want to eat. They may not want to lie down by quiet waters and go to sleep at eight. They just might want to check out the watercress down by the streambed. Or they might want to head out over the next ridge and see if there are any other flocks out there. Conveniently, machine parts don't get ideas. They just get to work, and they work according to specification.

Church members who don't comprehend this three-decade shift in leadership paradigms are frustrated that their CEO pastor is so self-absorbed. They were looking for a shepherd—albeit, one with a big name and a big flock. Instead, they ended up with a "my-way-or-the-highway" autocrat—a top-down aficionado whose ecclesiastical machine whirs only to the sound of his own voice and functions tightly within the parameters of his own limited vision.

One doesn't have to be on the pastors' conference circuit long to figure out that prime-time clergy (ages forty to fifty-five) are marinated in this kind of thinking. They have been told repeatedly that this is the only leadership model that will ensure success. (And make no mistake—in new millennium America, success equals the greatest number of seats filled on Sunday morning.) Theirs is a mono-vocal, mono-vision world—one that affords the most uniformity and thus the most control. It is a world of hyperpragmatics where the ends (church growth) can justify the most dehumanizing of processes.

Pity the member who questions the machine and develops any significant influence. Sooner or later that member will be disposed of—shunned, silenced, and quietly removed from any position of authority on staff, boards, worship teams, or within the most lowly of programs. Unwittingly this member has run headlong into an industrial age anachronism: "the great man with the plan" methodology. And he or she has lost.

But it is not only individual members who lose. It is God's kingdom and the waiting world that is being sacrificed, sacrificed on the altar of pastoral ego. The question is, how long can these antiquated, top-down systems last? As long as people will let them. In a push-back world, hierarchy can function only in the womb of passivity, which may be good news—at least on the survival level—for big religion. Because, if there is anything the entrepreneurial church is good at creating, it is compliant cultures—those Stepford-like minicities populated with otherwise savvy, creative human beings. Yet these otherwise savvy children of God somehow missed the memo: they have a brain, a voice, and a Jacobesque call to wrestle, not only with the living God, but with whatever institution claims to hold all truth inside its too perfect confines. Is it any wonder that megachurches proliferate in areas of the country where the church attendance percentages are well above the national norm?[8] This is not quantum physics. It's the law of supply and demand. Entrepreneurial churches thrive in the most churched areas of the country because they are populated with the already churched, not the unchurched. And their leaders know this, despite their incessant outreach-speak. They know who their real target market is. It is hothouse Christians. And if hothouse Christians are anything, they are passive.

With passivity an apparent requirement for participation in big-church America, it is no wonder that most new world citizens wouldn't put so much as a tire mark on our parking lots. Maybe they get what we refuse to get: *super-sized ecclesia is as much about power as it is about God.* With luxurious facilities bordering on the obscene, organizational hierarchies designed to feed pastoral ego, and constituencies of the robotically religious (who else would tolerate living in a machine?), it's not hard to figure out that one's story, creativity, and opinions aren't welcome. Newsflash: the "Forty Days of Honest Dialogue" campaign is *not* coming to your local suburban church-plex anytime soon. So much for relevance in a reflexive culture, the members of which will most likely keep driving past our edifices. No one has to tell a new world citizen that power-and-control religion is about monologue, not dialogue. It is about one leader's vision; one take on what God is up to in the community, the nation, and the world; one single, often blurry, and out-of-context frame in this speeding movie we call life.

Sameness as Terminal Illness

Passive systems are systems of sameness. Yet sameness is eventually terminal. Ask any biologist and he or she will tell you that diversity and the adaptability necessary to sustain it are exactly what is required for living systems to thrive. Eliminate even a few species from an ecosystem, and the system begins to fail. So it is in human systems. We need difference, not because it looks good to the outside world, not because it is mandated at some denominational level, but because it is healthy. We think, work, learn, respond, and create better in the midst of a rich tapestry of the human family. Richard Florida, in his book *The Rise of the Creative Class,*[9] researches those cities on the cutting edge of innovation, and they all have one thing in common: a high diversity of people groups and lifestyles. Surowiecki comments about our penchant for sameness:

> Groups that are too much alike find it harder to keep learning because each member is bringing less and less to the table. Homogeneous groups are great at doing what they do well, but they become progressively less able to investigate alternatives. . . . [They spend] too much time exploiting and not enough time exploring. . . . But, if you can assemble a diverse group of people who possess varying degrees of knowledge and insight, you're better off entrusting it with major decisions rather than leaving them in the hands of one or two people, no matter how smart those people are.[10]

Diversity may well be one of the primary keys to innovation, but it is hardly a lived value within entrepreneurial church circles, whether they are comprised of baby boomers or shaved-hair twentysomethings. In modern, mono-vocal religion, the lack of substantive influence by people of color, females, and singles is appalling. For instance, females make up well over 60 percent of the average entrepreneurial congregation's constituency, while their representation as leaders outside the realm of children's and women's programs is usually less than 1 percent. Those few who are given staff or lay positions in nontraditional areas are rarely more than glorified clerks or assistants. The female staff member may have a plaque on her door that indicates she is a respected part of the "team." She and her female volunteer cohort may even have their names in the bulletin as heads of programs, but they know what is really expected of them. It is to do the mundane, lower-level work of getting things done. Ultimately, it is to keep the lie alive—to feign diversity in a system that has no interest in actually embracing it.

The Neutralized Voices of Women

When it comes to women, what we are actually seeing within big-box church is the engineered neutralization of well over half of the human voices.[11] And it is the case, not just in entrepreneurial congregations with an average age of forty or fifty, but surprisingly, in church plants with an average age of twenty-five to thirty. To quote Einstein, "No problem can be solved from the level of thinking that created it." And that statement describes twenty- and thirtysomething church circles only too accurately. In the case of diversity, most young church leaders are blithely oblivious to their entrenchment in patriarchy and the command-control systems inherent to it.

The debilitating DNA of patriarchy—hierarchical organizational structures and their marginalization of the powerless—is tenacious, and to shake it loose will take an enormous amount of intentional, humbling work. But shake it we must, because the reality is this: hierarchy (command and control) fails to move the reflexive souls of new world citizens, regardless of gender or race. It simply ensures their absence. And in case we haven't noticed, there are now a plethora of spiritual experiences waiting for them outside the cloning parlors of big churchdom. Carole Gilligan is right: "Hierarchy always creates an underground."[12] These days, undergrounds simply vote with their feet and go elsewhere, somewhere they can talk back, wrestle, contribute, make a difference, have a voice, challenge Dan Rather, or join a prayer circle on Beliefnet.

If we really can't accept the reality of the flattened, antihierarchical world described in Thomas Friedman's *The World Is Flat*,[13] then perhaps we should take a look at Scripture and see what God had in mind. Jesus flattened the universe to reach it. God Incarnate—the Omnipotent, Omniscient, and Infinite—leaves the realms of glory, subjecting himself to human existence and pouring himself out for the sake of all creation. This is hierarchy confounded, power and position undone. And Paul's impassioned plea to the Philippians encapsulates this divine deconstruction of dominance so perfectly that, to this day, it is considered to be the great prayer of the church—one of the clearest and most compelling expressions of the gospel in any form. Yes, according to Jesus, the world is indeed flat. He flattened it himself.

> In your relationships with one another, have the same attitude of mind Christ Jesus had: Who, being in very nature God, did not consider equality with God something to be used to his own advantage; rather, he made himself nothing by taking the very nature of a servant, being made in human likeness. And being found in appearance as a human being, he humbled himself by becoming obedient to death—even death on a cross!
>
> Philippians 2:5–8 TNIV

Jesus's flattened world was no more clearly evident than in his relationship to women. He didn't draw them out just to comfort them or even to elevate them out of their oppression. That he did, but first and foremost, he drew them out for the sake of the kingdom. Their obvious discernment, strength, vision, courage, and ready response of faith made them the logical forerunners in the spread of the gospel. Who they were qualified them for leadership, which is exactly why Jesus trusted them (and trusted them first) with some of the greatest truths of his Person and ministry.

Jesus first revealed his identity as the Son of God to a woman—and an outcast woman at that (John 4). She responded (at great risk) by evangelizing. It took a woman to understand that Jesus was to be crucified, even though Jesus had told his disciples what was to happen (Matt. 26:6–13). She responded (again, at great risk) in profound grief and worship, anointing Jesus's feet with a perfume that had cost her everything and with her tears. Jesus affirmed her act as exemplary, as an act of leadership to the rest of the world. "I tell you the truth, wherever the Good News is preached in all the world, what this woman has done will be told, and people will remember her" (v. 13 NCV).

Finally, women were the first to see the resurrected Christ (Luke 24:1–12). Was that an accident? Hardly. Again, Jesus trusted that not only would these women believe, but in believing they would do the hard thing—risk not being heard and not being believed. Which, of course, was the case. The consequence of their obedient, apostolic act—encountering the risen Son of God and voicing what they had seen and heard—was not much different from what women today experience within the patriarchy of big-church. Those women who see and hear God well and speak about what they see and hear can expect, in too many cases, to be dismissed.

Many women see and hear God well. But they also tend to see people well and the systems of relationships people create, whether in personal or business spheres. Business experts are now observing the remarkable feminine tenacity in the fight for collaborative systems. Their larger vision seems to be long-term, organizational health, with many sacrificing reputation and easy advancement to flatten top-heavy, unresponsive structures. Peter Senge, one of the world's most respected voices on leadership and culture, is struck by the disproportionate number of women who are "making things happen," especially when it comes to durable, organizational change. He observes: "Women managers and executives are leading many of the most important sustainability innovations. . . . They seem especially willing to take on long-term issues that deal with imbalances in the system as a whole."[14]

Women also seem more comfortable with ambiguity, unpredictability, and crisis than their male counterparts. Not surprisingly, all three of these realities are inherent to the postmodern context. William Bergquist, in his groundbreaking book *The Postmodern Organization*, described the kind of leader that the postmodern world requires. And he places women at the forefront:

> What will be the nature of the newly emerging postmodern leader? He or she will be one who can master the unexpected, and often unwanted. He or she (and more often, it will be she) must be able to tolerate ambiguity. Most importantly, the postmodern leader will acknowledge and even generally anticipate the occurrence and impact of rogue events (i.e., those unforeseen incidents that occur from within the system or outside of it).[15]

Is the anticontrol, relational, intuitive edge Bergquist describes here the sole hegemony of the female? One would be hard pressed to find such a view among sociologists and psychologists. Even populist works underpin a more holistic perspective. Malcom Gladwell, in his bestselling book *Blink,*[16] proposes that relational/intuitive propensities—those necessary for effective systems thinking and certainly for handling irreversible change—are a common denominator of all humans. He contends that most of us, including many women, have simply learned to mute or silence right-brained information, especially in the modern era.

Muting Intuition

Psychologist Carol Gilligan is famous for her concept of muting—of editing the deeper, intuitive self. In her seminal book *In a Different Voice*[17] (see also her latest work, *The Birth of Pleasure*[18]), she traces the severe editing of the relational/intuitive voice in males to early socialization. This socialization culminates at about age eight, when boys adopt a more distant, objectified interaction with the world—one that replaces interdependence with independence, and relationships with objects. This socially mandated flight from the relational in young boys also results in a constriction of the emotional range, an enforced editing of what are perceived to be "weaker" emotional expressions: sensing, caring, attachment, compassion, grief, and so on. The result is what Gilligan refers to as "voicing-over": a pseudomale orientation to the world that is less attuned to the forces of connection and certainly less attuned to what we have come to know as right-brain operations. The strong attraction evangelical men have to neopatriarchal works, such as John Eldredge's *Wild at Heart,*[19] may actually be rooted in what Gilligan describes as the socialized amputation of the male relational/intuitive bent. In his book Eldredge actually romanticizes the all-too-familiar male caricature, the male cut off from the expressive and vulnerable self of early boyhood, the self-sufficient, invulnerable, impenetrable rescuer. Perhaps, when one has little memory of a complex self, caricature is the best one can hope for.

Editing the authentic self is not only a male problem. Much of Gilligan's work focuses on how girls edit themselves. She contends that girls begin the voicing-over process sometime around puberty. Anywhere from the age of ten to twelve, girls start a process of conscious silencing. But not only do they muzzle one sphere of knowledge as boys do, they muzzle both their rational and intuitive insights. The reason is simple. In our persistently patriarchal culture, females who know what they know and speak what they know—whatever the source of their knowing—are at risk. Early on, girls figure out that knowledge is power. And power, even in the new-millennium West, is still a male birthright. For a female, to know anything and then to speak what she knows is a fairly certain path to rejection. In "great man with the plan" circles, whether they are Dockers big-church or frayed-jeans hip, it is a sure path.

Yet what happens when women begin to release their voices? They begin to understand just how well they are wired to lead in the new "flattened" landscape. If the best leadership in the postmodern setting is connective, intuitive, and responsive at its core—if it is about the nativity of God's work in community versus captivity to one person's and one gender's ego and agenda—then the gutting of female influence in the kingdom is not only brainless, it is suicidal.

Female Christ-followers who possess true leadership skills do not need to lead because it is politically correct. Neither do they need to lead to assuage what is most often a millimeter-thin veneer of male guilt. Women with leadership abilities need to lead because, more often than not, they get this new world and they get it really well. In a world weary of hyperindividualism, top-down systems, pedestal personalities, and I-win-you-lose dichotomies, the natural feminine resonance with the flattened world—conversation, collaboration, participation, influence, presence, collective intelligence, and empowerment—has raised the cultural bar for what true leadership is and does.

Leadership in a truly flattened world has no precedents. Never in the history of humankind have individuals and communities had the power to influence so much, so quickly. The rules of engagement have changed, and they have changed in favor of those who leave the addictive world of hierarchy to function relationally, intuitively, systemically, and contextually. Male leaders—yes, even the male leaders of entrepreneurial churchdom—know this at their core. They realize they're playing a deadly endgame and that the hierarchical clock is ticking. More than that, however, they have a deep knowledge of another way of being, though they may rail against it, retreating for comfort into cardboard cutout versions of both leadership and masculinity. But if they're honest, they know they have tasted the new essence that is required of leadership now. They know it in the recesses of their boyhood memories and in the experience of intimacy, art, music, story, film, hospital prayers, and all that human beings do best, together. Those who are up to the challenge of the new world will draw on that deep knowledge. And they will look to the marginalized—including women—not as necessary evils in a politically correct world, but as their own leaders, mentors, and guides. The brightest will finally dump the myth of the great man, park their egos, and follow the one Great Man into the relinquishment of power.

16

THE SWEET PROBLEM OF INCLUSIVENESS

Finding Our God in the Other

SAMIR SELMANOVIC

Chomina, chief of the Algonquin tribe, lost all his men protecting an expedition of the French colonizers of Quebec as they traveled fifteen hundred miles to the Huron Mission. A cruel winter, a brutal attack, capture, and torture by another Native American tribe resulted in a mortal wound for the chief.

Sensing the end, Father Laforgue, Jesuit priest and leader of the expedition, said to the chief, "When I die, Chomina, I will go to paradise. Let me baptize you now so you will go there too."

"Why would I want to go to your paradise?" Chomina responded. "My people, my woman, and my boy would not be there."

The next day, as the chief lay dying in the snow, Father Laforgue made one more attempt: "Chomina! My God loves you. If you accept his love, he will admit you to paradise!"

"Leave, my friend, leave," Chomina murmured as he died.[1]

For many of us, the problem was not immediately apparent. Discovering the God of the Bible felt like puzzle pieces of all that is truthful and beautiful coming together. A flat world turned 3D, the grayscale turned

---

Samir Selmanovic grew up in a European Muslim family and served as a Seventh-day Adventist pastor and community organizer in Manhattan during 9/11 and its aftermath. A pastor, writer, teacher, advocate, and international speaker, Samir serves on the Coordinating Group for Emergent Village, on the Faith and Order Commission of the National Council of Churches, and on the leadership team of Re-church Network. He holds graduate degrees in religion, psychology, and education from Andrews University. Samir, his wife, Vesna, and their daughters, Ena and Leta, practice hospitality, advocate for Africa, admire Ena's writing, laugh at Leta's jokes, and cheer for Samir at marathon races. Contact Samir at www.samirselmanovic.com.

to color, as if someone had turned on the light. We were bathed in light. In time our eyes adjusted and we became aware of shadows.

It has always been that way. Every generation of those who decide to follow Christ learns that there are Bible texts to be reinterpreted, theologies to be reconstructed, faith communities to be reimagined. Those of us who are a part of the conversation about the emerging church believe such transformations are God's doing. And for our generation, the shadow is not to be seen in the flaws of Christian people or the dysfunction of Christian institutions, as flawed and imperfect as they may be. Our shadow is the idea of Christianity itself. Our religion has become a Christ management system.

We have experienced great joy in God's embrace of humanity through Jesus Christ. It has filled our lives with light. But Christianity's idea that other religions cannot be God's carriers of grace and truth casts a large shadow over our Christian experience. Does grace, the central teaching of Christianity, permeate all of reality, or is it something that is alive only for those who possess the New Testament and the Christian tradition? Is the revelation that we have received through Jesus Christ an expression of what is everywhere at all times, or has the Christ Event emptied most of the world and time of saving grace and deposited it in one religion, namely ours? And more practically, how can we have a genuine two-way conversation with non-Christians about our experience of God if we believe that God withholds his revelation from everyone but Christians?

Because we believe that there are no shadows in Christ, we want nothing less than to reinterpret the Bible, reconstruct the theology, and reimagine the church to match the character of God that we as followers of Christ have come to know.

When I put myself in the moccasins of chief Chomina, I feel God's Spirit asking me, "What would you choose, eternal life without your loved ones or eternal death with them?" Chomina knew his answer. He would rather die than live without his beloved. Moved by the Holy Spirit, people like Chomina reject the idea of allegiance to the name of Christ and, instead, want to be like him and thus accept him at a deeper level. This choice between accepting the name of Christ and being Christlike has been placed before millions of people in human history and today.

One does not need to believe in God before living in God's presence. God is present whether we believe in him or not.[2] And people do respond to him. Mark, a non-Christian friend of mine from New York, says that for him "to become a part of Christianity would be a moral step backwards." Yet, he would say things like this to me: "To live is to be given a gift. I believe that there is a transcendent sweep over our existence and it seems to me that humanity has been squandering this gift. One just needs to look at what we are doing to each other. But in the midst of the mess, I see grace of a new beginning all around me. And within me. I often fail to respond to it. I participate in the madness instead. Whenever in my inner life I do turn to this grace to look for a second chance, I am always granted one. I think I want to spend the rest of my life being a channel of that same goodness to others." This view embodies the doctrine of creation, sin, salvation, and new life. That's Christ, embedded in the life of Mark, present in substance rather than in name.

The Chominas and the Marks around us leave us wondering whether Christ can be more than Christianity. Or even other than Christianity. Can it be that the teachings of the gospel are embedded and can be found in reality itself rather than being exclusively isolated in sacred texts and our interpretations of these texts? If the answer is yes, can it be that they are embedded in other stories, other peoples' histories, and even other religions?

Idolatry of Christianity

Questions that seek to differentiate Christ and Christianity seem less and less absurd than they once did. Commonly defined, Christianity is "a monotheistic religion centered on Jesus of Nazareth, and on his life and teachings as presented in the New Testament."[3] It is worth being reminded that Christ never proclaimed, "Christianity is here. Join it." But Christ did insist, "The kingdom of God is here. Enter it."

The emerging church movement has come to believe that the ultimate context of the spiritual aspirations of a follower of Jesus Christ is not Christianity but rather the kingdom of God. This realization has many implications, and the one standing above all is the fact that, like every other religion, Christianity is a non-god, and every non-god can be an idol.

Acts of greed, hatred, and neglect of people aligned with Christianity that have littered the world throughout history are a result of their loving something else more than God. Sin is always a result of this displacement of one's heart. Someone or something else, a non-god, becomes the focus of one's love. An idol is generated when something grabs the functional trust of an individual or a social group. It happens when, in a relationship with God, something other than God becomes a non-negotiable value.

Has the supremacy of Christianity become our non-negotiable value? Every sin is a result of some faith commitment to things, people, or forces other than God, which are ultimately commitments to self. Religion, any religion, is not exempt from these dynamics of human experience.[4]

Scripture frequently describes other religions as idolatrous. Although worshiping idols would often result in violence, suffering, and degradation, these were only the symptoms of the larger issue God had with idol worshipers—their attempt to manage God. It was the sovereignty of God that was in question.

In the Old Testament, God repeatedly rebuked his followers for treating him as a manageable idol, someone they could actually avoid through the means of religion. Christians can conceive of things like money, sex, and power being idols. But the Christian religion itself being an idol? Certainly, if we proclaim that Christianity is immune from idolatry, then we have come to believe that, finally, God has become "contained" by Christianity.[5] We do believe that God is best defined by the historical revelation in Jesus Christ, but to believe that God is limited to it would be an attempt to manage God. If one holds that Christ is confined to Christianity, one has chosen a god that is not sovereign. Søren Kierkegaard argued that the moment one decides to become a Christian, one is liable to idolatry.[6]

Religion, whether in its traditional or personal forms, is the way we approach the power and mystery behind life, and since all humans have to approach the power and mystery behind life, we are all religious. This includes skeptics who say, "I don't believe in God. I don't have religion." That's a religious statement, a statement of dogma. Religion is a way we justify our existence, an explanation of why we matter. It is our "immortality system."[7] So for us to survive, for our meanings to stay intact, we have to dismantle or discredit the meanings that are contradictory to ours. No wonder that for many of us considering the possibility that Christianity could itself be an idol in the biblical sense of the word is a thought too traumatic to entertain.

Is our religion the only one that understands the true meaning of life? Or does God place his truth in others too? Well, God decides, and not us. The gospel is not *our* gospel, but the gospel of the kingdom of God, and what belongs to the kingdom of God cannot be hijacked by Christianity. God is sovereign, like the wind. He blows wherever he chooses.

Taking a Backseat

Christianity cannot regain credibility or recaptivate human imagination until it learns to exist for the sake of something greater than itself. People are rightfully afraid of any religion that will not accept its place at the feet of the Holy Mystery. If the Christian God is not larger than Christianity, then Christianity is simply not to be trusted.

In the eyes of an increasing number of people seeking God, Christian or not, Christianity has developed an inordinate sense of self-importance. In contrast, there is potency and beauty to a religion that is able to place the good of the world above its own survival.

Paradoxically, Christianity professes to trust the most peculiar deity of all religions, the God who has incarnated, become a servant, and died for the sake of something more important to him than his own life.

The future of Christianity depends on its willingness to serve something larger than itself. If Christianity is to be resurrected into a new life, it must aspire to be like the God it professes and take a backseat to something more dear than its own life. And what can be better than Christianity? The kingdom of God, of course. This kingdom supersedes Christianity in scope, depth, and expression. This is true regardless of whether we talk about "Christless" or "Christfull" Christianity. Even in its best form, Christian religion is still an entity in the human realm.

When we say that only Christ saves, Christ represents something larger than the person we Christians have come to know. He is all and in all. And Christ being "the only way" is not a statement of exclusion but inclusion, an expression of what is universal.[8] If a relationship with a specific person, namely Christ, is the whole substance of a relationship with the God of the Bible, then the vast majority of people in world history are excluded from the possibility of a relationship with the God of the Bible, along with the Hebrews of the Old Testament who were without a knowledge of Jesus Christ—the person. The question begs to be asked: would God who gives enough revelation for people to be judged but not enough revelation to be saved be a God worth worshiping? Never!

God enlightens every human ever born and opens a way for a relationship with him. The Bible says that if a person talks like an angel, but acts like a devil, his actions mean more than his words. His deeds trump his faith. In the same way, one can deny a faith that is evident in one's life.[9] My friend Mark from New York serves Jesus in substance rather than in words, living out a wordless faith in God.[10] This is only to say that there are no indications in the Bible that this dynamic applies only to individuals and not to groups. Religions live under the spiritual laws of the kingdom of God. Talking about other religions, theologian Miroslav Volf says, "God may employ their religious convictions and practices, or God may work apart from those convictions and practices. . . . That's partly how the giving and forgiving God works in Christians too, often using but sometimes circumventing their convictions and practices."[11] To put it in different terms, there is no salvation outside of Christ, but there is salvation outside of Christianity.

For the last two thousand years, Christianity has granted itself a special status among religions. An emerging generation of Christians is simply saying, "No more special treatment. In the Scripture God has established a criteria of truth, and it has to do with the fruits of a gracious life" (see Matt. 7:15–23; John 15:5–8; 17:6–26). This is unnerving for many of us who have based our identity on a notion of possessing the truth in an abstract form. But God's table is welcoming to all who seek, and if any religion is to win, may it be the one that produces people who are the most loving, the most humble, the most Christlike. Whatever the meaning of "salvation" and "judgment," we Christians are going to be saved by grace, like everyone else, and judged by our works, like everyone else.[12]

Becoming Master Learners

> Wisdom is so kind and wise
> that wherever you may look
> you can learn something about God.
> Why would not the omnipresent teach that way?
>
> St. Catherine of Siena

For most critics of such open Christianity, the problem with inclusiveness is that it allows for truth to be found in other religions. To emerging Christians, that problem is sweet. In fact, instead of being a problem, it is a reason to celebrate. We don't want to just tolerate the godliness of "the other" as if we regret the possibility. The godliness of non-Christians is not an anomaly in our theology. Instead of adding it as an appendix to our statement of beliefs, we want to move it closer to the center and celebrate it as the heavens certainly celebrate it. The gospel has taught us to rejoice in goodness we can find in others.

Moreover, if non-Christians can know our God, then we want to benefit from their contribution to our faith. Because God is sovereign, present anywhere he wants to be, our attitude of merely accepting the possibility of the salvation and godliness of others without an attitude of learning from them is simply lazy, a sin born of pride. Besides rejoicing, to celebrate means to learn about our God from others.

In fact we have been doing it every week in our churches. We use sermon illustrations from all aspects of life under the sun to illuminate the gospel of the kingdom of God, but we stop short of using and crediting such illustrations when they are part of someone else's religion, such as a life of Muhammad or a Zen story. Why? Is it because we are afraid we might find our God there like we find him everywhere else? Christ, the apostle John, and the apostle Paul were not afraid. They used the terms, concepts, and sources of the religions of the time to convey the meaning of the gospel. They could do it, and we cannot, simply because Jesus, John, and Paul were not about Christianity but about the kingdom of God.

This explains another phenomenon. If we believe that the ultimate method of spreading the Good News is through loving people, why do non-Christians so rarely feel loved by Christians? My thesis is that love accepts what others have to offer and we think non-Christians don't have much of anything to add to what is most valuable to us, namely the gospel. Although we accept their virtues with admiration and their brokenness with compassion, we do not seriously expect them to add to what matters most to us—our knowledge of and our relationship with God. We withhold from them the possibility of being our teachers. Without an attitude of learning, we have not entered a sacred "I/Thou" relationship. And that's why they hold back. The world is withholding from us what we are withholding from the world.

We want to provide for them what they lack, care for their needs, and teach them what they need to know. This position of a giver affords us a sense of control. But true love means knowing how to take. You love your grandma when you take her recipe; you love strangers when you need their company; you love your parents when you need their advice; you love your children when you need their forgiveness; you love your friends when you hear their stories. We don't truly love someone until we take what they need to give us. Although we often think of God as self-satisfied, needing nothing, God does honor us by needing us. This need of God for us is symbolized in the Sabbath commandment that has no other purpose than creating a space in time when God can enjoy our full attention, when a lover can simply be with his beloved. Rabbi Abraham Joshua Heschel explained once how the greatest human need is to become a need. God *needs* us to participate with him in healing the world.[13]

We too love others not only by giving but by taking. I was a Muslim, then an atheist, then a Christian. I became a follower of Christ because another Christian found the footsteps of God in my story and my religion of the time. He loved me by learning about God from my story. Before teaching me, my friend took what I had to offer.

The followers of God are not called to be the master teachers of God, but to be master learners. Pursued correctly, this attitude does not relativize what we believe. In fact it radicalizes what we believe because it establishes God as Sovereign one, one who "shines in all that's fair."[14] Humble learning and strong convictions are not mutually exclusive because humility is not a sign of weakness but of strength. Genuine regard for what others can add to our faith does not compromise our Christian commitment but rather expresses it. That's why evangelism is to be a two-way street. If we expect others to learn from us and be changed, we must first allow for a real possibility that we have something to learn from them and be changed by what we learn. It is fear and not the strength of our convictions that stops us from learning about our God from other religions.

Identity Worries

If we accept the possibility that other religions have redeeming stories or truths in them, then what is going to become of our identity? Would this kind of reckless humility drive us into one big stew pot of religions where the meat of the gospel can get lost among the potatoes and carrots of other religions?

Humility is the most powerful force in the kingdom of God. One needs only picture God kneeling before his creation in the person of Jesus washing our feet (see John 13). Through the humility that is at the heart of the incarnation and atonement, God evangelizes us (see Phil. 2:4–11). That's why humility holds such promise for the future of Christianity. It does not exclude evangelism but vastly improves its prospects.[15]

Humility is the ultimate expression of courage. In the context of the kingdom of God, a sheer display of power is simply too weak to be effective. We have created a false tension between keeping our Christian identity intact and approaching the world in humility. Humility is to be our identity. When we open ourselves to be taught by "the other," we don't become less the followers of Christ but more so.

We have come to the place where we have accepted the depravity of individual human beings and the necessity of repentance for every person, but the moment we group ourselves into Christian denominations, or the Christian religion at large, the doctrine of depravity suddenly vanishes from our consciousness. In fact, behaving like we hold all the truth about God and doing away with healthy self-doubt is the ultimate form of conformity—because every religion has a superiority complex—and thus a loss of a true identity. In the world as a whole, no group or religion is repenting of anything much today. That's why being "chief repenters" would not be a loss of identity; it would be a first step in becoming "chief learners" and the renewal of our identity as a Christian community. We are to be those who convert first, those who lay down their arms and submit to Sovereign God, those who put nothing before the kingdom of God, even if it is our beloved religion.

My friend Mark from New York asked me more than once, "Why do you Christians want Christianity to win all the time? You don't seem to know how to live in a world where you aren't in charge." This made me think about the history of Christianity and its aspirations to be in charge. Looking back nostalgically to the times when Christianity was an empire, we tirelessly monitor our power, our growth, our numbers, our financial success, our political strength. Maybe the time has come for Christianity to lose.

To lose one's life is to gain it. It would not be the first time that God has broken out of religion, which carries his message, and made something new. If God found it good for his followers to break out of the confines of a religion two millennia ago, why should we expect God not to do such a thing in our time? Maybe Christianity should be thinned out and broken up, spent like Christ who gave himself for this world.

If we seek first the kingdom of God, then maybe even our beloved religion, saved from ourselves, will be added to us.

17

ORTHOPARADOXY

Emerging Hope for Embracing Difference

DWIGHT J. FRIESEN

MARIE: I'm a little bit country.
DONNY: And I'm a little bit rock and roll.

The Christmas of 1976 my sister and I received tandem gifts. She received a Marie doll, and I got Donny—purple socks and all. Clad in disco glitter with their television variety show topping the charts, Donny and Marie were my introduction to paradox. Okay, I'll grant that Marie being "a little bit country" and Donny being "a little bit rock and roll" may not be on a par with Penrose's triangle, Schrödinger's cat, Russell's antinomy, or even the drawings of M. C. Escher; nonetheless, Donny and Marie Osmond introduced this seven-year-old to the possibility of rightly holding difference within a relational context.

"Paradoxes," says philosopher Roy Sorensen, "are questions (or in some cases, pseudoquestions) that suspend us between *too many* good answers."[1] It seems that most often one solution to a paradox looks compelling when considered in isolation, but paradoxes thrive when equally matched solutions dance together. The modern age was no friend to paradox. Any paradox was fodder for modernity to flex its logical and empirical muscles. Mystery was out; facts were in. Paradoxes literally became mind games, puzzles to solve rather than tensions to live in. Paradoxes signified a flaw in logic. Competing truth claims were an assault to the evolution of the human mind, tensions

---

Dwight J. Friesen teaches practical theology at Mars Hill Graduate School, is the founder and community-curate for a metro-Seattle simple church, is active locally and nationally with missional and emerging church movements, and serves on the Faith and Order Commission for the National Council of Churches. He is often asked to speak on themes of missional relationality, network theory, the social self, relational images of God and other expressions of interconnection, and kingdom living. Dwight, Lynette, and their son, Pascal, live in Bellevue, Washington.

that would have to be resolved; paradox was the fly in the ointment of the rational mind.

The postmodern turn is finding that this paradoxical fly in the ointment of modernity may in fact be the balm of Gilead. From quantum physics to medical sciences, from philosophy and religion to social sciences, paradoxes are increasingly being explored with a sense of hope that truth may be best experienced when the tensions between contradictory claims are held rightly. This sense of hope does not derive from looking for the tension between the dueling parties to be relaxed or resolved. It is a hope that imagines leaning into the tensions in such a way that life flourishes. Jürgen Moltmann, in his groundbreaking book *Theology of Hope,* writes:

> A thing is alive only when it contains contradictions in itself and is indeed the power of holding the contradictions within itself and enduring it. It is not reflection, recalling a man's own subjectivity from its social realization, that brings him back to possibilities and therewith his freedom, but this is done only by the hope which leads him to expend himself and at the same time makes him grasp continually new possibilities from the expected future.[2]

As I began to prayerfully consider my own "manifesto of hope" for the Emergent Village within the kingdom of God, I went right to what Moltmann refers to as "contradictions." Just as he highlights the necessity of contradictions for life, so I declare that embracing the complexities of contradictions, antinomies, and paradoxes of the human life is walking in the way of Jesus. The more we lean into the tension between competing truths, the closer we are to the heart of God. Territorial battles around theology cannot be seen as Christian work. Christianity is not a divine call to root out difference, nor is it a religion with the purpose of resolving paradox in a "once and for all" manner; rather the call of Christ is to live as a bridge, a link, a reconciling agent, rightly holding paradox with humility, faith, and love. Christ is the bridge not only between death and life but between black and white, male and female, Jew and Gentile, Republican and Democrat, conservative and liberal, modern and postmodern, I and thou. Wherever there is an impassible divide, we find Christ bridging the chasm with arms wide open; in just that place are followers of Christ, with their arms wide open as well.

In these few pages I am proposing orthoparadoxy as the ethic, methodology, and theology for life within Emergent Village.

> The paradox of reality is that no image is as compelling as the one which exists only in the mind's eye.
>
> Shana Alexander

> In life, the issue is not control, but dynamic connectedness.
>
> Erich Jantsch

What Is Orthoparadoxy?

The concepts of ortho*doxy* and ortho*praxy* are familiar, at least to many religious people. Ortho*doxy* is generally understood as right beliefs (*ortho* = "right" or "correct"; *doxa*- "thought," "teaching," or "glorification"). These right beliefs tend toward authoritative theoretical and theological claims, such as creeds, doctrines, and dogmas. Ortho*praxy* is generally understood as right practices. Orthopraxy is the customary use of knowledge or skills, distinct from theoretical knowledge. Often orthopraxy refers to the practice of the faith, especially to corporate and private worship, such as liturgies, life rules, and prayer books. My hope in writing this chapter is to further the dialogue of what right beliefs and right practices look like in emerging Christian life.

As important as both right beliefs and right practices might be, neither was Jesus Christ's primary mission, and neither is the primary ministry of God's people. In the incarnation, God became human as a continuation of God's hope for creation. God's hope for creation is peace or *shalom*—wholeness. This wholeness conjoins God, humanity, and the cosmos in a flourishing life, which simultaneously honors individuation and oneness.

John, the beloved disciple, tells us that Jesus understood his mission as bringing life and life to the full (see John 10:10). A full and flourishing human life, as evidenced by the life and ministry of Jesus Christ, is a reconciling life with God, others, creation, and self. The ministry of God's people has always been understood as a ministry of blessing—from God's call to Abraham, with the promise that Abraham and his descendants would be a blessing to the nations, to Paul's charge to the church in Corinth: "All this is from God, who reconciled us to himself through Christ and gave us the ministry of reconciliation" (2 Cor. 5:18). Orthoparadoxy is an effort to make God's main thing the main thing for all the people of God: reconciliation. Not sameness or agreement but differentiated oneness—where the fullness of one can be in relationship with the fullness of another. Orthoparadox is right paradox—holding difference rightly. Orthoparadox seeks to hold difference, tensions, otherness, and paradoxes with grace, humility, respect, and curiosity, while simultaneously bringing the fullness of self to the "other" in conversation, not to convert or to convince but with the hope of mutual transformation through interpersonal relationship.

Orthoparadoxy is the Triune life of God: one God while simultaneously three differentiated social persons, moving together in a coeternal Divine Dance of service for the sake of the other. This Divine Dance is the hope of the kingdom of God, as reflected in Jesus's prayer for us just before going to the cross, that we would be one as he and the Father are one (John 17:20–21). Genuine difference and genuine oneness, the life of God as the life of God's creation: this is orthoparadoxy.

My emerging manifesto of hope for the world is that followers of Christ embody an orthoparadoxical ethic, theological method, and theology. Let's begin by looking at an orthoparadox ethic; *how* do we hold difference rightly?

> My way of existing conveys my final answer.
>
> Emmanuel Levinas

> What therefore God has joined together, let no man separate.
>
> Jesus Christ

Toward an Orthoparadox Ethic

An ethic is a theory of living. As I've mentioned, inviting people to fullness of life is how Jesus described his mission in the world; this fullness or abundant life, Jesus announced, is life in the kingdom of God. Jesus did not announce ideas or call people to certain beliefs as much as he invited people to follow him into a way of being in the world. Before followers of Christ received the label "Christians," they were referred to as "People of the Way." The *Way* was Christ's way of being.

The various streams of Christianity emphasize different facets of the way of Christ in the world. The Eastern Orthodox Church emphasizes living in mystery and tradition, the Roman Catholic Church emphasizes an ethic of submission to the unitive function of centralized authority, the Protestant ethic protests abuses of authority by emphasizing the priesthood of all believers, and the evangelical ethic has emphasized evangelism and conversion. Obviously the above does not do justice to any of these rich traditions, but it serves to demonstrate that every person and every community has a particular ethic—a way of being in the world.

Part of the hope signified by the existence of the Emergent Village is an ethic of orthoparadoxy. An orthoparadox ethic seeks to hold rightly the tension of difference with differentiation. Differentiation is our ability to live separately from others, without being separated. It allows us to hold strong beliefs and convictions without shrinking away from them when we encounter another perspective; instead, we are able to offer the gift of our beliefs and convictions to the other as an act of love within a relational exchange. Differentiation is the capacity to offer the fullness of one's story, face, and voice to another in interpersonal relations. An orthoparadox ethic rightly holds differences, tensions, and paradoxes in reconciling movement toward oneness with the other.

When orthoparadoxy becomes our way of being in the world, the kingdom of God is manifest. The very Triune life of God finds expression in human relations with one another, creation, and God. To walk in the way of Jesus is to bring the fullness of one's individuated self in humble service of the other. The hope is not to defeat, debate, condemn, or even convert the other; rather the hope is to live reconciled with the other, not avoiding differences but seeing them as an expression of the largeness and diverse beauty of God.

> The movement of faith is unceasing because no explanation it offers is ever finished.
>
> Jacques Ellul

> We must know where to doubt, where to feel certain, where to submit. [The person] who does not do so understands not the force of reason.
>
> Blaise Pascal

Toward an Orthoparadox Theological Method

I propose that an ethic of rightly holding difference, paradox, and tensions must shape our theological method. A methodology is an attempt to be conscious of the rules of engagement to which one submits.

Orthoparadoxy represents a conversational theological method that seeks to graciously embrace difference while bringing the fullness of a differentiated social-self to the other. Through the methodology of orthoparadoxy, competing ideas, practices, and hermeneutics are seen as an invitation to conversational engagement rather than as something to refute, reform, or revise. In fact, ideas, practices, and hermeneutics are not seen as things in themselves; they are seen as inseparably *linked* with the whole biography of the person who presents, embodies, and brings perspective. With curiosity, a person seeking to hold the other in orthoparadox strives to enter the other's story, traditions, location, history, and so on in the belief that he or she will be impacted and changed by the encounter and with the hope that both may be transformed. Orthoparadoxy is less committed to solving or resolving apparent antinomies, contradictions, differences, and paradoxes and more committed to relational engagement, allowing for the other perspective(s) to impact and transform the self.

By declaring orthoparadoxy a *conversational theological method*, a dialogical form of ongoing, open communication is underscored. Conversation is mutual engagement in pursuit of wisdom. Anyone with access to the Internet, television, radio, and newspapers encounters more information than has been available at any other time in human history, but we risk ignorance because we tend to receive information passively, relying more on experts than on our own experiences to make sense of what we take in. Talking with others is a way out of this bind. Conversations move beyond claims and arguments toward understanding that is beyond ideology; conversations encourage us to probe the complexities of our world. Through ongoing conversation we learn to trust the Holy Spirit's presence in our lives, trusting that God is with us, helping us evaluate the information and the exchange.

Conversation brings people together. The hope is not to win or even to convert the other to your perspective, but for both to be transformed through the engagement. One of the exciting moments in any conversation is when you find yourself saying something with conviction that you hadn't previously realized you knew or believed. This kind of relational engagement is less about knowledge and more about wisdom. The act of talking with another is often far more important than the content of the conversation. This is not to discount the content of a conversation but to place a premium on encountering difference. Conversations matter because the people with whom we converse matter; thus, conversations offer a human face—created in the image of God—to what otherwise might be reduced to an abstract idea. This kind of engagement is less about knowledge and more about wisdom.

Without a movement of good faith toward the other, conversation is impossible. As such, faith is a type of relational currency. Conversely, to lose faith in another is to give up on the conversation. Here is the paradox of a conversational methodology. Those people we most need to be in conversation with are the very people in whom we most quickly lose faith. Faith is the relational lubricant that facilitates a smooth exchange between people. Without it, conversation seizes up, grinding to a halt.

As the need to be right is a great threat to conversation, so failure to bring the fullness and beauty of a differentiated self to the conversation is equally a threat. The theological method of orthoparadoxy surrenders the right to be right for the sake of movement toward being reconciled one with the other, while simultaneously seeking to bring the fullness of convictions and beliefs to the other. Current theological methods that often stress agreement/disagreement, win/loss, good/bad, orthodoxy/heresy, and the like set people up for constant battles to convince and convert the other to their way of believing and being in the world.

> It would seem very strange that Christianity should have come into the world just to receive an explanation.
>
> Søren Kierkegaard

Toward an Orthoparadox Theology

Here is my working maxim of a theology of orthoparadoxy: *the more irreconcilable various theological positions appear to be, the closer we are to experiencing truth.* As Søren Kierkegaard said, "The paradox is really the pathos of intellectual life and just as only great souls are exposed to passions it is only the great thinker who is exposed to what I call paradoxes, which are nothing else than grandiose thoughts in embryo."[3]

Theology is generally understood as reasoned discourse concerning God, the God/creation relationship, and religion. The hope of orthoparadox theological engagement is not so much to solve the big questions as much as to better equip people to understand who they are, when and where they are, while imaging a glorious future together, with the Father, through Christ, and in the Holy Spirit. Orthoparadoxy sees all theological claims as working thesis statements of the community of God's people constructively engaging with God in Christ by the Holy Spirit, with the many varied traditions of the church, and in our particular cultures, geographies, and political and economical contexts. Orthoparadox theology may be understood as supporting a form of ecumenism, which broadens the conversation beyond the church to include and engage cultural voices. Therefore, in orthoparadox theology propositions and truth claims are more important than ever but not as litmus tests of correct belief or practice; rather, truth claims become launching pads for differentiated conversational relationship, marked by mutual exploration, humble submission, deference, and wonder.

Orthoparadox theology is less concerned with creating "once for all" doctrinal statements or dogmatic claims and is more interested in holding competing truth claims in right tension. It is nearly if not entirely impossible for anyone to embrace rightly another person who holds to claims that compete with one's own, which is precisely why the development of a robust theology of holding difference, paradox, and otherness is so essential. Orthoparadox theology requires a dynamic understanding of the Holy Spirit. Without the reconciling presence of the Holy Spirit actively drawing together those who would naturally divide, there is no possibility for humanity to experience the kind of oneness that Jesus enjoys with the Father. Thus the emerging hope of Christianity is not found in a modernist claim to intellectual certainty any more than it is found in a moralistic way of being in the world; it is found in our walking with the Holy Spirit of God as reconciling agents.

The certainty necessary for making decisions and for guiding one's life is not found in abstract theological propositions but is found in the mystery of interpersonal relations. Any honest thinker is cautious regarding claims to certainty, but such caution makes no sense to the lover. The lover finds rest in the tacit knowledge that he or she is loved. This orthoparadoxical tacit knowledge is reflected in Paul's words to the church of Rome: "God's Spirit testifies with my spirit that I am his child" (see Rom. 8:16). This is the kind of theology that orthoparadoxy seeks to fan into flame.

Orthoparadoxy is a useful way of understanding the early Christian councils and the creeds that came out of those long conversations. Those conversations were held when Christ-followers representing divergent solutions to a theological paradox gathered to explore a way forward together. Those people most vested in the discussion met and thoroughly explored the various positions and most often created a paradoxical statement. Of course not all perspectives or positions ultimately ended up in their final paradoxical statements. In fact some positions were communally determined to be wrong, yet all serious perspectives were engaged.

Today we look at our creeds less as a final authority on truth and more as a conversation guide; our creeds don't stop conversation, rather, they reveal the trajectory of our ongoing conversation. In exploring our creedal history, it seems wise to reflect beyond simply the statements they produced, to also consider the generative, gracious, and differentiated encounters they were. As a result of these long conversations, most Christ followers paradoxically hold that God is three and God is one, that Jesus Christ is fully God and fully human. Christian theology and biblical teaching are filled with paradoxes: God is both immanent and transcendent; followers of Christ are both sinners and saints; one must die to live; the greatest is the least; and loving our enemies is the way of Christ. And then there are many theological questions still on the table for discussion, like determinism and free will or salvation by grace and salvation by works, just to name a couple.

At times it may be necessary for a person to explore a possible solution to a paradox apart from the other possibilities. So we can imagine a person frolicking in Calvin's TULIP fields (total depravity, unconditional election, limited atonement, irresistible grace, perseverance of the saints) for a season before returning to the place of conversation. After all, much can be learned through analytical methods that ignore the larger context for a season. But such study is incomplete in itself. Such study is like the spiritual discipline of retreat in that it removes itself from its larger context to reflectively listen so as to reenter society better able to live into the particularity of the larger context. So the gift of playing in the TULIP fields is not realized in the TULIP fields but is found in humbly bringing the beauty experienced there into conversation with others.

One of the problems with paradoxical theology is that it does not feel as solid as we would like; in fact it produces more tensions than it resolves. Thus when we encounter another perspective on a theological issue, we tend to defend the claim with which we've been most comfortable. Orthoparadox theologians seek not to defend their claims as much as present the fullness of their convictions and beliefs as an act of service. Christ always comes to us and says, "Surrender your confidence in anything but me—trust me." In response to theologian C. S. Song's statement, "Truth . . . cannot unite the ununitable; only love can," Lesslie Newbigin said, "But it is not love which encourages people to believe a lie."[4] This is orthoparadox conversation in action.

The problem with orthodoxy or authoritative dogmatic claims is that they are conversation stoppers. Rigid orthodoxy doesn't leave room for genuine questions borne of new contexts or new technologies. Rigid orthodoxy loves rules; Christ tends to break such rules. People rely on religions; Christ bids us to trust him. Christ invites us to lay down that which we think we can and should rely on to become humble servants, hosting meals of bread and wine to a hungry and thirsty world—not religiously but out of divine love. Orthoparadoxy sees the theological conversational process less as a goal unto itself and more as serving the people of God (personally and corporately) to live full and particular lives with God, with one another, and with creation.

> Relationships are not just interesting; to many physicists, they are all there is to reality.
>
> Margaret Wheatley

> I have found the paradox, that if you love until it hurts, *there can be no more hurt, only more love.*
>
> Mother Teresa

Denouement

This brief introduction to orthoparadoxy is my manifesto of hope for living within emerging Christianity. To some readers it may sound like little more than esoteric mumbo jumbo, for others these proposals may feel like conversation stoppers despite my hope for the opposite response, and for still others it may spark hope for a way of living as a link or bridge wherever division has reigned. As you come to the end of this chapter, I imagine the So what? question moving to the front of your mind.

So what? may in fact be the most important question we ask of all our beliefs. I invite you to lean into that question as you consider your beliefs, your practices, and the interpretive lens through which you see the world. What if you saw connections where you had seen otherness? What if you saw conversation starters where you once saw theological disagreement? What if you sought to embody an ethic of orthoparadoxy rather than separation? What if Christ-followers became known as a reconciling people?

My hope and prayer is that this chapter can ignite further conversation with all followers of Christ who are seeking to bless the world with their presence. Developing a life of orthoparadoxy, which fosters relationships by allowing strong conviction to remain in dialogue and surrenders the will to exclude on the basis of those same convictions, may sound impossible. Let there be no doubt, seeing *connections* where we once saw *difference* will require nothing less than divine intervention; may it be so.

A Few Questions for Further Conversation

- What kind of authority do the Christian Scriptures have from an orthoparadox perspective?
- How does orthoparadoxy address the problem of evil?
- If I hold that murder is wrong while someone else has a different perspective, am I supposed to simply be in conversation with the other?
- How might evangelism and conversion be understood in this paradigm?
- What happens if I seek to bring the fullness of my convictions to another, while also seeking to enter the other's perspective, yet the other person is not willing to reciprocate?
- How are people transformed?

> Something is on the way out and something else is painfully being born. It is as if something were crumbling, decaying and exhausting itself, while something else, still indistinct, were arising from the rubble . . . we are in a phase when one age is succeeding another, when everything is possible.
>
> Václav Havel

> A perspicuous representation produces just that understanding which consists in "seeing connexions."
>
> Ludwig Wittgenstein

18

HUMBLE THEOLOGY

Re-exploring Doctrine While
Holding On to Truth

DAN KIMBALL

I remember a youth pastor's pained expression when he told me he was leaving his church. He said he loved the church and loved the people and loved the staff, but he was feeling more and more out of place at the church because he couldn't talk about theology. He shared how he loved to read and would try to start discussions about theology in church staff meetings. But from his perspective, discussing theology wasn't received well. The staff would eagerly discuss new methodologies of ministry and new models for how to do ministry, but they did not want to discuss any different or new theological ideas.

The Secret Bookshelf

He explained that if he discussed anything that was outside of his church's specific doctrinal positions, he would get suspicious looks that meant "Why are you asking this?" or "You're not going liberal on us, are you?" Because of this reaction, he had to start what he called a "secret bookshelf" at home. He said he needed this bookshelf because if other staff saw some of the books he was reading, he could get in trouble. I asked him what books were on this shelf and I can honestly say they were not that controversial. They were, however, books that were outside of the norm of the specific denominational beliefs of his church. I did not sense that this pastor had a bone to pick or was rais-

---

Dan Kimball is the author of several books including *The Emerging Church* (Zondervan, 2003), *Emerging Worship* (Zondervan, 2004), and *They Like Jesus, but Not the Church* (Zondervan, 2007). He is one of the pastors of Vintage Faith Church, a recently planted church in Santa Cruz, California. Dan holds a master's from Western Seminary and is currently pursuing a doctor of ministry degree at George Fox Evangelical Seminary, where he also serves as adjunct faculty mentor. Dan is married to Becky, has two daughters, and drives a rusty 1966 Ford Mustang. (Dan's website: www.vintagefaith.com; Dan's blog: www.dankimball.com)

ing theological questions to be an irritant with his church staff. He was simply an honest student of Scripture who wanted a forum for theological discussion where he had assumed he was safe and even encouraged to have one.

I often think of this pastor and his secret bookshelf. This may be an extreme situation, but I think the reality of this pastor's dilemma is probably quite common among many in the evangelical world. We feel comfortable talking about ministry methodology and all types of innovative and new ideas, but when it comes to theology, we can sometimes be very uptight and rigid. If we find that someone holds any theological position other than that of our church or our particular denomination, our protective defenses go up. Anyone questioning any facet of our particular theology is often perceived as trespassing into dangerous territory that should not be entered. In the very place where we should feel free to have safe, open, and even fun theological discussions, sadly, this is the place it can quite often be most dangerous.

Re-exploring Theology as a Strength Not a Weakness

I believe that theology and doctrine are extremely important (see 1 Tim. 4:16; Titus 1:9; 2:1). In our church we hold to specific theological beliefs and we do have a doctrinal statement. I am aware of the extreme limitations of doctrinal statements and how they don't represent all that a church or person believes, but it is actually very helpful for people to be able to read our church's basic core beliefs. As a church, we could be called a Nicene Creed church in terms of our beliefs. I recognize that the Nicene Creed was written at a specific time in history when the church was grappling with specific questions about the relationship of Jesus to the Father and Spirit. But as a church we believe we can revere certain things as truth no matter the particular cultural or historical context in which they originated.

Recently I was joking and said that I am a fundamentalist because I hold to certain fundamental beliefs. If someone believes in the resurrection of Jesus or believes that God exists, then they actually have a fundamental belief or two. So in that regard, most of us are fundamentalists to some degree or another. Yet I understand fully the limitations of the word *fundamental*. That word is negatively loaded due to what "fundamentalism" has become. So I use the word very, very rarely. I am simply saying that I do hold to fundamental beliefs, such as what is in the Nicene Creed and other primary doctrines of the faith (the deity of Jesus, inspiration of Scripture, the substitutionary atonement, the bodily resurrection of Jesus, salvation through Jesus alone).

However, having said that I hold to some fundamental beliefs doesn't mean that I stop exploring theology. I want to be continually discussing, learning, reading, and thinking seriously about all varieties of theological thought. I want to be constantly exploring which theological beliefs have changed throughout church history, which ones have remained consistent. There are many unknowns and mysteries in theology. We should be able to continually think and learn about theology with open hearts and open minds. It is not a weakness to explore theology outside what we've been taught in our specific church or seminary. It's not a weakness to admit there is a lot we just don't know. I see that as a strength, not a weakness. Weakness is when we simply close our minds and become afraid to explore different ideas, which may mean we are afraid to be challenged or discover something new.

For me, theology is incredibly important and I love opening a Bible, discussing and even arguing among friends about differences of opinion on things. I love being challenged theologically by ideas I may have not thought of before. As I have looked at certain things from a different perspective over time, some of my views have changed. Theology is a living, relationally dynamic thing—it is not stagnant. Theology impacts everything we do in our churches. What a church believes theologically should be very prominent in all that a church practices. All of our churches' methodologies should be an expression of our theology. Understanding how methodology is shaped by theology is critical.

I can't say that I used to be as open to discussing differing theological viewpoints with people. Honestly, I didn't feel the need to discuss theology because I thought my theology was all nice and clean and packaged and systematically figured out by smart people from the 1500s and the church I went to. Neither have I always grasped the critical importance of understanding the intertwining of theology and methodology in our churches. I didn't realize how decisions about methodology cannot be made in a void, without understanding the theology behind the methodology. Let me share some of my story.

Diving into Methodology and Models of Ministry

I grew up outside the church, so I didn't have any preconceived notion of what church or ministry was supposed to be. I got involved in a wonderful, contemporary Bible church and was drumming for the choir and was also the volunteer coleader of the college ministry. Eventually I was asked to become the youth pastor. I had absolutely no concept of youth ministry. I had never been in a youth group before, so needless to say it was ironic when the senior pastor asked me to consider leading the youth ministry after the former youth pastor left. I felt inadequate, especially since the previous youth pastor at the church was a super-athlete/charismatic big-smiler/tall, energetic cheerleader type with a mullet haircut (this was in the late 1980s). I was the total opposite of him. I was the nonathletic (sports to me is bowling and shooting pool), introverted type. But I was passionate about doing whatever I could to introduce Jesus to those in our emerging culture, which included youth, so I said yes.

As I jumped headfirst into becoming a youth pastor, I called up other churches who had youth ministries to find out what they were doing. I wanted to know what "worked" for them. I visited Willow Creek and Saddleback and a few others to learn how to "do" youth ministry and to look for "models." Saturating myself in methodology, I began serving away with my mind and heart swirling with ideas for messages, dramas, videos, games, and summer camps. With a massive amount of published and packaged youth ministry materials out there, I became happily entrenched in youth ministry methodology and was doing whatever "worked" so that youth would become disciples of Jesus. I read all kinds of books on how to speak to youth, books on finding movie clip videos for a meeting, discipleship materials for youth small groups, dramas for youth, retreat ideas, songbooks and new worship CDs, PowerPoint, and on and on. It was great! You could find almost anything you wanted. As a youth pastor, I could indulge in all the how-tos of youth ministry, and thanks to all these products, ministry ideas and, of course, the Holy Spirit, the youth ministry grew. Parents were happy, the senior pastor was happy, and I believe that God did bless the ministry.

Uncomfortable despite "Success"

I was in a thriving church and immersed in an exciting, growing youth ministry, and my focus was very much on helping people with their felt needs. Most youth or adults in the church weren't asking direct theological questions; but youth were asking questions about dating and relationships, and parents were asking about how to deal with a troubled teenager and the other normal struggles of life. So setting up teaching series, classes, and various programs to address these issues helped. It worked well; a lot of lives were changed. I saw God do wonderful things through felt-need teaching, and most people came to the church because of these needs. As long as these things were happening, my ministry was seen as "successful."

However, over time and due to several reasons that I don't have space to develop here, I became more and more uncomfortable with my primary focus on felt-need ministry and models and methods of ministry.[1] I started to be more aware of how much the church and our youth ministry focused on improving and developing methods of ministry. We taught systematic theology in classes, so it wasn't as though we were not clearly teaching core doctrines. That wasn't what was disturbing me—it was not thinking about the holistic theology behind all the pragmatic methodology that was causing me to be unsettled. This is what caused me to enter *phase 1* of beginning to rethink things.

Phase 1: Rethinking Methodology

Youth leaders are usually accustomed to the idea that while methods change, the message stays the same. That is exactly what I was focusing on and doing—exploring new methods to communicate the message. Usually what people mean by "changing the methods" is "changing the worship service." Usually the "message" is the gospel message about salvation and heaven after we die if we put faith in Jesus. Most churches, as they begin "changing the methods," change the worship service or the youth group meeting. What we generally "change" first is the music, then we add PowerPoint, videos, candles, and whatever else will help communicate to people. These are actually very valid things to do. But when you allow yourself even more freedom to think and pray through change, you naturally go beyond just the worship service and "styles." Communicating the gospel in a changing culture is not just about what music you play and what videos you use and whether or not you have couches or candles in the room where you meet.

So this began opening me up to larger and more important questions, beyond just the immediate methodology questions. We can't just rethink the worship gathering "style"—we have to move beyond just the hour or hour and a half that we meet together each Sunday. I began wondering how the worship gathering itself fit within someone's process of following Jesus and the life of the church. I began wondering why the method of raising your hand to make a decision for salvation during a worship gathering was used. I began wondering, *Where does this come from? Why do worship bands stand up in the front like a pop concert and sing five songs every week? What does this communicate about the meaning of "worship"? Who came up with the idea of separate services so that teenagers and their parents and families attend worship gatherings separately, dissecting the family every Sunday morning?* These questions, which started within the context of youth ministry, eventually moved me to *phase* 2 of my rethinking process, which extended past youth ministry.

Phase 2: Rethinking Ecclesiology

Once you start rethinking the origins of various methods of ministry in the church, it is only a matter of time before you have to revisit the theology of church, our ecclesiology. All of what we do in our churches and methods of ministries do not stand on their own; they are part of a local body of Christ. For instance, the theology and methodology of a youth ministry is dependent on the methodology and ecclesiology of the local church of which it is a part. So, as a youth and young adult pastor, I had more questions that I needed to ask because what I was doing was not in isolation but part of the larger church.

So the questions started coming, such as: What is the "church"? Is it a meeting people go to? If we think of the church more as a meeting and a place theologically, shouldn't that shape what we do? Is the church the building or the people? Why do most people say they "go to church" or "attend a church"? Aren't we supposed to "be the church"? What is a "pastor"? How did we end up turning what was originally listed as a spiritual gift and role of shepherding into a formal hierarchical title that is generally only used for paid seminary-educated people? Some are even called "senior pastor," "executive pastor," and so on. Where did the concept of a senior pastor come from? Why do we use business titles in an organic family like the church? What was the New Testament church like, and does it resemble at all most churches today? What does this communicate in terms of our values as a church? Isn't how we set up the room an expression of how we think about community? Is community a bunch of pews or seats all facing one speaker? Why is singing the way most people in a church define "worship"?

I got dizzy with all these questions, and the scary part was not knowing anybody who had the same questions. It seemed like everyone just assumed this is the way "church" is supposed to be, and no one questioned anything. Originally I felt pretty alone, only to later find there were others thinking and asking these same things all around the country. But once I started asking these kinds of key questions, it was only a matter of time before I had to move from thinking about ecclesiology to thinking about even more basic issues of theology.

Phase 3: Rethinking Theology

Rethinking ecclesiology naturally led to rethinking theology as a whole. Do I believe what I do theologically because I was initially taught very certain and compelling answers during the formative years of my faith? In retrospect, in the early years of our faith we generally are given only one specific theological viewpoint depending on whom we are learning from and what they believe. So in my case, it was later in my young adulthood that I discovered there are other orthodox viewpoints from throughout church history about some of the nonfoundational issues that also had very good arguments supporting them. I began realizing that maybe some of our neat, clean, and packaged theology is actually more messy and complex than we like to admit.

So the questions started coming. Will my senior pastor be upset if I begin exploring other views of the end times? I understand that Jesus died for our sins, but was salvation and the gospel only about going to heaven when we die? I began wondering about how the way I thought of salvation determined how I went about evangelism. What did the word *salvation* mean throughout the Bible? There were so many interesting questions to wrestle with. Sure, I learned about all these things in seminary and in church from sermons, but I never really wrestled with them. For the most part, I was told what to believe with such enthusiastic certainty and confidence that I didn't question anything.

However, slowly but surely it began to dawn on me that our constant focus in the church was so primarily about methodology and what "works" that it limited the degree of our theological discussion and exploration. Of course, all of us want to make disciples, but sadly we have too often focused on methodology without thinking carefully about the theology or lack of theology behind it. When I began to feel the importance of thinking about theology, it caused me not to be afraid to ask questions about the theological implications underlying our methodology. I was embarrassed to realize that I and most church leaders I knew didn't really ask questions about the theology behind the methodology. I was amazed that I had gone so long without questioning it all.

Not Being Afraid to Think about Theology

Going back to the story I started with, no one should have to install a secret bookshelf for fear of being put under suspicion for reading various ideas and concepts of theology. If we aren't open to talking and discussing different theological opinions on things, are we afraid that we might discover something we can't answer? Or is that the fear, that not answering something might be a weakness?

As I explained earlier, although I do have specific core and fundamental beliefs that I hold to, I also appreciate the diversity of beliefs that Christians have. I strive to be open to listening and exploring all types of theological thinking. I don't see this as a weakness but a strength. It is actually exciting, fun, invigorating, and stimulating both intellectually and spiritually to be in discussions about theology and different thoughts about it today. It stretches our thinking; it causes us to dig deeper in the Bible; it causes our minds to quicken in joy at the marvel and wonder of God. But not everyone sees it this way, and in fact some find it threatening.

My Doctrinal Statement Can Beat Up Your Doctrinal Statement

One of the more embarrassing things about being a Christian today is being associated with other Christians who are so rigid in their theology that they go into a "defend and attack" mode with anyone who says something different from what they believe, even about the more minor doctrines. Please understand that I believe doctrine is very, very important. As I shared earlier, in our church we do have a doctrinal statement. But I wonder if we sometimes go too far developing such detailed doctrinal statements and absolute conclusions about certain beliefs that exceed the core and fundamental issues. It seems that some of us who go into detailed doctrinal statements get very defensive if someone believes otherwise about even small issues. We can subtly take on a "my doctrinal statement can beat up your doctrinal statement" type of attitude. Now, if anyone I know was questioning the resurrection of Jesus, I would go into a very strong form of defend mode. This is the cornerstone of our faith. There are times when I think we may need to take very strong stands about what we believe on critical issues, such as the resurrection, salvation through Jesus alone, the atonement, and the inspiration and authority of Scripture. But there is certainly a place for talking about theological beliefs that are situated outside of one's own church or denomination.

It's interesting, however, that some of the more aggressive "defend and attack" Christians out there, who generally won't openly discuss and explore theological beliefs besides their own, are the ones who hold more strongly to imputed sin and stress constantly how sinful we are. The irony, of course, is that if we are inherently sinful, how can we be so darn certain that our particular interpretation of the Scriptures and our theological positions are the absolutely correct ones?

Some Closing Thoughts

Finally, I want to encourage thinking about a few things related to how we as fallible human beings go about responding to various theological ideas. Following are a few things that I try to remember and practice.

Always remember that methodology flows from theology. I eventually realized our methodology flows from our theology, not vice versa. I hope we will constantly be thinking through the reasons we do what we do and what theological roots support our church practice. I can no longer teach anything or use a form of media or launch a new program without thinking through the theological meaning behind it and what it communicates theologically. As a pastor, I also want to be creating a culture of theological thinking within the people of the church. I try my best to constantly be explaining the theological "why's" behind whatever we are doing in the church.

We can hold certain beliefs as truth and not feel arrogant or close-minded when we do. Yes, there is mystery and, yes, there are a lot of unknowns, but we can still confidently say we do know certain things that God revealed to us (see John 8:32; 14:6). Holding to doctrine is critically important. I shared some of what I think fits in this category, and I am not ashamed nor do I feel "unemerging" in saying that I hold to and will even defend some core or fundamental beliefs. Again, I understand we need to unpack the words *fundamental* or *core*, but for simplicity's sake these words communicate the heart of what I'm trying to get at. We don't have to feel close-minded or overly dogmatic when saying we hold to certain truths. Jesus himself said he was truth.

It is not a weakness to be open to theological rethinking. At the same time we hold to certain truths, it is also a wonderful thing to be open to discussing all types of new thinking and rethinking and to be willing to learn. Discussing and rethinking theology is exciting. It is not a weakness to be open to hearing other viewpoints and even to be challenged in what we may believe. In fact I think it is a weakness when we are not willing to do this, as it may mean either we don't have confidence in what we believe or we are afraid or close-minded (in a negative way) and unwilling to discuss anything.

Approach theology with humility. We all need to really grasp that we approach the Scriptures and theology with our own personal biases and backgrounds. We should also never forget that we are sin tainted, imperfect human beings. Recognizing this should cause us to have some humility in our approach. Yes, we have the Spirit to guide us, but even so, there are many godly, wonderful, Spirit-filled people who sincerely study and pray and ask the Spirit to guide them, yet they come to different conclusions.

Be loving and gracious to others when you disagree. Throughout the New Testament we are constantly reminded that a sign of being a follower of Jesus is our love for each other (John 15:17). In Galatians 5:22–23 we are taught that we should bear the fruit of the Spirit: "But the fruit of the Spirit is love, joy, peace, patience, kindness, goodness, faithfulness, gentleness and self-control." When we have disagreements among ourselves, do we demonstrate these characteristics in how we speak about each other and in our attitudes toward one another?

I am not saying we should passively let anyone say any theological idea he or she wants to say without argument. I argue and debate with friends about theological issues all the time. But I hope I do so with love and with gentleness and respect. I hope my words do not wound or slander those with whom I may not fully agree. I am all for openness, discussion, and disagreeing—but I want to do so in a manner that honors how Jesus told us to love one another.

Ultimately, our methodology is not about new innovative things. It's about Jesus. Our theology is not about being fresh and innovative. It's about Jesus. All we do is really about Jesus and our lives being shaped into what he taught about and lived. My prayer is that in the emerging church this will be our ultimate goal. The more we study and discuss methodology and theology, the more we should be seeing the fruit of the Spirit in our lives as a result. We should be interested in methodology and theology not for inquiry's sake, but to be like Jesus and for the sake of the gospel.

19

LEADING FROM THE MARGINS

The Role of Imagination in Our Changing Context

"*The world is changed. I feel it in the water. I feel it in the earth. I smell it in the air.*" Do you recognize this quote? It is from elf queen Galadriel in the opening scene of the film adapted from Tolkien's classic book *The Fellowship of the Ring*. I am not the first to use this quote in reference to the emerging church. In the foreword to Brian McLaren's book *A Generous Orthodoxy*, theologian John Franke quotes it.[1] I feel more than a bit unoriginal in cribbing it, but it is such a poetic statement about the nature and reality of change that I am willing to let the statement's visceral imagery and power push aside any doubts I have about using it.

The world has changed. This is a fact. And this is how Franke uses the quote in the introduction to McLaren's book—reckoning the reality of the change as something that has occurred. The quote's unique power for me, however, is not simply the way Galadriel reckons the change *as* a fact—a past tense occurrence. While it is an effective illustration of that point, its real power for me is in *how* that fact is experienced. It is an intuitive and somatic reckoning. It is not mere cognitive acknowledgment. In her gut and through her sensory experience of the world, she knows the environment has altered. She *feels* it. To expect a listing of empirical data demonstrating environmental transition in the ecosystem of Middle-earth misses the point, especially at the beginning of an epic fantasy saga. Some things you know simply by being alive and attentive,

---

Tim Keel is the founding pastor of Jacob's Well. He is married to Mimi and together they have three children: Mabry, Annie, and Blaise. Tim received a BFA in design from the University of Kansas and a master of divinity from Denver Seminary. Tim is an avid reader and loves to learn, write, and teach. He is passionate about creating spaces for people to connect to God, themselves, and others. Tim also serves on the board of directors for Emergent, a growing generative friendship among missional Christian leaders seeking to love our world in the Spirit of Jesus Christ (http://jacobs wellchurch.org/tim).

and some things can be expressed only through poetry. This reminds me of another story.

During World War II, Europe was plunged into the horror of battle on an unimaginable scale. With only the tail end of Vietnam and two Gulf wars in my memory, I have a hard time wrapping my brain around a multidecade military engagement in theaters of battle all over the world where millions of people died. This chaotic time in world history is the setting for a story about a community of monks living in Greece on Mount Athos. If you have never seen the Mount Athos monastery, pause here and do a quick search for an image on the Internet. I have done just this and am now looking at a picture of an ancient, fortresslike structure built on a mountain promontory over the ocean.

For those in the Orthodox faith, it is a holy mountain. The monks of Mount Athos live there in isolation and understand their vocation as prayer on behalf of the world. Elder Paisios of Mount Athos explains, "The monk flees far from the world, not because he detests the world, but because he loves the world, and in this way he is better able to help the world through his prayer, in things that don't happen humanly but only through divine intervention. In this way God saves the world."[2]

This understanding of vocation was especially true during World War II. At one point the young monks of the community approached the abbot. It was not the monastery's practice to stay up on current events, especially through reading the newspaper. But because of the extraordinary events of the war raging around them, they asked their superior for permission to read the paper for news so that they might pray more effectively. The abbot granted their request, but chided them saying, "Remember, though, that one can know more of what is happening in the world by remaining in one's cell and praying than by reading newspapers."[3] In our totally connected world, this concept is not only different, it is totally alien and nearly incomprehensible.

Both this quote and this story suggest and illustrate an alternate way of accessing reality beyond the simple discovery and announcement of facts through direct observation of data. This is important. The world *has* changed. And of course, it will continue to do so, but it is my conviction that it has changed in ways that are altering our basic understanding of reality, and thus the ways in which we *access* reality are in the process of changing as well. *How* we *know* is changing or, better, expanding.

We know, and I believe *have known* for quite some time, that the world has changed. But we have known it in the same way Galadriel knew that Middle-earth had changed. Before we ever became aware of the notions of postmodernity, globalization, postcolonialism, and a hundred other "posts," we knew something was changing. We could *feel* it. Unfortunately, our ability to acknowledge that reality was beyond us. Unlike Galadriel and the abbot of Mount Athos, our instinctive and spiritual capacities were in a state of atrophy. We stopped listening to what our gut and our body and our spirit communicated to us. Or maybe we never listened in the first place. Those intuitions were not reliable or at least not verifiable enough to recognize. Instead, we came to rely on knowledge accessed in far more reliable ways, ways that were found outside ourselves.

A Domesticated Faith

The missional context of our culture is undergoing a transformation. To respond, pastors and lay leaders must develop new competencies as well as attract and release leaders who already have these competencies in place. Unfortunately, most of our systems and structures are ill-prepared to deal with this new environment and the opportunities and challenges it presents. The modern age was ruled by science and structures of control. In that environment the humanities were relegated to the margins. In the postmodern milieu, the humanities are asserting themselves, not in terms defined by science but with a language all their own—creative, artistic, intuitive, organic, prophetic, and poetic. New structures and systems are emerging to facilitate and sustain life and ministry in ways that are appropriate to this new environment. Leadership must undergo transformation in this new context as well. To ignore this reality simply means to doom the church to more bad leadership, emerging or otherwise.

My purpose in writing these things is not to denigrate facts, data, or cognition, but to say that in the world we live in *now*, facts alone are not adequate. They never were. And the artists, poets, prophets, contemplatives, and mystics among us have been witnessing to this from the margins for a long time. Artists and poets and others in our midst are in tune with the collective, intuitive, and spiritual. They have honored and then honed their senses and intuitive capacities in a way that allows for a radical engagement with the environment, with reality, to reflect, respond, and create something that is true and vital and defining. They are leading us somewhere.

Like the monks of Mount Athos, these marginalized prophets have labored in obscurity, offering their gifts to the world from the edges. They have functioned as a sort of minority report that witnesses to a different landscape, an alternate view of reality that up until now we have been willing to ignore. While we are in little danger of seeing the world around us go monastic (though we should note the emergence of neomonasticism), we live in a world that is undergoing a radical transformation and beginning to account for and respond to the reassertion of creativity, imagination, and intuition as legitimate and valued currencies of exchange. For many of us in the church, missing this fundamental shift *is* a danger that we must be aware of because, as I assess the environment in most churches today, we are not equipped or prepared to reckon in this version of reality.

The world we find ourselves in is no longer the world of mere facts, data, and cognition. It is no longer a world dominated by modern, linear, cognitive, Western paths of knowledge. It is the world of postmodernity, globalization, and postcolonialism, but also of quantum physics, the nonlinear, networked systems, and increasing Eastern influence. The West has colonized the rest of the world so long and so effectively that we have grown accustomed to our power and influence. We are shocked to discover that when a route is open to another culture, influence is not a one-way street.

Missionary Lesslie Newbigin returned from India to the United Kingdom after thirty-five years of embedded, cross-cultural mission work. Using the experience, knowledge, and tools inherent to cross-cultural engagement, he found that Jesus and his gospel had been domesticated in the West. To domesticate something wild, you capture and tame it to keep it under control. Newbigin's assessment was that the gospel had lost much of its power in the West because our understanding of it was too conditioned by unquestioned cultural assumptions of what reality is and how it is accessed. We took the world of the Spirit, of Scripture, of creation itself, and submitted it to Western, scientific rationalism. The only reality we allowed ourselves to see was the reality filtered through a small, culturally defined grid. In other words, we read the gospel, but we didn't allow the gospel to read us. We dictated the terms and received an anemic faith stripped of its wildness. Now when animals are domesticated in captivity, they sometimes lose the ability to produce offspring.

If they do regain the ability to reproduce, it is often under artificial and controlled circumstances. You see the analogy, I'm sure.

Leading from a New Place

I believe that the emerging church phenomenon is but one small example of an alternative attempt to engage reality. The emerging church strives to refathom who God is, what the gospel is, how we access and read Scripture, what it means to be human, and how we generate a common life in the midst of creation in response to these realities. We are seeking freedom from captivity to a mindset that does not seem true to life as we experience it nor capable of incorporating our emerging understandings of reality.

Let me give you one practical example of how this plays out. Witness the increasing dependence of pastors and leaders on pollsters and demographers to tell them what is happening in their own environment. Every few years a new book comes out in which a pollster unearths some new, groundbreaking take on what is going on culturally and how the church must respond. Witness the increasing loss of local imagination and the phenomenon of scanning the spiritual horizon for "success." Then witness the publishers rushing in to capitalize on this phenomenon and marketing the newest method for "winning" (if that isn't a culturally conditioned word, then I am not sure one exists) the culture for Christ. Finally, witness exhausted and bored pastors and congregations fed up and frustrated by the next new thing but at the same time discipled masterfully in the art of technique reproduction. This is reflective of a mounting leadership crisis in the church.

At the same time, leadership is the subject of a lot of discussion and hand-wringing in emerging churches. Previous iterations of church in the West have been shaped largely under the organizational metaphor of "corporation." As a result, leaders are often viewed (and view themselves) as CEOs or some variation thereof. Thus leadership structures often operate in one direction: top down. We have used, almost exclusively, structures of command and control. Certainly these commitments produce a kind of effectiveness. But have we asked what they eliminate? The corporation metaphor wipes out much of what I was describing before—the creative, imaginative, intuitive, and organic. Much of what we are seeing in the emerging church derives from a rediscovery of these sensibilities and capacities. But they do not function well within top-down, command-and-control structures.

In early expressions of the emerging church, many wanted to jettison the notion of leadership altogether. But while this sentiment may be understandable given the environment, it is ultimately naive and foolish. Leadership simply is. There is good leadership and bad leadership. There is leadership that is contextually appropriate and helpful, and there is leadership that is irrelevant and outdated. There are helpful metaphors for the identity and leadership of local churches, and there are metaphors that have lost their currency because they were born in a world that no longer exists.

The character required for leadership has not changed. It is *a*contextual. I will say that more explicitly: biblical leadership still requires (and will always require) discipleship in the way of Jesus Christ. But this discipleship involves being radically incarnational and engaged in the world that is before us in the power of the Holy Spirit for the sake of the world. In the midst of the fact of change, this fact does not change. Yet apart from this, we must allow our imaginations to run free.

Please don't misunderstand. I'm not saying leaders today must be masters of creativity and intuition. Increasingly, and perhaps most important, they must be able to create, nurture, and sustain environments where those capacities can be birthed, fed, and empowered among the people of God. I think perhaps the best way of saying this is that leaders must become environmentalists in the sense of those who create and shape environments. They must nurture organizational ecosystems that are diverse in life and resources. Leaders in the emerging world must be able to help create, shape, and nurture environments where life can emerge and grow organically. Leaders must shift out of attitudes of command and control and into postures of humility, engagement, listening, and collaboration. The irony is that these emerging understandings and postures of leadership are more demanding, rigorous, and challenging than anything we previously understood and rejected. They are also more fun.

Shades of Gray Matter

One of the many ways to illustrate this transformation is through an understanding of how the human brain functions and how that correlates to what is happening in our surrounding culture. Recently we have seen the emergence of right brain–related research. In education we talk of "multiple intelligences" and how important it is to engage children holistically when we seek to educate them. For a long time we have inhabited a world dominated by the left hemisphere of the brain.

The left hemisphere is traditionally associated with the kinds of activities that could be characterized as literalness, sequence, and analysis. The right hemisphere of the brain is associated with context, emotional expression (a different kind of intelligence increasingly in demand), and synthesis. Daniel Pink describes it this way:

> Until recently, the abilities that led to success in school, work, and business were characteristic of the left hemisphere. They were the sorts of linear, logical, analytical talents measured by SATs and deployed by CPAs. Today, those capabilities are still necessary. But they're no longer sufficient. In a world upended by outsourcing, deluged with data, and choked with choices, the abilities that matter most are now closer in spirit to the specialties of the right hemisphere: artistry, empathy, seeing the big picture, and pursuing the transcendent.[4]

Clearly, Pink is describing the environment as it relates to ventures previously understood as secular. But this is an unfortunate and inaccurate distinction: school, work, and business are simply collections of people in systems seeking to respond to the context in which they exist. The church is also a collection of people in a system seeking to respond to the context in which it exists. And so we can take some cues from Pink's words because we share this context. Our seminaries have entire ministry and theological training programs designed exclusively around the left hemisphere of the human brain. They are training men and women for a world that no longer exists. We must begin to engage our brain's right hemisphere and make room for those for whom the right hemisphere is native landscape. Even so, we will not be well served by a new dichotomy that polarizes in the opposite direction. Rather, we must seek the integration and reconciliation of both the left and right brain. Pink says as much:

> Let me be clear: The future is not some Manichaean landscape in which individuals are either left-brained and extinct or right-brained and ecstatic. Logical, linear, analytic thinking remains indispensable. But it's no longer

> enough. These [right hemisphere] abilities have always been a part of what it means to be human. It's just that after a few generations in the Information Age, many of our high concept, high touch muscles have atrophied. The challenge is to work them back into shape.[5]

Amen, and amen.

Galadriel was right: the world has changed. Unfortunately, I see a disconnect between the world where people live and the world where people worship. It is my hope that these two worlds can be reconciled in Christ for the sake of the gospel—God's work in the world. We need men and women who have previously been on the margins to come forth and lead us. In focusing so exclusively on our cognitive capacities, we have lost our imagination. We need mystics. We need poets. We need prophets. We need apostles. We need artists. We need a church out of the margins, drawn from the places and filled with people and shaped by competencies formerly thought to be of little account. In fact, perhaps it is from such "marginal" communities as these that influence will begin to spread outward into communities that have been domesticated in the modern world and thus rendered docile. We need a wild vine to be grafted into the branch. We need a church from the margins—a minority report that sees the unseen. We need alternate takes on reality. We need a different kind of leader—one who can create environments to nurture and release the imagination of God's people.

20

DIGGING UP THE PAST

Karl Barth (the Reformed Giant) as Friend to the Emerging Church

CHRIS ERDMAN

Dusty, musty, old things. That's what I loved as a child. My father was an archaeologist, and I spent my first few years playing in the dust, smelling the tang of juniper and sage, searching out what little shade I could find from the scorching sun of Colorado's desert southwest, sheltering in musty caves and amongst the ruins and ghosts of the past. The cliff dwellings of Mesa Verde National Park were my playground; bones, potsherds, and ancient scrap were my toys. It's little wonder that I thought I'd grow up and spend my life in places like this, fascinated by the stuff of the past, attracted to the dead.

Last summer, Julie and I took our teenage sons back to the mesas and canyons of Colorado for a weeklong archaeology camp—introducing our sons to the stuff of their family's past. We did it, not just so they can know their family history, but because our family history teaches us to believe that the road to the future runs through the past. Old, dead, and discarded things have much to teach us; we believe they are guides for the future.

As I see things today, I'm not, as a pastor, all that far from the vocational interest of my childhood. I still love dusty, musty, old things. I still dig around in the dirt, paying careful attention to things others overlook. I'm a theologian who handles old texts. I'm a pastor who believes the best way to shepherd the living is to help them learn from the dead. In short, I still believe that the road to the future runs through the past.

In Emergent circles I sometimes find a nagging suspicion about the past—specifically, the near past—born of our heightened sensitivity to

---

Chris Erdman serves as senior pastor at University Presbyterian Church, Fresno, California—a conventional congregation increasingly being made unconventional by the signs of "emergence" around and among its people. He also teaches preaching and missional leadership courses at the Mennonite Brethren Biblical Seminary. His newest book, *Countdown to Sunday: A Daily Guide for Those Who Dare to Preach*, is forthcoming from Brazos Press in 2007.

the compromises of the church within modernity. We're working to birth something new—new theology and new ecclesial forms that are free or at least loosened from uncritical compromises with the modern ideologies make us anxious. Sometimes the past is problematic (at least the past that's closest to us, where we see such troubling compromises); other times, the past is our companion (many of us find great encouragement from the thought and practice of the ancient, premodern church).

I hinted at some of this to Brian McLaren recently when we were between sessions at a meeting where Brian was teaching and exploring the broad contours of his "generous orthodoxy," his "broad ecumenism." I suggested to Brian that his theological project, while charting new territory in our day and age—thrilling some while antagonizing others—has some kinship with what I considered an important and enormously creative part of the near history we often overlook. "You're not far," I told him, "from the theological project of Karl Barth." In fact, Brian's kind of theological innovation is part and parcel of the Reformed tradition—a tradition that many in Emergent circles have dismissed as hidebound, doctrinaire, resistant to the impulses of our movement, an impediment to our vision. Having said such things, Brian was intrigued, not a little encouraged, and asked if I'd spend a little time explaining my comment more fully and publicly.

In what follows, I not only explain myself but hope to testify to the gifts a particular part of our near past can bring to us who are friends of things Emergent.

Who Was Karl Barth?

On August 1, 1914, the First World War broke out. Karl Barth was pastor in the tiny Swiss village of Safenwil. A large number of the villagers were called up to war; Barth was not among them. Instead, he worked among his remaining parishioners, whose husbands and fathers were off to war, cutting and bailing hay for weeks on end, preaching on Sundays, and fuming about it all until one woman came to him after a Sunday service and asked him to speak for once on something other than the war. But Barth didn't know what else to speak about . . . until he learned that ninety-three German intellectuals, including all of his theological teachers, had issued a manifesto supporting the war policy of the German Kaiser. Barth was devastated. He hung his head in shame and lamented, "They seemed to have been hopelessly compromised by their failure in the face of the ideology of war. . . . Thus a whole world of exegesis, ethics, dogmatics and preaching, which I had hitherto held to be essentially trustworthy, was shaken to the foundations."[1]

The bankruptcy of the liberal theological tradition that was Barth's own sent him, bewildered, to begin all over again theologically. But where was he to begin? In between making hay, keeping up with the news, and preparing sermons, he started again (as any good German speaking pastor would) reading Kant. Dissatisfied, he turned to Hegel. They were both dead ends. Then he and Eduard Thurneysen, a pastor in a nearby village, tried something much more obvious. "We tried to learn our theological ABCs all over again, beginning by reading and interpreting the writing of the Old and New Testaments, more thoughtfully than before. And lo and behold, they began to speak to us. I sat under an apple tree and began to apply myself to Romans. I began to read it as though I had never read it before."[2]

In 1918, Barth published his interpretation of Romans and it was a bombshell on the playground of the church and its theologians. It broke completely with the tradition of theological liberalism and took God seriously, arguing that God is not humanity writ large; the wholly otherness of the kingdom of God was the essential turn Barth made, and that in turn relativized all else.

I wonder if that's not what many of us sense and hope for—the freedom of God and the church from the ideological captivities that make God a commodity to be bought and sold, and the church an institution that gobbles up resources, panders to cultural whims, and resists the renewing, emerging winds that feel like life to us.

This break with religion as the cult of humanity isn't the only thing Barth did. He wrote gobs and gobs of theology, thousands and thousands of pages alone in his monumental *Church Dogmatics*. What I like most about this Reformed theologian is his insistence that the theological enterprise must never be the sole realm of academic theologians. Rather it is the work *of* the church and *for* the church. He liked to refer to himself as simply a pastor, nothing more, but nothing less. He also believed the theological imperative was never finished. Each and every volume of his *Dogmatics* reveals an astounding freedom and innovation to reengage the tradition and the Bible, reinterpret them for our times, and always ask fresh questions.

Writer William Blake once said, "Improvement makes straight, straight roads, but it is the crooked roads without improvement that are the roads to genius." Such was Karl Barth. He wrote and wrote crooked, undomesticated theology, but in it we have a theological model or method so needed in our times. For us Emergent folk, it is a model—a tradition—that ought not only intrigue us but encourage and envision us.

Two Reasons for Digging Up the Past

Now to the reasons I'm digging up the past, urging us to pay attention to the gifts of the dead for the future of the living. I do so believing that digging up the past, working among the bones and potsherds and scrap of what others too easily discard as irrelevant, might provide us with some useful material for entering the future before us.

The Present State of Emergent(cy)

Many Emergent pastors and theologians know that we are working not only with a new and emergent theology, but that we do so from a situation of emergency. The work is vitally important in this post-Christian, postmodern, post–9/11 world. We work with a sense of urgency and hope that what we're about will form the church—whatever it might look like—as a faithful witness in the century to come.

Karl Barth found himself in such a situation at the beginning of his pastoral ministry. The First World War threw him into a tailspin, but one in which he found new wings. In 1916 he wrote: "We must begin all over again with a new inner orientation to the primitive basic truths of life: only this can deliver us from the chaos arising from the failure of conservative or revolutionary proposals and counter-proposals. . . . Above all, it will be a matter of our recognizing God once more as God . . . this is a task alongside which all cultural, social and patriotic duties are child's play."[3]

By 1932, more fully engaged in the theological work that began in crisis, he continued to see the pastoral task as one done in a perpetual state of emergency—never static, never dull, never fixed, always open. This is precisely why Barth is a friend to us who also find ourselves in such a condition. In the first volume of *Church Dogmatics*, he issues this challenge:

> How disastrously the Church must misunderstand itself if it can imagine that theology is the business of a few theoreticians who are specially appointed for the task. . . . Again, how disastrously the Church must misunderstand itself if it can imagine that theological reflection is a matter for quiet situations and periods that suit and invite contemplation, a kind of peace-time luxury. . . . As though the venture of proclamation did not mean that the Church permanently finds itself in an emergency! As though theology could be done properly without reference to this constant emergency! Let there be no mistake. Because of these distorted ideas about theology, and dogmatics in particular, there arises and persists in the life of the Church a lasting and growing deficit for which we cannot expect those particularly active in this function to supply the needed balance. The whole Church must seriously want a serious theology if it is to have a serious theology.[4]

Many of our own theological statements echo Barth's understanding of the theological challenge. We now, like Barth then, are dissatisfied with the established and entrenched theology that has produced our present crisis. We seek another way; we want to "begin all over again," to work in a state of "constant emergency" in order to subvert and convert so many "distorted ideas about theology" that hold the church captive. We also know that this vital work must be done with broad involvement of ordinary church folk (and perhaps, nonchurch folk as well). We know that beginning again cannot simply mean repeating the perspectives of an entrenched elite who may well be compromised by that all-too-common conservative impulse to protect the institution that guarantees their retirement benefits (this is true on the Right as well as on the Left). Barth knew that theology was always threatened by politics—both ecclesial and secular—and he, like us, worried that theology can too easily "conform to the ruling regime."[5]

The Theological Freedom We Need

When I suggested to Brian McLaren that his work reminded me of Barth's nearly a century ago, I had in mind a story Barth tells in his concise *Dogmatics in Outline* (a tiny little primer in his theological reconstruction of Christian faith). *Dogmatics in Outline* is a series of lectures given in the postwar ruins of the once stately Kurfursten Schloss (castle) in Bonn, Germany, during the summer of 1946. He began his lectures at seven in the morning, "always after we had sung a psalm or a hymn to cheer us up." By eight o'clock, "the rebuilding of the quadrangle began to advertise itself in the rattle of an engine" as the engineers went to work on "the ruins" around them.[6]

This is the place in which theology is done—for Barth in the rubble of World War II and for us in the rubble of our postmodern, post-Christian, and post–9/11 world. A theology for the future is reconstructed in the place of deconstruction, and it must be performed in genuine freedom.

Barth began his theological reconstruction in the rubble, and it was that rubble that gave him new freedom. It was a freedom to innovate, but not without being moored to the past. If you read Barth, especially the small print in his vast *Church Dogmatics*, you realize what kind of dialogue he maintained with the past—not unlike the "broad ecclesiology" McLaren champions.

In his first lecture, Barth lays out the task or method of dogmatics, that is, theological reconstruction:

> Dogmatics is the science in which the Church, in accordance with the state of its knowledge at different times, takes account of the content of its proclamation critically, that is, by the standard of Holy Scripture and under the guidance of its Confessions.[7]

In his theology, Barth reveals (and revels) in an astonishing freedom, but it is a freedom that is always tethered. He is like a jazz musician who knows the score so well he can freely improvise but without the foolishness of those naive, would-be musicians who think they can soar in ecstasy without knowing their chords or being tutored by the tradition itself. In fact, I suggest that it was his love for Mozart that may have nourished or at least have provided a metaphor for this freedom. Says his biographer:

> At one point, Barth bought a gramophone, which "virtually became a centerpiece at home, and a large number of Mozart records, which can often be heard in my study. Following a tendency which I had even as a small boy, I have now concentrated completely on Mozart and have established that in relation to him Bach is merely John the Baptist and Beethoven, Origen, if not the Shepherd of Hermas." Barth's objection to Johann Sebastian Bach, otherwise so loved by theologians, was his all too deliberate, all too artificial "desire to preach," while Mozart attracted him because he was free from such intentions and simply played.[8]

If we are to have the kind of theology we most need today, this is the kind of freedom we need. But it is not a freedom *from* the tradition. Rather, it is a freedom to live inside the tradition, but never simply to repeat it. Ours ought to be critical while being playful, wild without being reckless (though those who don't understand may think we are). And we must be free of that "all too artificial desire to preach"—that desire to prove something, to challenge, even to cut a new path that can, frankly, undermine our service to the Word of God. Instead, we'll revel in the chance to "simply play," but we can do so only by knowing our chords, embracing the tradition, even while we improvise on its richness.

Finally, I think we must be willing to change our minds. And here we also have the witness that is Karl Barth. In 1956, his birthday allowed him to take stock of nearly fifty years of theological work. Critics talked about a new Barth, one who'd changed his mind. "It's true," Barth said, "that I have learnt some things on the way. At least I hope so. The way to not grow old, and to stay young with advancing years, is to continue to learn."[9]

> As far as I can recall there was no stage in my theological career when I had more than the very next step forward in mind and planned for it. On each occasion this step developed from the steps which I had already taken, and followed from my view of what was possible and necessary in each changing situation. I saw myself as the man who I had become so far. I used what I thought that I had learned and understood so far to cope with this or that situation, with some complex of biblical or historical or doctrinal questions, often with some subject presented to me from outside, often in fact by a topical subject. It was always something new that got a hold of me, rather than the other way around.[10]

His work was extemporaneous, free, meandering, playful.

Theology is done in a perpetual state of emergency; it is free improvisation on the tradition inside our new setting. These are two great gifts Karl Barth gives us; they are, in large measure, exactly what we're about in our friendships across the Emergent world. While we're digging up the far past in our worship liturgies and our sense of the renewal of Christian practices, let's not avoid the gifts given us by this witness from the near past many of us might sooner ignore.

Cultivating a friendship with this thinker—not in the grave long enough to gather much dust, but long enough to be forgotten or ignored—might well strengthen our nerve and stiffen our resolve to be the theologian-pastors the church today so desperately needs.

HOPE

PART 5

Hopeful Activism

The Jesus Way in the Realities of Life

Tony Jones

I live in a suburb. I say that by way of confession. I don't know that I *want* to live in a suburb, but I do. I'm surrounded by white people, all of whom make a decent (or more-than-decent) living. I could list the litany of suburban possessions—what's in our driveways and backyards and savings accounts—but that would depress you and me both.

I spend a fair amount of time reconciling myself to the fact that I live in a suburb. And I don't take my suburban existence as an excuse for seclusion or retreat. I think I'm about as involved in the life of my suburb as I have time to be. But it's still a suburb, and thus it still is affordable to only a certain type of person. And it seems to breed a certain outlook on the world that makes me more than a bit uncomfortable.

So I'm glad to rub shoulders with the people who have written the following chapters. Each one of them, in her or his own way, is provoking me to a more authentic existence. By that I mean a more introspective existence, for I am firmly convinced that the old Socratic saw is right:

"The unexamined life is not worth living." I'm also a firm believer in the other old proverb, from Thoreau, "The mass of men [and women] lead lives of quiet desperation."

To immerse oneself in the thoughtful reflections of those who are pushing issues that can make us uncomfortable is the only way to live forward into the life that Christ commends. Let's be honest: in my suburbs the racism is subtle and hidden, talk of sexuality and gender stays locked in the bedroom, and there's not a Native American for miles. So how do I overcome the shortcomings of my own surroundings? Only by being proactive and listening to persons like Deb and Ken and Randy and Anthony and Rudy and Karen.

Please don't think me patronizing in this little intro. I'm not just blowing smoke. This is a real issue that a lot of us need to confess. Many of us spend a lot of time reading blogs or deconstructing movies or updating our iPods when we should be neck deep in the realities of life that these authors are talking about. How we manage all this is crucial. It's crucial for the future of the emerging church. Indeed, it's crucial for the future of the church. And I know that it's crucial for my children. If I screw up these lessons, I've really dropped the ball.

"I'm a follower of Jesus." It's such a pithy little phrase. But like so many pithy phrases, it becomes virtually meaningless without some serious self-reflection. And the more I dig and the more I confront the realities exposed in the chapters that follow, the more humble I am about uttering that phrase.

21

A POUND OF SOCIAL JUSTICE

Beyond Fighting for a Just Cause

RODOLPHO CARRASCO

A lot of Christian service groups visit Harambee Ministries, a Christian urban ministry that I direct in Pasadena, California. I love to read them the fifth chapter of the book of Amos. For dramatic effect, I use *The Message* version of the Bible. It leaves little room for interpretation of the writer's intent. For example, take Amos 5:21–24 (Message):

> I can't stand your religious meetings.
> I'm fed up with your conferences and conventions.
> I want nothing to do with your religion projects,
> your pretentious slogans and goals.
> I'm sick of your fund-raising schemes,
> your public relations and image making.
> I've had all I can take of your noisy ego-music.
> When was the last time you sang to me?
> Do you know what I want?
> I want justice—oceans of it.
> I want fairness—rivers of it.
> That's what I want. That's all I want.

I read this aloud to visitors, and then I pause. I follow with the story of how Harambee was established, why, and what we do now to love people in our community in the name of Jesus. But the Scripture makes its own point, and I have to be careful not to dilute that point, not to pull the punch, not to water it down. So I wait. Then I move forward

---

Rodolpho Carrasco is executive director of Harambee Christian Family Center in Pasadena, Calif. Harambee provides afterschool programs and a private, Christian school that emphasize personal responsibility and indigenous leadership development. Rudy's articles on urban ministry, youth development, and racial reconciliation have appeared in *Christianity Today*, the *Los Angeles Times*, and other publications. He serves on the board of directors of the Christian Community Development Association and World Vision U.S., and is a member of the Hispanic Scholarship Fund's Alumni Hall of Fame.

with a personal attempt to amplify a centuries-old text. The best I can do is punctuate these Scriptures with a summary statement. On any given occasion I might say:

> God is serious about justice.
> God is very serious about justice.
> Ain't God worked up about the plight of the poor?
> God gets bent out of shape when it comes to justice for the poor.
> God is impolite in his passion for the poor.

Any one statement will do, because each is true. And these truths are bad news for Christians. The above verses from Amos contrast the common religious activities of Christians today with God's desire for justice. The concept of justice is not unpacked in this section. We are left to wonder what "oceans" of justice look like. We can get a clearer sense of what the writer means when we look elsewhere in the fifth chapter (v. 11 Message):

> Because you have run roughshod over the poor
> and take the bread right out of their mouths,
> You're never going to move into
> the luxury homes you have built.
> You're never going to drink the wine
> from the expensive vineyards you've planted.

At the very least, justice means doing the opposite of running roughshod over the poor and taking bread out of their mouths. Before we engage justice-preserving solutions, let's sit under the spittle of bitter biblical condemnations a little longer, because they reverberate throughout Amos. See chapter 2, verse 7: "They grind the penniless into the dirt, shove the luckless into the ditch." Or chapter 8, verse 6: "You exploit the poor, using them—and then, when they're used up, you discard them."

Amos is not the only place you will find God's anger over injustice. Pick any biblical prophet. Here's an interesting one—Ezekiel 16:49: "This is the sin of Sodom. She was arrogant, overfed and unconcerned." Ezekiel is describing the destruction of Sodom, well-known in Genesis 19 as a symbol of judgment on sexual perversion. But the sex sin is dealt with in Ezekiel as a secondary matter. The first thing Ezekiel gets across is the people's guilt in being arrogant, overfed, and unconcerned. That chills me, because "arrogant, overfed, and unconcerned" pretty much describes me. Toward those who are arrogant, overfed, and unconcerned, God is not merely perturbed, annoyed, saddened, perplexed, bewildered, or brokenhearted, he's enraged, like a vendetta-seeking Hollywood action hero. Back to Amos 9:3–4 (Message):

> If they dive to the bottom of the ocean,
> I'll send Dragon to swallow them up.
> If they're captured alive by their enemies,
> I'll send Sword to kill them.
> I've made up my mind
> to hurt them, not help them.

What are we supposed to do with that? I ask sincerely, because the direct content of those verses does not fit my image of a loving God. And though I'm puzzled, I'm not fool enough to disregard the warning. The Almighty is cranked up and hopped-up about how the weak are victimized. While we may not know exactly how to respond, try reading these and other biblical judgments and coming away unconvinced about the *need* to respond.

Responding to Injustice

Thankfully, Amos does not just unload; he tells us what to do. His answer is true and right. But there's a problem. True and right as his answer may be, it is also fuzzy, lyrical, poetic, and downright enigmatic: "Let justice roll on like a river, righteousness like a never-failing stream!" (5:24).

It's a start. But it's not very helpful in this day and age. I mean, show me "justice rolling on like a river." Take me to this never-failing stream of righteousness. You might as well give me a pound of social justice.

However elusive, the biblical injunction is nevertheless on us. Given the anger of the Almighty on this topic, we would do well to follow the advice the apostle Paul gave so succinctly in one of his letters: "Work out your salvation with fear and trembling" (Phil. 2:12).

I do not have a pound of social justice to give you, but I can share my community's efforts at enacting godly justice. Harambee, established in

1983, is an urban ministry with the goal of reaching children, youth, and families with the saving knowledge of Jesus Christ and his atoning death on the cross, and with the promise of new life as his disciples. As we minister through Harambee, we are painfully aware that we are in a context of poverty, generational sin, historic racism and injustice, pervasive cynicism, and despair. We seek to preach the truth of Jesus Christ with words and to demonstrate that truth with our own actions. As we pursue godly justice, as we see justice enacted in our community, we see that justice ministry can be a profound tool for building trust with neighbors who long ago may have given up trusting God, their neighbors, or themselves.

A note: you have entered a highly anecdotal zone. If you want an introduction to social justice, a reasoned reflection on different approaches to social justice, or more specific challenges to social justice issues for today, there are a number of great books and resources out there.[1]

I've been formally working for justice for sixteen years now, and what I'm learning is that the best stuff comes from your own personal experience, knocking your own head, and seeing surprising developments after the smoke clears. There's a lot to learn from plain old experience. That's the reason it can be more profitable to sit with an old head, an old schooler, someone who has been around the block, even if that person is older, retiring, not in touch with popular culture, and perhaps not the greatest communicator. I can't find the things I hunger for in a book or a formal lecture. So I hope to share with you a little bit of what has quenched my thirst and sated my hunger.

Born in East LA

Harambee's founder, Dr. John Perkins, wrote a book in 1981 called *With Justice for All*.[2] In the first chapter, "Evangelism Is Not Enough," Perkins describes how his heart was broken by the rural poverty of Mendenhall, Mississippi. School dropouts, terrible living conditions, drunkenness, absentee mothers and fathers, and teen pregnancy defined the community. He had moved to Mississippi from California to evangelize his own people, after reading Romans 10:1–2 and recognizing that his people had "a zeal for God, but it is not enlightened." While living in the community, meeting the people, and getting to know the problems, he realized that "the Gospel, rightly understood, is holistic—it responds to man as a whole person; it doesn't single out just spiritual or just physical needs and speak only to those."[3] From that initial understanding, Perkins led an effort to live out the words of Micah 6:8: "He has showed you, O man, what is good. And what does the LORD require of you? To act justly and to love mercy and to walk humbly with your God."

The ministry in Mendenhall was centered around a local church. And surrounding the church there was a gymnasium for youth activities, a Christian elementary school, a law office, a health office, and a thrift store and cooperative farm for economic development. They evangelized young people and families in their community. They taught them how to walk as disciples of Jesus who live out their faith in all areas of life, public as well as private.

I read *With Justice for All* when I was a student at Stanford University. It resonated with my own life experiences, and I felt as though I was finally seeing the Bible come to life. I hadn't seen the Christians around me living the way the early disciples did, and so, like an arrogant, hotheaded, better-than-thou, I purposed in my heart to blow off the Christians in America because they weren't living out their concern for the poor. When I read the Perkins story, I decided that Perkins was the one Christian leader to whom I would listen. What an extremist!

When I came to faith in Christ, I was ten years old. It was in a Baptist Sunday school class, and the story that Sunday was about the walls of Jericho coming down. I refrained from pulling the hair of the girl next to me just long enough to hear Joshua's rallying cry: "Shout! For the LORD has given you the city! The city and all that is in it are to be devoted to the LORD" (Josh. 6:16–17). I heard that and wondered, *God cares about cities?* Right then I made a deal: "God, I will follow you, because one day you are going to do something about East LA." I was ten years old and bargaining with God and telling him what he was going to do. Right then I said yes to the Christian project, to this Jesus-my-Lord-and-Savior thing, because he was going to do something about East LA.

East LA was a burden for me because I had been born in East LA and loved East LA, but I'd also fled from East LA. My mother died when I was just about to turn seven, and my father was not in the picture. We were poor—I remember getting in trouble for destroying our food stamps. My mother was buried at Resurrection Cemetery, and it was left to my sister Yolanda to raise my brother, Andrew, my sister, Silvana, and me. The first thing Yoli did was to get us out of the dangerous East LA neighborhood of El Sereno. Getting out, getting far, fleeing—that's what we did. But though I feared some of the people on the streets of East LA, I also loved the place.

Early childhood psychologists and Jesuit priests share a saying, which goes roughly like this: "Give me a child until he is seven, and I will show you the man." Something profound about the human psyche is formed by the age of seven, and I had spent the first seven years of my life in East LA. When I learned about the cry of Joshua at Jericho, my childish heart believed that God would do something about East LA. "Something" meant turning people into followers of his Son Jesus, and it also meant changing the community so that it was a less fearful and dangerous place to live. (I told you it was a simple vision.) From that time on I was focused. I had a plan, which was to get a college degree, learn to read the Bible and interpret it by myself, and live in East LA and be a Christian. I had no idea what I would do to support myself; God would take care of that as he had taken care of the prophets of old.

Even after I moved out of East LA, the taste of injustice, and the call to do something about it, lingered. It lingered through my teen years and followed me to Biola University and then Stanford. Every step of the way I encountered very few people who were unnerved by the biblical mandate to love the poor and act justly wherever we went.

That's the reason John Perkins was a godsend to me. On an InterVarsity Christian Fellowship–sponsored trip to Mississippi in the summer of 1989, I served in ministries that he had started and turned over to people from the community. The next spring, one week away from finishing my last class for my undergraduate degree, I heard Perkins speak on my campus. Afterward my friends and I shook his hand. Then he invited us to work with him in Pasadena, where he had started another ministry. When I graduated from college, I hustled to work with my hero. I imagined that I would work two years with Perkins, learning everything I could from this black Christian leader, and then take what I had learned to Mexican-dominant East LA. I hadn't planned to take a detour in the black community on my way back to East LA. But the more I got to know Perkins and the peculiarities of justice seeking among blacks in America, the more I imagined that there were valuable things that Hispanics could learn from our black brothers and sisters, so I jumped in with two feet.

Sixteen years later, I'm still here. Everything I thought I would encounter in East LA is here in Northwest Pasadena—Hispanic people, Hispanic challenges, and Hispanic dreams. But God gave me more than I asked. He turned my dream of "helping out" and "making a place less dangerous" into something more specific and effective.

Doing Justice

When you think of Harambee, think of the movie *The Matrix*. Think of the visible, seen world and the unseen, deeper reality.

Our visible reality is a set of outreach and development programs under the umbrella of Harambee Ministries. We have an after-school program where children and teens can have fun, get help with their homework, hear Bible stories, pray with their peers, and engage in extracurricular activities—like vocal music, art, dance, karate, and computers—all in a safe environment. We have a private, Christian elementary school and a preschool. A teenage jobs and college prep program, called Junior Staff, challenges teens to step into their God-given opportunities. Summer programs, internships, and trips to faraway places minister in unique ways to the people of the community. We emphasize racial reconciliation—people building deep relationships across ethnic lines because of the saving work of Jesus on the cross.

The unseen reality starts with the detail that the majority of our staff live in the community that we serve. We are embedded. We are "deep cover." We are neighbors. We *are* the community. We believe that living in the community we seek to serve is critical to our efforts to make disciples for Jesus Christ. Also we are committed to living in the community for a long period of time, because the problems we are confronting do not have instant solutions. This dynamic of living in a justice-needy situation for a long time helps us see our work more clearly and therefore to focus our efforts more effectively.

This is important because the justice that people need is a moving target. For me, engaging this moving target involves thinking about justice as both "eternal vigilance" and an onion. Perkins says that justice is eternal vigilance. You will never arrive at justice, or at a point when justice has been completely fulfilled, until the day of the Lord. You will never complete all the tasks laid before you that fit the category of justice.

If you take your hand off the plow (yes, I'm a city guy using a farming metaphor), the gains you made in the fight for justice may be reversed while you are off doing something else. Fighting for justice doesn't fit a timetable—the battles emerge in their own timing, when we do not expect them, when we are not prepared.

To Perkins's formulation that justice is eternal vigilance, I would add that justice is an onion. You peel back one layer, successfully complete one task of justice, and find that there is more, much more, sometimes devastatingly more, to do. Here's an example. I know these apple farmers in southeastern Washington State, a Christian couple named Ralph and Cheryl Broetje. Years back, in the 1980s, Cheryl came on an area of their property where migrant laborers were living in horrible conditions. These were the very laborers who made the farm successful. She was burdened by what she saw. The Broetjes' response was to take their own resources, somewhere in the neighborhood of five million dollars, and clear off a section of their land, build one hundred homes, pave roads around those homes, put in a gas station and a convenience store, open a school and a gym and a church, and otherwise try to meet the needs of the community in their midst. Families rented the homes at very fair and affordable prices. How incredible! I haven't heard of many responses to injustice like this.

Soon the Broetjes encountered another challenge: Many of the teen children were not in school because they had to take care of their smaller siblings, as both parents were out working, usually in the apple farm. So there was a need for day care and for making sure youth were getting a proper education. That led the Broetjes to get involved in family and community life and in longstanding issues like alcoholism, gangs, and domestic violence. The Broetjes couldn't just abandon the entire endeavor, because they had become personally involved in the lives of the people they worked with and sought to serve. Today the Vista Hermosa community is growing and thriving, with great challenges, because an entire body of people has joined with the Broetjes to seek justice for their neighbors.

An experience like that will make you or break you, but the one thing it won't do is leave you as you are. Often North American Christians say that it's not as challenging to be a Christian in our context as it is elsewhere, because we live in a Christian nation and are prosperous. We don't have the threat of discrimination or persecution hanging over us as do many of our fellow believers around the globe. Well, if we commit ourselves to justice as the prophet Micah says, if we keep peeling back the layers of the onion, and if we don't shy away when we encounter deeper challenges, I don't think we'll say that anymore.

We've seen a lot at Harambee over the years, and because we have seen so much, we stress the development of individuals, usually poor individuals, over activities to change society. Here's why. I've seen initiatives for justice come and go. One season it's a campaign for fair housing. Another time it's increased funding for inner-city schools. There may be a fight against gangs and crime. A major grant to improve health services rolls through town. The list is endless, and all these initiatives are important. I did not say that we don't engage social change, only that it carries a secondary emphasis. It is secondary because the development of a needy individual does not follow the timetable of a cause or a campaign.

For example, imagine a ten-year-old boy who does not know his father, is being raised by a single mother, does poorly in school, and has a lot of friends in a gang. The boy gets involved in a mentoring initiative to keep kids out of gangs. The program is active for two years and does a great job, but then the program is defunded. The boy had a great two years of intervention, but he still needs help, because now he is twelve. His need did not end just because the program ended. Then a fair housing initiative goes through town, some advances are made, and his family is able to move into more secure, affordable housing, but the boy still has no father. Perhaps he hasn't gotten any better at school. The success of the mentoring initiative and the success of the housing initiative still do not meet all of this boy's needs.

Programs will never replace people who love a person over the long term. Programs, no matter how well-planned or well-funded, can't do what a committed person can do—a principle easily overlooked, even by those of us who preach it.

At Harambee we invest in the lives of individuals, and in others who are personally invested in individuals. After sixteen years of ministering at the corner of Howard and Navarro, I've learned that living in a stable, relatively good family is a person's best chance at experiencing justice. The best way for a child to get out of poverty is for his single parent to get married. We know that from social science and from evaluating the results of welfare reform. I've seen it in my own community. One set of brothers was doing decently at school and managing to stay out of trouble. Then their single mother got married and their achievement level shot up.

The Need for Committed People

After investing yourself in justice for others, you may wonder at what point you can stand back and say, "I did my part; it's up to the Lord now." I want to push you. Theologically, if you are from a more Reformed tradition that emphasizes God's sovereignty in all things, it's all up to the Lord, so whether we do our part or not, the Lord will have his way. I'm not sure Amos would go with you on that. Somewhere someone has to do something. Yes, the Lord will provide. But that provision is tangible. What the child doesn't receive at home is going to have to be instilled or replaced, somehow, by someone.

I know this because I grew up in double jeopardy, with neither father nor mother. Years later I'm a college graduate who has won awards and was once approached by the White House about taking a position there. I'm probably digging a hole for myself on Judgment Day because of my pride, my hubris, but let me say that a lot of people would like to see a lost inner-city kid turn out like Rudy Carrasco. I think about my life a lot. How did this all happen? I know that the Lord literally replaced the things I didn't have. At key points in my life, he filled the gaps with his people. I needed a father and a mother during my childhood and teen years. I got to college and wished for a father to navigate me through turbulent waters. On my wedding day my heart cried out for my father and mother. When my first child was about to be born, I spent the entire ninth month of my wife's pregnancy in deep existential angst, wishing for my father to comfort me and tell me I would be okay, that I wouldn't screw up my kid like, well, like he had by not being there for me.

Each step of the way, the Lord provided one of his people—extended family, friends, teachers, Bible study leaders, mentors, bosses—to help me. Christians filled with the Holy Spirit were there to guide me on the path to wholeness. None of us is completely whole until the day we are transformed and in the presence of Christ, but still, I feel pretty whole. God has poured great things into my life through other people who were there.

That's what is on my heart when I think about justice, when I think about the emerging church being committed to justice. It gives me joy—yes, the word is *joy*—when I think about how so many of my peers are committed to justice for the poor around the globe. It's a big, big deal that it is one of our core values. I want what happened in my life to happen all over again in the lives of countless little Rudys floating—lost, bewildered, hanging on—in America. And I want my friends and those who listen to me to remember that justice goes way past causes like the environment, the economy, education, and foreign policy. When the protest is over, when the program has concluded for the day, in the stillness of private life, the person in need of justice still needs justice, in the form of love and friendship. Perhaps justice, in the end, is giving a person everything that God wants for him or her to have, not just material or social goods but the quiet assurance that, "Before you were born, I knew you—and loved you. I still do."

22

EMERGENT KISSING

Authenticity and Integrity in Sexuality

KAREN E. SLOAN

Greet one another with a holy kiss.

Paul, in letters to the Romans, Corinthians, and Thessalonians

I have a confession: recently I have not been confessing my sins to other people. In particular, it can be daunting to confess sins related to my sexuality. But, in the past, I have been in church settings that safely encouraged me to share about my sexual brokenness. Within small prayerful groups, I've journeyed from the shame of hidden sexual sin to healing through specific confession. Every time, the response of a group was to assure me of Christ's cleansing forgiveness and to pray for God's ongoing healing in my life through the working of the Holy Spirit.

These times have been a meaningful way of ministering to the challenges of living well in my body. Yet I rarely hear of churches that deeply consider how we can love God with our bodies, part of which is being authentic about the realities of sexuality. When we gather as the church, we bring our minds, spirits, and bodies. Church communities that don't model appropriate intimacy by providing for redemptive confession and physical affirmation, fall short in helping us love God with all of who we are. Handshakes, hugs, and kisses are a significant part of church, alongside being known and confessing sin.

A reason that I ceased confessing personal sin is that I have been lacking structure that encourages me to live out the instructions, "confess your

---

Karen E. Sloan, a minister in the Presbyterian Church (USA) with an MDiv from Fuller Theological Seminary, can often be found praying in Catholic churches. For the past few years she has hung around the Dominican order and monastic life, resulting in her recent debut book *Flirting with Monasticism: Finding God on Ancient Paths* (InterVarsity Press, December 2006). Karen delights in hosting conversations about old and new monastic life. She regularly leads others in experiencing monastic practices, such as Liturgy of the Hours and Examen. (More about this journey can be found at www.flirtingwithmonasticism.org.) Her wide-ranging interests have also led to involvements with Desert Stream Ministries, Christian Formation and Direction Ministries, the Presbyterian Center for Mission Studies, Evangelicals for Middle East Understanding, and Godly Play. And from years of looking at antique furniture with her mom, she is drawn to anything from the Arts and Crafts period with a fascination for that movement.

sins to each other and pray for each other so that you may be healed" (James 5:16a). With several transitions and moves in the past two years, I have not been able to find, or form, a church community where people are authentic about sexual sin. This leads to an unspoken worry. Am I ignoring places of vulnerability that are subtly tempting me to retreat from my commitment to healthy sexuality?

Watching Kissing

When I was around five years old, I specifically remember being at my aunt's house as our families watched *The Sound of Music* together. I was embarrassed and uncomforable seeing Maria and the Captain smooching extensively toward the end of the film. As far as I was concerned the scene could not be over fast enough. This was the early '80s, kissing was not something I was used to seeing on television. Sensitized by this memory, I wonder how children today are impacted by the increase in sensuality as they, often alone, watch television and spend time on the Internet.

It's not that kissing itself is appalling. Seeing friends greet each other with a hug or a kiss is joyful. But how can it be beneficial to be a close-up observer of others' extended moments of physical intimacy?

One setting in which it is an enormous joy to see kissing is at the conclusion of a wedding service. It is a holy moment. Earlier this year when I officiated a wedding, rather than using the traditional statement, "You may now kiss the bride," I asked the groom and bride, "Will you bless us with a kiss?" Their kiss was a symbol of the life partnership which they had just vowed through their words and the giving of rings. Because they will share an exclusive, sexually intimate relationship, the moment of kissing ideally foreshadows the man and woman coming together in God's instruction that they "be fruitful and multiply."

Preaching Kissing (and What Married Kissing Leads To)

Searching for Christian community after completing college, I attended a young adults group that did several talks on decision-making. The only mention of sexual intimacy was a short admonishment that the Bible says, "Don't have sex other than with your spouse." The young adults group could have used more guidance, yet how often are positive visions of human sexuality proclaimed in church settings? How often do we talk about one-night stands in fellowship groups, or oral sex in youth groups? How often do we talk not only of our spirit but also of the realities of living in a physical body? Healthy sexuality is not about harsh repression or reckless expression. It is found, instead, in an honest self-awareness of both the good elements and the sinful elements of sexuality. Honesty such as this can provide opportunities for those in church communities to seek out healing toward living out God's best intention for human sexuality.

Having heard hundreds of sermons, mostly in evangelical churches, I can recall only one brief tangent in a sermon years ago that continues to inspire me to value sexual fidelity. That Sunday, the preacher was an associate pastor near retirement, and I don't remember the main point in his sermon. But during a throwaway comment, a bright flash came into his eyes as he paused to challenge the younger listeners: "All of you young people who think the sex you're having is wonderful, you have no idea how much more incredible it is to be sexually intimate with the person you've been married to for several decades of life together." More than these words, his entire gleaming countenance convinced me of his belief in this reality that the best sex comes with years of family life, raising children, and grandchildren. When I heard him say this, and whenever I recall the memory of it, I still yearn to live a life of self-control so I too can experience the joy of sex that is discovered only by decades of faithfulness in marriage.

My mother's parents shared such a marriage. As an adult, it is now obvious to me that their marriage had a rewardingly high amount of physical intimacy, even during their later years when they were also frequently babysitting grandkids. However, I was far more impacted by watching my parents' painfully difficult marriage, which mercifully ended in divorce when I was in high school. Examples of vibrant marriages among various mentors and friends are great treasures to me, and their occasional references to sharing a fulfilling physical relationship are reassuring. Their lives are dramatically different from the many, many stories of sexual brokenness that our culture tells far more often.

It's sad when those in church settings are not comfortable being honest about their sexuality. Outside churches, our culture bombards public spaces with unholy sensuality. From the pictures on magazine covers in the checkout lines of grocery stores, to the billboards along freeways that advertise "adult" bookstores and "gentlemen's" clubs, it can be difficult to resist the temptation of sexual fantasy and more than fantasy. Placed as lights in the midst of these unsatisfying allurements, Christians must propose a better vision of sexuality.

Never Kissing?

Working with Catholic priests is teaching me to value celibacy—the commitment to remain unmarried and refrain from any sexually charged intimacy. Though a new monastic awareness has led me to learn a great deal from ancient Catholic orders, I also resonate with the uncertainty of Reformation leaders like Martin Luther regarding the wisdom of vowing to permanent celibacy. Yet it concerns me when church communities strongly encourage, if not require, all of their leaders to be married.

Sometimes the circumstances of a person's life are better suited for celibacy. Some are called to live a lifestyle of self-giving that would not be possible with the additional demands of a spouse and children. Churches must not teach only about the goodness of sexual intimacy in marriage.

It was a disappointment during seminary that taught me this lesson. Due to overlapping class schedules, a classmate I'll call Ray and I ended up spending time together. Tenderhearted, humorous, and attractive, Ray drew many to him, including me. During the second year of seminary, when Ray was around, an internal monologue borrowed from *The Sound of Music* often ensued. In my desire for naïveté, I would quote Maria: "Couldn't keep his eyes off me?" Grounding myself in reality I would then quote the Baroness's response: "Come, my dear. We are women. Let's not pretend we don't know when a man notices us." So when he invited me to visit a youth group meeting he oversaw, I decided to go and be open to whatever might come of it.

Arriving late, I stood in the back of the completely dark seating area, watching what was going on in the front of the large room. A youth band played for a while, followed by an energetic talk by Ray. As the students were dismissed to smaller group discussions led by college volunteers, the room's lights were turned on. Ray now saw me, our eyes met in hopeful expectation, and he made his way over. Walking me around the church's buildings, as he checked in with the various group discussions, he introduced me charmingly to his life outside our classes. And he shared more personal stories from his own journey, drawing me to want to know him more. Later, when the students left, I went with the volunteer leaders to a nearby coffee shop. Ray's skill in pastorally caring for the volunteers was evident as I watched them hang out and talk through the youth group meeting.

It also became apparent that he was not choosing to talk with me more that night. As it became late, I eventually said farewell and began the long drive home. While driving, I thought about how fun the evening had been. Seeing Ray minister increased my admiration of him, yet it was undeniably obvious that youth ministry was the focus of his life. His eyes would wander to me during class, but all he was offering me was an invitation to become more involved in his ministry world. One evening was enjoyable, but with all the other commitments in my life, I knew I was not called to invest more time at that church.

Later I figured out from Ray's comments that one of the reasons he reached out to me was pressure from church leaders who wanted him to "settle down with a nice girl." His denomination expects that everyone will benefit from marriage. But as a full-time student in a full-time ministry job, Ray had no room in his life for dating. Following up with Ray, I invited him to visit me at the church where I ministered. I was only a little sad that he never made the time to do so. I wonder how someone like Ray would have benefited from being intentionally supported in living celibately during such a full season of his life. Even when there is a longing for the intimacy of marriage, it can be a better choice to refrain from striving for marriage. A celibate lifestyle is healthier for some callings.

The Church's Failures

Beyond fostering church communities where healthy sexuality happens, there is also a need for greater honesty about the struggles to live out the commitment to sexual integrity. Recent surveys reveal that the majority of church leaders, married or celibate, fail to be faithful in keeping their vows. Though sexual misconduct among Catholic priests has been prominently reported in the mainstream media, it was still surprising to come across research done by the *Los Angeles Times* that around two-thirds of priests fail to perfectly keep their vow of celibacy.[1] Even after learning of these findings I was startled at a presentation on research about the rate of adultery among conservative evangelical pastors. Collecting data over a span of years, the studies suggest about two-thirds of pastors while in ministry will be sexually intimate with someone other than their spouse.[2] Both studies indicated that only rarely does the sexual misconduct become public knowledge. Common sense tells me that far less than two-thirds of Christian leaders acknowledge their sexual unfaithfulness.

Unfortunately, I know this from firsthand experience. At the church where I have been a member for many years, I've seen several associate pastors leave the church because of what has politely been called "the zipper disease." Sometimes there was a public announcement of what occurred, but more often pastors would simply disappear suddenly in hushed silence and rumors. By doing no more than removing the pastor who acted out within the church's system, avoiding any larger process of healing for the church community, the church allows this pattern of sexual sin to be repeated every few years. Though well-intentioned in wanting to respect the privacy of individuals and spare the pastor's family embarrassment, the church has missed opportunities to be authentic about brokenness and to experience genuine healing. From this I learned that where there is intense pressure to be perfect, it becomes very difficult to be honest about sin.

And it has been painful to discover that this kind of situation is not a new development in the centuries of church history. In many times and places, Christian leaders made it more of a priority to hide sinful behavior, rather than choose to heal through appropriate confession. Out of a seemingly honorable desire to prevent scandals and preserve God's reputation, heinous choices have been made. The solution to struggles with sexual integrity cannot be: "Make sure that no one else in your community knows what you are doing."

Freedom is not found in avoiding public confession. Ultimately it is impossible to keep others from seeing the effects of sinful behavior on a person's heart. And if unclean hearts are ignored, emphasizing outward displays of cleanliness will not lead to health in the church. In today's context where cynicism is high and developments in technology further reduce the possibility of hiding, authenticity is a nonnegotiable of meaningful Christian life. What does it mean for church communities if many church leaders are hiding or justifying their sexual failures, rather than confessing them? A leader's level of self-awareness and confession will often determine whether or not space is created for others to grow in these essential practices.

And if the lives of Christian leaders are not modeling authenticity, including an honest self-awareness of their sexual sins, how can what they're preaching be good news? Of course, there is much more to the Good News of Jesus Christ than the call to live out healthy sexuality. Yet this aspect of God's redemptive work is central in contexts where the gift of sexuality has been so terribly abused. It is wrong for Christian communities to overlook the pervasive impact of rampant sexual brokenness on younger generations.

Kiss and Tell: Reforming Church Cultures

What would it mean for conversations about the church emerging to include authenticity about the joys and struggles of healthy sexuality? What if, instead of hiding sexuality in the darkness, church communities were characterized by an exposing light of confession and the fertility of healing?

Alongside developing individual commitments, including marriage and celibacy, church communities need to be places of healthy and culturally appropriate touch. To varying degrees all people need nonsexual, physical affirmation. In Paul's letters, which among other things are a record of the beginnings of the church, we see repeated exhortations about holy kissing. Traveling in the Mediterranean region, I often received the friendly greeting of being kissed on one, or both, of my cheeks. Adjusting to it involved a few awkward moments, like when I sought to give a hug and received the surprise of kisses on both my cheeks! It is likely that this type of kiss is being commended in Paul's letters. Such kissing is comparable to the cultural practice I am most used to, a hug of welcome. Cultures have diverse ways of greeting with physical touch. If such appropriate greetings occur well whenever Christian communities gather, it is a significant act of ministry, a practicing of what the church has been directed to do in Paul's letters.

To be the church is to embrace fellow sisters and brothers in Christ with the love that transforms our brokenness. For what remains hidden and unexamined will hinder, if not destroy, much good ministry in the world, the body of Christ, the local church community, and the lives of individual people. To the extent that churches practice confession, tell stories of satisfying fulfillment, and pursue healthy sexuality, the church will be a vital contrast to the many stories of brokenness told in the world around them. A poignant way to announce that the kingdom of God is near is authentic sexual integrity. May God's grace enable us to live this out!

23

OUR REPORT CARD IN THE YEAR 2057

A Reflection on Women's Rights, Poverty, and Oppression

DEBORAH AND KEN LOYD

Twenty-eight-year-old Luke, drunk, jumped into the Willamette River. He wanted to go swimming. Jesse, his street friend, tried to talk him out of it, but it didn't work. As Jesse scrambled to borrow a phone, Luke began to realize the terrible mistake he had made. Thankfully, the police boat arrived in time to save Luke's life.

The following Sunday Luke stumbled down the sidewalk toward me, eyes vacant. I (Deborah) was so relieved to see him that I reached out, grabbed his shoulders, and excitedly exclaimed, "Luke! Don't die!" He smelled of stale alcohol and months without personal hygiene. Luke fell into my arms like a little child and began convulsing with sobs. In his gravelly, pirate voice he whispered, "I don't want to die."

Luke is still drunk 24/7 but he wants to change. His street friends who have moved indoors have agreed to allow him to sleep in their backyard until he makes headway toward sobriety. There is hope for Luke because positive peer pressure from the community will eventually change him. We will give him second and third and fourth chances—whatever it takes. That's what Jesus would do. Should we, his family, do any less?

Deborah Loyd is a writer, conference speaker, and a founding pastor of The Bridge Church in Portland, Oregon. She holds a master of exegetical theology degree from Western Seminary and is currently working on a doctorate of ministry. Deborah teaches biblical ethics and inductive Bible study at a local Bible college. She is married to Ken and together they have four children and two granddaughters.

Ken Loyd is a founding pastor of The Bridge Church, author of *They're Gentiles for Christ's Sake* (Bridge Publishing, 2001), and conference speaker. He is also pastor of 25, a church for homeless youth in Portland. Ken founded and directs 141PDX, a nondenominational coalition of churches, people, and businesses dedicated to serving the homeless youth of Greater Portland. He has a bachelor's degree in political science from the University of Washington.

"I don't want to get socks or hoodies or pastries or any of that stuff from you anymore. I want to be part of your community and earn money and buy that junk and give it away with you guys." The words tumbled out of Josie in a torrent. Tall and beautiful with flaming red hair, green eyes, and a smile that would melt the hardest heart, Josie was in her early twenties. She was an alcoholic and also an epileptic. On the streets for years, she knew her way around but had an engagingly innocent air about her.

My (Ken's) conversation with her took place in downtown Portland, Oregon, on a warm spring evening, a Thursday. Sunday, Josie was dead. Too much alcohol, a fall while climbing down off a bridge, a seizure, and she was gone.

We did a memorial for her in a park, attended by her street family, friends, and relatives. Following the informal service, we set about helping Tim, her partner, pick up the pieces of his life and move forward. Today he is a trusted friend, lives indoors, and has a good job. He serves Jesus, the church, and anyone who needs help.

Come to Church with Us

It's Sunday morning in North Portland. The streets are lined with SUVs and other expensive vehicles belonging to tourists in town for the day. They are here for brunch at one of the many fine bistros on Mississippi Avenue, then off to peruse the upscale shops that have opened in the last two years. Our neighborhood, once the most run-down area of the city, is now one of the trendiest.

As we approach "our" building, rented for four hours each week, we encounter the smokers encamped around the front door, impervious to the cold. They welcome wary visitors enthusiastically. There are suburban teens and twenty-somethings, street kids dressed mostly in black with their "houses" (backpacks) in a heap beside them, some older folk just out for a chat, and a smattering of other types, ages, and colors; all economic groups are represented, but mostly we are poor.

Once inside it seems at first glance as if we've entered the world of Barnum and Bailey. We're a colorful bunch. As the music cranks up in volume, some sit silently, their eyes shut. Others dance frantically. A few stand, sometimes raising their hands to an invisible God. Here and there someone weeps with pain or joy or rage. The music subsides and a chorus of voices, desperate voices, fills the void as the people take the lead.

Sharing time. The language is raw; honesty is the rule as the people talk about what's going on inside. The crowd, always attentive, punctuates the speaker's words with laughter, compassionate silence, smart remarks, profanity, and applause.

One or more give the main message, which regularly includes God's amazing love, his acceptance of the broken, and his purpose and better future for all who want it. Jesus is at the center of every sermon.

When "the talking" is over, we have a meal together. The meal is sometimes provided by groups from suburban churches who serve and then join us to eat. As people begin to leave, we encourage them to pick up the vegetables, fruit, meat, bakery goods, canned food, and other wonderful items donated by Trader Joe's. Do you need clothes? Come over to the house afterward, and we'll see what we can dig up.

The Bridge is a community where those further down life's path choose to hold the broken, caring for them and tending to near-fatal wounds. We hold them until they don't hurt so much. We hold on until they have the ability to become something other than what they have been. The Bridge Church has become a place with a reputation, a Jesus reputation. Ours is a rich community where side by side we are free to be ourselves without the pressure of conformity, where each one can work out his or her issues, the poorest of the poor, middle class, and wealthy—men and women, Mohawks and briefcases, skateboards and minivans.

The Challenge

"Oh, you do *that?*" some say. "I admire you, but I could never do *that*." Don't admire us; we are the fortunate ones. And, yes, you can do *that!* You can care for the poor and oppressed and fight for equality for women in your own neighborhood, church, and city—if you choose to act. What you do will, of necessity, look vastly different from what we do. It will reflect your locale and its culture. It will make as much sense to you as The Bridge makes sense to us.

Why aren't more Christians involved in social justice? Are we callous and uncaring? We don't think so. We *can* both learn and do.

First, we must come to *recognize* that great inequity in the distribution of income, opportunity, and access to power exists all around us. We must agree that there is a problem and train ourselves to see it.

Second, we must *seek out* those who have slipped through the cracks in our society and elsewhere. If they remain invisible to us, they will never really matter to us. If, however, we come face-to-face with individuals who have fewer resources than we, if we walk and talk with them, we will begin to care.

Finally, we must *act*. Restructuring our traditional churches to reach out and include those previously ignored may work well in some situations. In others the answer will be to create new missional, inclusive communities where service and the battle for equality for all are the foundational attributes.

Fifty years from now, in the year 2057, will history be kind to the Emergent movement, or will our report card be mediocre (or worse)? The choices we are making today about the issues of women's rights, poverty, and oppression will determine more than anything else how we will be viewed. We may bring some change to the theological landscape, but we will be *defined* by what we have *done or not done* in regard to these three central issues. Our legacy will be one of triumph or continued failure. The choice is ours alone. The very existence of Christianity as a viable force in the Western world hinges on our response to injustice.

Women's Rights

The overwhelming majority of boardrooms and bedrooms in the world are filled with a profound disrespect for the value of women. "Enlightened" Western culture and the most primitive of societies share the shame of this inequity. More often than not, on a world scale, the name of a deity and a sacred book are invoked to perpetuate the status quo. The oppressor is always eager to point out the benefit of his benevolence to the oppressed. The only variables seem to be the breadth, depth, and extent of the pain inflicted and whether the disrespect is out in the open or hidden behind a thin veneer of genteel civility.

Here is what this looks like in America: women receive less education than men, are found more often at the lower levels of the employment ladder, and are paid less than men for the same work. They are poorly represented at the highest levels of power and decision making in church, business, and government.

Women are poorer than men in every age group, but the disparity is greatest for the very young and the very old. They make up 85 percent of the victims of domestic violence and an even higher percentage of the victims of sexual abuse. They bear the brunt of child rearing in the aftermath of abandonment, divorce, or the death of a spouse. Women-led households earn less than one-half of those with two parents and are less likely to have access to adequate nutrition, housing, and health care.[1]

Have gains been made in women's rights? Yes, at least in America and the developed world. In most of the Third World the battle has barely begun. Will we lend our time, energy, and resources to right these great injustices, both near and far away?

When we founded The Bridge in 1998, one of our distinctives was the demand that women be afforded equality in every area of endeavor. As we looked through that lens and educated ourselves in women's issues, it was only natural that, over time, we became aware of the related issues of poverty and oppression.

Poverty

We love the poor in our faith community. Our average income is $13,500 per year, less than half of the norm for our city. It's not that we don't have wealthy or educated individuals in our community; we do. The poor just seem to gravitate to us in greater numbers than the rich and famous. Perhaps it is because we have trained ourselves to see their beauty; indeed, to see the beauty in each individual, rich *or* poor.

The most current statistics tell us that the concentration of our nation's wealth has continued to shift upward, with 33.4 percent being held by 1 percent of the population. The top 10 percent of households in our country hold more than 71 percent of the wealth. Conversely, this leaves the bottom 40 percent holding less than 1 percent of the nation's wealth. Wealth, or the ability to hold on to earnings, is the prime indicator of our standard of living. And the gap is ever widening.[2]

If these statistics translate across the board, 40 percent of the church in the United States is suffering from poverty. Still, unless Christians are particularly intent on doing otherwise, we will continue to worship with those most like ourselves. We would like to suggest that homogeneity is the curse, rather than poverty. Mutual exposure will benefit us all. Why is this so hard for the church? How do we change the church; how do we change us?

Eyes that cannot see and ears that cannot hear (see Isa. 6:10): this is how the prophet Isaiah described Israel who could no longer feel the pain of injustice. Could the same indictment hold true in the church today? The poor and the marginalized stand on our street corners, sit in our coffee shops, and attend our churches, but we are not yet trained to see them.

The church needs an attitude adjustment and a change in thinking. The poor will always be with us. How amazing is that! We could be welcoming them with open arms, with accepting hearts drawing the mission field through the doors of our churches. The poor and the outcast give us the opportunity to fulfill the mission that Jesus charged us with: visit, feed, heal, and clothe. What a blessing to the body of Christ! Rather than seeing them as a bad report card or a mission failed, we could see them as objects of God's grace.

New life flows through the veins of those of us who dare to risk our comfortable worlds for the wild frontier. God calls us to action, he calls us to serve, he calls us to love in the most substantial ways: with our time, resources, and gifts.

Oppression

Webster defines *oppression* as burdening or keeping "in subjection by harsh and unjust use of force or authority." This definition helps us see that men and women everywhere and in all eras have oppressed others by using inaccurate stereotypes to deny basic rights to those who differ from them in race, gender, tribe, religion, appearance, lifestyle, or culture. The oppressors use military might, legal power, economic superiority, and/or other forms of coercion to maintain their advantage. Tragically, as the tables turn (and they often do), the downtrodden abuse their former overlords in the same manner that they were once abused. Revenge, if not sweet, is at least common.

Genocide, fueled by tribal conflict, is currently occurring in much of Africa. The loss of life is in the millions, yet the Western world is largely unaware of what is happening there. Why? At least part of the answer must lie in the fact that our governments have no perceived self-interest in those nations because they pose no terrorist threat, are not in a strategic position that would benefit us militarily, and do not sit atop oil reserves as do nations in the Middle East. Is this an overly cynical view? Probably not.

Throughout Asia and South America multiplied millions are held in economic slavery as they toil in horrendous conditions to supply the wants of the people in the wealthier nations. The richest 20 percent of people on earth account for 81 percent of private consumption expenditures, while the poorest 20 percent purchase 3.5 percent.[3] This is oppression, not by government decree, but by the individual actions of many.

Slavery, child prostitution, racial inequality, imperialistic wars; the list goes on. Is there any hope of ameliorating oppression? We think so. The opportunity is before us. If we choose to turn our focus outward, beyond our walls, and reallocate our human and financial resources, we will have immense impact and display the love and justice of Jesus Christ to a world that has lost hope.

A Brighter Future

One of the primary commonalities of the new missional communities we have encountered is a willingness to actually engage with humanity and grapple with the real issues that arise from that contact. We are no longer content to rise up and be against something every three decades or so and then scamper back to our carefully protected fortress-churches. We are choosing to educate ourselves on what is really happening in our neighborhoods and around the world. We are recognizing our responsibility to strive to bring holistic freedom and salvation to all humankind. We dare to think new thoughts and dream new dreams. We choose to extend God's kingdom into new areas, not being content to limit our role to the narrowest conceivable definition of "spirituality." We are choosing not to spend our financial resources primarily on ourselves, both as individuals and communities, but, instead, we are reducing our consumption to have more to give to those who have less. We are daring to believe that equality of opportunity can become a reality for all.

Many centuries ago Isaiah wrote these words of promise to those who would respond:

> Is not this the kind of fasting I have chosen: to loose the chains of injustice and untie the cords of the yoke, to set the oppressed free and break every yoke? Is it not to share your food with the hungry and to provide the poor wanderer with shelter—when you see the naked, to clothe him, and not to turn away from your own flesh and blood? Then your light will break forth like the dawn, and your healing will quickly appear. . . . If you do away with the yoke of oppression, with the pointing finger and malicious talk, and if you spend yourselves in behalf of the hungry and satisfy the needs of the oppressed, then your light will rise in the darkness and your light will become like the noonday. . . . you will be called Repairer of Broken Walls, Restorer of Streets with Dwellings.
>
> Isaiah 58:6–12

God and his Son Jesus have a special affection for the marginalized, ignored, and unwanted. There are a growing number of people within the Emergent movement who have become aware of the opportunity to advance God's kingdom *by our own behavior* toward women, the poor, and the oppressed. We are consciously tearing down the fortified walls of our church communities and spilling out into our neighborhoods to love and care for those less fortunate than us. It is our privilege to join hands with those throughout the world who are fighting for social justice. We don't reach *down* to our fellow human beings but *across*. We are committed to rise to the challenge simply because, in good conscience, we can do no less. We are, after all, the hope of the world.

24

PRACTICING PENTECOST

Discovering the Kingdom of God amid Racial Fragmentation

On the day of Pentecost, Jesus poured out Spirit power on his followers, as he had promised. The purpose of this outpouring was to empower them to bear witness to Christ's kingdom. This outpouring of the Spirit is one episode in God's story of the redemption of a fallen and broken creation. The Spirit falls and a people of varied cultural/ethnic backgrounds come together in worship and are empowered to bear witness to a new order of things inaugurated by Christ's death and resurrection—and the outpouring of the Spirit himself. To be in Christ, according to the apostle Peter, is to be among a people where Pentecost is a sign that the end of the age has come.

If we are to take seriously the Bible's witness regarding Pentecost, we must take another look at the racial divisions that continue in the body of Christ. We must look at the beliefs and praxis that appear to be thoroughly wedded to what the New Testament refers to as the "present age." I believe the imagery and language of Pentecost provide a practical guide to discovering the kingdom of God amid racial fragmentation. Practicing Pentecost is about participation in the *missio Dei* (the mission of God). It is about being *missional* in relation to racial and cultural divisions that continue to hinder the unity of the Spirit and the bond of peace that should characterize Christ's body. Practicing Pentecost is about participating in the shalom of God—a peace that inspires local *ekklesias* (churches of assemblies) to embody a racial and cultural unity while also resisting death-dealing exclusionary Powers. These death-dealing and divisive Powers perpetuate a profound rebellion against the

---

Anthony Smith lives in Charlotte, North Carolina, with his wife, Yashica, and four children, Isaiah, Israel, Abraham, and Deborah. He attends Warehouse 242, a missional community in the Charlotte area where he is engaged in racial reconciliation and social justice ministry. He also co-organizes an Emergent cohort in Charlotte. He facilitates the blog "Musings of a Postmodern Negro" and serves on the national Emergent Coordinating Group.

redemptive will of God. The church becomes complicit in this rebellion when it perpetuates long-standing racial divisions and hostilities that are ultimately an affront to God's intent: *a new humanity where God dwells.* Christ's body is a part of a new creation. It is to be a *sign, foretaste, and instrument* of God's coming kingdom.

In practicing Pentecost we will not only discover God's kingdom, we will also discover the various ways in which we are subservient to and complicit with the very Powers that crucified Christ. We will discover that the more we lack a Holy Spirit–empowered worship and fellowship, the more we are being determined by what the apostle Paul describes as the "principalities and powers" (see Eph. 6:12). The Powers would have us believe that we are better identified by race than baptism. The Powers would also have us believe that we are better identified by our particular demographic than by the Eucharist. When we fail to unmask and resist the Powers on this issue, we dilute our baptism and fail to discern the body rightly. When we avoid practicing Pentecost, racially and culturally speaking, we are a people who desperately cling to the old age and refuse to participate in the dawning of a new world begun by Christ.

A Fundamental Issue

Dealing with the racial segregation of Christ's body in overt biblical language such as Pentecost is not an attempt to bring external issues into the fold and give them Christian garb. Looking at this issue through the prism of Pentecost equips us to think more redemptively about it. Pentecost also challenges us to stop seeing this as an *optional* issue. This is especially true for those of us in the emerging church conversation, which is often associated with deep concern about the church's complicity with the bad habits of modernity.

Oftentimes the issue of race is seen as an issue for those who have an interest in it. Very rarely do we see it as a fundamental issue—an issue that is deeply grafted into the heart of the gospel's call. That some of us see the issue of race as optional only reveals how wedded our theologizing is to the old age that crucified Christ. The issue of race is not optional. We must engage. We must claim the reality of racial fragmentation and the quest for racial/ethnic harmony in the body as a part of the core of the gospel. We must wrestle the concern over racial realities away from conservative and liberal ideologues and political pundits. We need to recognize that this issue is, at heart, a gospel issue.

Anglican priest Kenneth Leech in his book *Race* describes what we must do:

> My view is that the Church will never make progress in this area until we see opposition to racism as being central to biblical faith, incorporated at the heart of the liturgy and life, repeated regularly in creedal commitment. This must involve regular and serious theological preaching, as well as discussion, good collects, hymns, songs, pictures, and spiritual direction which will help to shape the character of the Christian person. It must involve taking seriously the fact that racism distorts and damages the life of the spirit. For racism is not simply a mistaken political option. . . . It is in fact an alternative gospel.[1]

Leech reminds us that race is a salvation issue in that God's people are being "rescued" or "saved" from sinful racialized practices—ways of being, ways of seeing, and identities that add fuel to the fire of a racialized culture. It is an eschatological issue in that we as a people are to be a foretaste of God's future. The church is called to bring the future into the present. There is an already/not-yet aspect to the church's racial/ethnic reality that we are called to embody in the here and now. It is also a pneumatological reality in that Christ sent his Spirit to create a community that reflects, or images, the life and character of God. The Spirit empowers the church with courage and wisdom to reflect the inner trinitarian life of God. It is to be a reconciling body of people that reflect the "oneness" (not sameness, which much talk of racial/ethnic reconciliation often comes down to) of Father, Son, and Spirit. In fact Jesus prayed for this very reality (John 17:20–21).

The apostle Paul once described the body of Christ as a people "upon whom the ends of the ages have come" (1 Cor. 10:11 NKJV). The *Gospel and Our Culture* series has produced a book titled *Stormfront: The Good News of God* that expounds on the New Testament's use of two ages:

> As that group of people on whom the ages have met, Christ's followers live much as did the saints of Israel who came before them, not hidden away in a safe place, removed from harm's way. They are instead gathered together by God to live under constant threat of a powerful thunderstorm (to continue this image from the Old Testament), generated by the meeting

of the ends of the ages in and through their participation in the crucified and risen Lord. This even divides the present age, over which sin and death have the final say in human affairs, from the time to come, when God will be all in all, creation itself will be liberated from its bondage to decay, and life rather than death will have the final word for all creatures. As Andre Trocme puts it, "Jesus is the central event of history, because de facto man is not the same after Jesus Christ as before."[2]

This two-age schema provides a way to discuss the issues surrounding racial divisions in the church. In many missional-emerging church[3] circles you will find this language used to describe the North American church's captivity to consumerism, nationalism, and so on. The issue of race has gotten very little commentary from within this framework. I believe this is in part due to the fact that race is an existential reality and a social construction that has a different history than the other realities discussed in missional circles. The way race has played itself out in our North American context is unfortunate given its particular origin in the Western world.

Roots in Modernity

I would like to propose that the racial divisions we see in our North American church are a profound practice of secularity that has its roots in modernity, specifically the age of Enlightenment.[4] In *The Goodness of God*, theologian and ethicist D. Stephen Long has a section titled "Family as Source of Idolatry and Division: The Invention of Race." In this section he sets forth a brief survey of the invention of race and the origins of modern racism:

> Racism represents the sinfulness of clinging to the old aeon even when the old aeon is a modern invention. The reality of cultural differences leading to violence against others is ancient, but the racism that privileges biology over baptism is a peculiarly modern heresy. Perhaps this is due to the rise of the empirical sciences, with their dependence upon the brute facticity of nature as providing the narrative descriptions that render our lives intelligible. Once nature appears to us as self-evident and "on the surface," the category of race arises. The cultural differences that separate persons are no longer viewed as cultural differences. In other words, Athenians, Spartans, and Ethiopians no longer oppose each other because they are

> Athenians, Spartans, and Ethiopians. Instead, differences of race are given a universal basis that sublimates the cultural differences behind the legitimating discourse of science. Consequently, the brute fact of biology becomes more determinative over our lives precisely because we no longer recognize differences as cultural and subject to revision, conversion, and defense.[5]

Dr. Long (who is actually practicing Pentecost in this section of the book) points us to Cornel West, religious studies professor at Princeton University, in his seminal book *Prophesy Deliverance*. In his essay "Genealogy of Modern Racism," Dr. West connects modernity and race:

> I will try to show that the idea of white supremacy emerges partly because of the powers within the structure of modern discourse—powers to produce and prohibit, develop and delimit, forms of rationality, scientificity, and objectivity which set perimeters and draw boundaries for the intelligibility, availability, and legitimacy of certain ideas.[6]

According to West, *modern* racism doesn't have its origins in the hills of Georgia but in the esteemed voices of the Enlightenment (for example, Carolus Linnaeus, Montesquieu, Voltaire, Hume, Thomas Jefferson, Kant et al.).

I am not an academician but a practitioner discussing this, but in reading Long and West I cannot help but see a connection between the emergence of modern racism and the emergence of a globally dominant white culture that had and has significant influence in the shape of the North American church. Toward the end of modernity and at the beginning of what many are calling after-modernity or postmodernity, white supremacy is thought to have been thoroughly debunked and set aside, especially in many North American churches. We assume, wrongly I think, that we have moved past the consequences of the principality of racism. But it is obvious that racial divisions still exist in our churches today. A racially divided church is the norm in our day rather than a peculiarity. This is due to the North American church's marriage to the old aeon, from which we are told Jesus came to save us.

Racial Penance

But enough of theory and talk! What do we do? We practice Pentecost, and more specifically we practice what I would like to call *racial penance*.

Why penance? D. Stephen Long talks about the lost art of penance in Christianity and the misunderstanding of it in many Protestant circles (especially evangelical circles):

> The history of penance gave rise to Christian ethics. Once Christian ethics seeks to be ethical apart from the practice of penance, it ceases to be intimately connected to Christianity. James Dallen has explained the importance of the rite of penance by noting that penance is not a claim for moral superiority but a way for people to be reconciled with the community of faith and thus constantly be renewed to their baptismal pledge.
>
> Sin is never merely a private affair; neither is its remedy. Just as sin affects the whole community of faith, likewise its remedy is entrusted to that same body. Paul referred to this when he wrote, "If anyone is detected in a transgression, you [plural] who have received the Spirit should restore such a one in a spirit of gentleness" (Gal. 6:1 NRSV). Restoration is the work of the Spirit. On Pentecost, the Spirit reversed the divisions created by language, restoring unity. Our differences are not transcended through a forged unity. Each still hears in his or her own language, but the divisiveness and violence that accompanied those divisions is redeemed. Through baptism the Spirit maintains "the unity of the [body] in the bond of peace" (Eph. 4:3). Likewise, in repentance the Spirit works to restore sinners to the community of faith and thereby restores the community itself. This work of the Spirit is present in church so that it might discern and heal our sin.[7]

Penance is essentially communal practices intended to bring restoration and healing. The purpose of such practices is to create space in the community for God's Spirit to bring about unity in the body. The term "racial penance" refers to specific practices done to bring about racial healing in a community of Christians. The *telos* or goal of racial penance would be to create kingdom spaces where Christians can become shaped into persons that witness to Christ's victory over the principality of race and its disordering work of racism.

Returning to the narrative of Acts on the day of Pentecost, I want to point out a few things that happened when the Spirit fell on the early Christians' corporate worship: (1) They were together in worship. (2) They spoke in tongues (declaring the works of God in different languages and cultural idioms). (3) They boldly bore witness to the new aeon brought about by Christ's resurrection. This event provides a clue into how North American Christians can practice Pentecost and racial penance.

The fact that we have racially divided corporate worship is more than just a matter of personal taste and cultural differences. It is the legacy of the disordering work of the Powers along racial lines. We need spaces where these realities can be brought out in the open—where Christians can embody the restorative work of God. We need a space where Christians of different racial backgrounds bring their culture's gifts of worship as a witness that the Powers do not have the last word on this matter. This would be a testament to Christ's victory over the Powers in their rebellion against God's intent to restore creation.

In the local Emergent cohort I help coordinate in Charlotte, North Carolina, we are creating a space where we practice this undivided kingdom. For instance, right now, we are reading Dietrich Bonhoeffer's book *Life Together*.[8] (Bonhoeffer actually sat under the tutelage of a black pastor in New York City during his sojourn in America.) Our next book will be Howard Thurman's *Jesus and the Disinherited*.[9]

On the day of Pentecost we are told the saints "spoke with other tongues." Personally I do not believe this to have been a matter of unknown tongues, or *glossolalia*, which is a prominent feature of Pentecostalism.[10] It is worth noting, however, that the more diverse congregations in America tend to be of a Pentecostal strain. One thinks of the ethnic diversity that was present during the Azusa Street Revival at the beginning of twentieth-century America. I believe the "speaking with other tongues" consisted of Jews speaking in different languages known to others who were gathered there. Practicing Pentecost would thus mean the creation of spaces, like my cohort, where Christians can learn the language, history, culture, and nuances of other races—a place where we can become theologically multilingual.[11] The text reads:

> "Parthians and Medes and Elamites, those dwelling in Mesopotamia, Judea and Cappadocia, Pontus and Asia, Phrygia and Pamphylia, Egypt and the parts of Libya adjoining Cyrene, visitors from Rome, both Jews and proselytes, Cretans and Arabs—we hear them speaking in our own tongues the wonderful works of God." So they were all amazed and perplexed, saying to one another, "Whatever could this mean?" Others mocking said, "They are full of new wine."
>
> Acts 2:9–13 NKJV

The key verse here is "we hear them speaking in our own tongues the wonderful works of God." In the midst of this corporate gathering, Christ-followers of different cultural and ethnic backgrounds heard their neighbor speak their language concerning the mighty acts of God. Of course this was a miracle wrought by the power of the Holy Spirit, but I see the shape of something that can be done by Christians in a similar situation today. Once again this would require space for Christians of different races to come together and hear each other speak of the mighty acts of God in another person's language or linguistic-cultural framework. In other words, we need to learn how to speak about God in the language of the worlds others inhabit. This does not necessarily mean literally speaking another language, although this would be a good thing. It means learning about the works of God in another person's racial history. Can I talk of how the story of God has played itself out among my European brothers and sisters, my Latino brothers and sisters, my African brothers and sisters, my Asian brothers and sisters? Can my white Christian brothers and sisters narrate for me the work of God among Africans and Diaspora Africans starting with Coptic Christianity up to the present? Are we cognizant of the nuances of how God has operated in others' ethnic and cultural histories? Are we aware of the complexity of such histories? What comes out of this is the skill to see God in my neighbor. I begin to have a deeper appreciation (and, if need be, a critical appraisal) for other voices than the ones that have come out of a particular stream of the Christian tradition. I begin to be comfortable quoting John Calvin and James Cone in the same sentence. Can I appreciate God working in different Christian contexts that may not give pride of place to esteemed doctrinal formations such as the five solas (*Sola Scriptura, Solus Christus, Sola Gratia, Sola Fide, Soli Deo Gloria*) of Reformational Christianity? Such acts of penance will create a people who are appreciative of what God has done in other histories and peoples down through the centuries. Practicing this level of penance will require a boldness or courage that can only come as a gift from the Holy Spirit.

After the day of Pentecost, Acts tells us in different places about the "boldness" with which the apostles gave witness to Christ's resurrection. Often the word used here is *courage* or, in the Greek, *parrhesia*. The word *witness* in the Greek is the word *martus* from which we get the word *martyr*. Commonly we use this term to describe one who has been killed because of the way he or she has lived out the faith. For a Christian, being a witness may lead one down that path. God knows the many Christians who have been martyred throughout the centuries.

What does it mean to give witness to Christ's resurrection, especially as it relates to the racial divisions that exist in the church today? It means that Christians must be willing to "die" to the old aeon characterized by sin and death. This may mean that some Christians will have to die to the racial disordering of the old aeon. In their witness or dying to the old order, they will be going after the new order of things brought about by Christ's resurrection. On a racial and cultural plane, this new order of things was exemplified on Pentecost. They will not be concerned about the relevance or the marketability of such an undertaking. They will be willing to die to the flesh (*sarx*[12]) and be led by the Holy Spirit. Such a witness amid racial fragmentation in the body of Christ will require a courage that can be given only by the Holy Spirit.

Practicing Pentecost will hopefully awaken some of us to the reality that we are being ever tempted to perpetuate some of the bad habits of modernity, specifically the racial hierarchy that came out of seventeenth-century Europe that used pseudoscience and Constantinian Christianity as justifications for white privilege and nonwhite subjugation. There is much of this heritage that persists in North American Christianity—not as overt as in the past but a bit more subtle. You see it in the aesthetics of worship, in the theological voices being referenced, and in the call to relevance as a justification for racial homogeneity. We cannot be self-deceived into thinking that we have properly and more fully named modernity's grasp on the church. Those in the emerging church cannot be self-deceived into thinking that we have faithfully named North American Christianity's captivity to the bad habits of modernity without touching the persistence of racism in our postmodern world.

One of the valid criticisms of the emerging church conversation has been the dominance of white maleness. This is not a startling revelation for many of us. This just reveals how much of American Christianity is deeply wedded to the racialized heritage of Western culture. The difference that Emergent makes is that we are equipped to be suspicious of human metanarratives, foundationalist epistemologies, consumerism, individualism, and formulaic ways of being church that have blinded us to the reality of racialization. We have been equipped to see how racist Christendom has been in its guardianship of white privilege and exclusionary practices. Just as we have been trained to be vendors and consumers of religious or "spiritual" goods and services, we have also been discipled to maintain, often unknowingly, the symbolic universe of ecclesial whiteness. In the emerging church I see a humbled form of North American Christianity. I have hope that God is shaking things up in Christendom with this conversation—in this generative friendship of missional Christians.

Oh, God, grant us the courage to resist the Powers in their work of racial disordering and the desire and wisdom to practice Pentecost!

25

RESTORING HONOR IN THE LAND

Why the Emerging Church Can't Dodge the Issue

RANDY WOODLEY

The Haunting

wasn't it 1492 when Columbus sailed the azure ocean?
salty water lapping shores separating neighbors
come into our house—there is no honor in dispelling a neighbor
but unruly neighbors are a curse and bad religion is a plague
came the call from every corner with mangled crosses and dubious preachers
came, you came to our land . . . our lives . . . our homes

"virgin land," mother earth milk & honey flowing from her breast—you saw fences
"virgin trees," Sequoia mammoths decorating a vast green park—you saw timber
"virgin nations," going . . . gone—left from a greater civilization—but you did not see me
land . . . trees . . . "ours" you say—and the nations? just a blight on your conscience
cut the land, cut the trees, cut the nations . . .
this is the clarion Christian call
rape the land, rape the trees, rape the nations . . .
ignore my blood and tears when you pray

i am a red Indian, a raped virgin—you make me a "noble whore"
thrown into a dark corner with the trees, and the land, and the "lost" civilizations
my spiritual reservations are the places you relegate to me
compartments fit for non-human species—churches made from acreage and board feet

good Indian—come to church, makum' god happy
good Indian get job, makum' government happy

Randy Woodley (PhD candidate) is a Keetoowah Cherokee Indian in ministry among First Nations for more than two decades. An author, pastor, teacher, lecturer, poet, and activist, Randy and his wife, Edith (Shoshone), consult and mentor through a school and community they established called Eloheh Village for Indigenous Leadership and Ministry Development. Randy is the author of several books and articles, including *Living in Color: Embracing God's Passion for Ethnic Diversity* (InterVarsity, 2004).

good Indian keep quiet . . . subdued . . . silent
quietly turn your vile abuse, your bitter loss onto yourself and other
  bad Indians
then . . . you makum' everyone of us Americans very happy
'cause we got your land
  and we got your trees
    and never forget . . . never, ever forget—that we got god—
  so we got your souls!

where do the souls of dead Indians go?
where *does* one go after rape and torture, robbery and slavery,
  disease and genocide?
perhaps we join the land and the trees
lingering with the spirit of Jesus on earth to curse savage Christian
  civilizations
we die early and we die often . . . but we die slow
and, we die knowing a secret that you don't even care to know

that your land will not rest
and your trees will make only crooked crosses
and your children will breathe their last breaths in despair
. . . groping for an identity that you could not steal for them
  . . . grasping for an honor that always alluded them
    . . . clinching for a God . . . and land . . . and trees . . . and
  nations that were never theirs

and herein is the lesson . . . gifts can't be stolen
and love takes flight where control makes its nest
and Jesus? O, Jesus . . .
You crucify Him anew with every sacrifice that we make to
  accommodate you
wasn't it 1491 when there was no haunting?

Randy Woodley

The Haunting Continues

In some ways every innovative church movement in each new generation finds itself as the heir apparent to the repulsive legacy of historic colonialism/neocolonialism—and this will always continue the "haunting." Yet as the colonial spirit wavers and dies, the expectation of our world is that people will have enough integrity to replace the old, paternalistic ways of relating with new ways. The emerging church is actually well positioned to take up this task, but it is not an easy one. To lend integrity to the past responses of the church, the same "colonial predicament" must be addressed once more, namely, What do we do about the indigenous people and their land?

I liken the typical evangelical response to the problem to a loaf of old bread. When pricked, crumbs of indifference fly off in every direction, exposing some moldy core of apology, often paraded via a staged reconciliation event. These faddish experiences only perpetuate an appearance of reconciliation. In effect what these charades accomplish is to absolve the perpetrators from all culpability while they continue to keep the injured party in a helpless (now seemingly hopeless) state of victimization. After such a farce, the present state is worse than the former because the crimes have been made bona fide by being addressed and "dealt with" in the public arena. And if the "Indian problem" ever comes up again, it will be glazed over as a fait accompli.

After such an event, it matters little to those in the church that America's 563-plus First Nations are still among the most marginalized in our society. Rarely do the daunting statistics have the names and stories of the victims attached to them when considered by evangelical reconcilers. The statistics appear to be surreal because those listening have no relationships with the victims. Consider a profile citing these findings:

- alcohol mortality is 770 percent greater than for all other ethnic groups combined;
- accidental deaths are 280 percent higher;
- suicides are 190 percent higher; 1 in 6 adolescents has attempted suicide;
- 52 percent finish high school;
- 17 percent attend college and 4 percent graduate from college;
- 2 percent attend graduate school;
- 45 percent live below the poverty level;
- average unemployment is 45 percent and several reservations are as high as 90 percent.[1]

To continue understanding the effects of colonialism and Christianity among America's indigenous people today, one writer reports:

> The Indian health level is the lowest and disease rates the highest of all major population groups in the United States. The incidence of tuberculosis is 400 percent higher than the national average. Similar statistics show that the incidence of strep infections is 1,000 percent higher, meningitis is 2,000 percent higher and dysentery is 10,000 percent higher. Death rates are shocking when Indian and non-Indian populations are compared. Influenza and pneumonia are 300 percent greater killers among Indians. Diseases such as hepatitis are in epidemic proportions, with an 800 percent higher chance of death. Diabetes is almost a plague.[2]

The life span of a Native American is twelve years shorter than that of the general US population.[3]

As populations, including Native Americans, age, there is a likelihood of developing chronic illnesses like arthritis or heart disease, which can impact both life span and quality of life. For example, the Native elders are 19.5 percent more likely than the general population to experience arthritis. Similarly, Native American elders are 48.7 percent more likely to experience congestive heart failure, 17.7 percent more likely to report high blood pressure, 17.5 percent more likely to have experienced a stroke, 44.3 percent more likely to report asthma, and 173 percent more likely to be afflicted with diabetes.[4]

These statistics reflect the crisis provoked mainly by the loss of land (that other Americans now enjoy), which led to the erosion of traditional identity, the breakup of family through forced government and church-sponsored residential boarding schools, the effects of naive missionary efforts, and the official stance of the government and the church concerning the practice of Native American religious traditions and culture.

In terms of missionary advancement, some estimate that less than 5 percent of our Indian people claim to be Christian.[5] All of this paints a grim picture of the future for our Native American people. Seen even more clearly to those of us ministering and living among our people, each of these statistics is a name, a family affected, a memory—each statistic is a story that takes a lifetime to tell.

As a Keetoowah Cherokee Indian, I wonder: *Do these stories even matter to the emerging church?* And most of all, I wonder, when the subject of land comes up: *Will the emerging church simply excuse itself from the table?* If so, colonialism will have once again found a home in a new church movement.

Why should the plight of America's indigenous peoples be a concern to the emerging church? It's not just for the sake of justice, integrity, and Christ's witness, but because the very land that was stolen through genocide is still under your feet. The government will continue to operate under its colonial constraints and surprise no one for its lack of concern for First Americans. If justice will ultimately be served to America's First Nations, it won't come through the United States government. But the church—which has in most cases been the co-conspirator of the genocidal impact (such as in the case of residential Indian boarding schools, which had a higher death rate than some Nazi concentration camps but lasted longer)[6]—has a new opportunity amid an emerging generation of people who may wish to live in real and lasting partnership with America's host people (Native Americans). How can this happen?

It begins with this generation. If, through relationships with Native Americans, the core of this emerging generation can be influenced to live in harmony, a lasting change may occur. This change has implications in every area of life from how we treat one another to how we sustain the earth. The emerging church may be the last great chance for true reconciliation with America's indigene. Native Americans and the emerging church share a number of values that could serve as a foundation for dialogue and reconciliation. A brief discussion of some of these values follows.

An Opportunity for the Emerging Church

Honesty

"White man speak with forked tongue" is a cliché, to be sure, but one that developed out of reality. Both Native Americans and those in the emerging church seek honesty in relating. Hidden agendas and political maneuvering will end conversations abruptly.

Building of Community

Our tribes (Nations) are communities. First Nations are fast losing the structure of community but still trying to maintain the values, in spite of eroding families and social dysfunction. The emerging church is trying to build community but has little experience with our understanding of communal values. Perhaps we can help one another.

Authentic Relationships

Friendship among those in the modern church was often illusive. A new generation has arisen without the foundational skills needed for making and keeping friends; yet this same generation possesses strong relational desires. Relationships are what Indians do best.

Service among the Poor

Among the emerging church there is a strong ethic of service among the poor. As Native Americans, we are the poor, yet we must learn to see the needs of others beyond ourselves. In a partnership approach, not only can First Nations be ministered to, but we can discover partnerships of dignity that break dependency cycles. In turn, the emerging church can learn ways to lend dignity in place of the pervasive, paternalistic alternatives.

Inclusiveness

Especially in matters of worship and religion, America's First Nations are tolerant to a fault. Women have equal places of honor in many of our cultures. The poor, the disabled, the marginalized are all seen as "part of the tribe." Our elders are viewed especially as a precious resource and given respect. Absent in Native American culture is a drive toward homogeneity that exists in the dominant society. This drive, present in American church culture, is most often expressed through control and regulation during worship. First Nations experience worship in many ways. Celebrating these differences can be good therapy for the emerging church.

Process

Among our Indian people it is important that everyone have a voice. Decisions are usually made by consensus, and our tradition has been to always consider how our decisions will impact the next seven generations. I believe this type of process is more appealing to this generation than present authoritarian and tightly controlled means.

Holism

The result of a dichotomous worldview has caused the modern church to relegate ministry to only certain areas of life, especially when ministry has a strong "knowledge based" component. First Nations do not suffer from such a worldview and, therefore, ministry is not categorized but is integrative in its approach. Restoration of ministry to the whole person is likely another fruit that can be borne if sincere attempts are made to learn from Native Americans.

The Harmony Way

Both the emerging and Native American communities seem to respect and seek these values. In fact the precolonial voice of Native Americans could keep the emerging church honest as it seeks to find an authentic voice in postcolonialism. At the same time, our Native American values are currently fading. As more of our elders die and colonialism continues to take its toll by eroding our values and traditions, the emerging church can serve to remind us to restore our hope in a way of life based on truth and respect for others. The parallel concepts that underpin both the emerging church and Native American lifeways are biblical shalom and the Native American Harmony Way.

An understanding of shalom has been one of the most neglected concepts in the modern church. The rendering of this word as "peace" in most translations of the Scriptures is anemic and inadequate. One should not underestimate the importance of shalom, for without this base of understanding, it is impossible to understand God or humanity. Shalom is the very DNA of God. The Trinity operates from a heart of shalom. The Scriptures begin in Genesis and end in Revelation with shalom pointing as the "true North." Shalom is God's greatest intention for all of humanity and Jesus Christ is the "once and for all" shalom bringer. Without shalom there is no "kingdom," for the very kingdom that Jesus comes to restore is a shalom kingdom.

The Scripture uses shalom in the Hebrew at least 225 times. *Eirene,* the Greek equivalent, is used 94 times. A quick (nonexhaustive) list of words in Scripture that can be used to express shalom includes peace, restoration of creation, prosperity, respect, justice, truth, acceptance, equity, restitution, reconciliation, salvation, integrity, intimacy, growth, well-being, restored relationship, and a place where God is in charge.

Walter Brueggemann describes biblical shalom:

> That persistent vision of joy, well-being, harmony and prosperity is not captured in any single word or idea in the Bible; a cluster of words is required to express its many dimensions and subtle nuances: love, loyalty, truth, grace, salvation, justice, blessings, righteousness. But the term that in recent discussions has been used to summarize that controlling vision is *shalom*. Both in such discussion and in the Bible itself, it bears tremendous freight—the freight of a dream of God that resists all our tendencies to division, hostility, fear, drivenness, and misery. *Shalom* is the substance of the biblical vision of one community embracing all creation. It refers to all those resources and factors that make communal harmony joyous and effective.[7]

Native Americans have a similar concept that can be collectively expressed as the Harmony Way. Each tribe has a different word or phrase expressing the Harmony Way, but the core of the principle is the same. Sometimes the word *respect* is used in English to summarize the First Nations' view of Harmony. Often symbols such as the circle are used to express our Harmony ethic. The nature of the Native American Harmony Way and biblical shalom are almost indistinguishable. By keeping an understanding of these two parallel concepts at the center of discussion, the emerging church and First Nations will have a richness from which they can draw meaningful dialogue.

Emerging Theologies of Place

Perhaps the most important understanding that First Nations can lend to the emerging church is that of a theology of place, land, and creation. It has been difficult for the American church to develop a theology of place with a stolen continent as a foundation. Such an understanding would have no integrity or credibility, as seen in the case of Manifest Destiny.

In our Native American understanding, the Harmony Way is not an ethereal concept. Jesus, as the Creator-Son, is the one who brings the Good News of the relational aspects of the Trinitarian God to earth by creating a *place*. Eden was a place where human beings were first placed to enjoy the fullest possible sense of *place* on earth. God's original intention was to allow humans to relate in the parameters of this garden existence, a *shalom* garden. A Native American understanding might be that the garden culture is the original human culture from which one could come to know the Creator in a personal way and understand God as one who relates in and through community.

The divine community relating with human beings in the garden becomes the model for all human societies including Native Americans. It is this story to which Native Americans can relate, because it is the same story we already know in our own context and in our own *place*. As a Keetoowah Cherokee Indian person, I have been given an understanding of how my people came to be on the particular land that the Creator reserved for us since the beginning of time. The same can be said of every Indian nation. Our Keetoowah story is a story of true covenant between our nation and the Creator. Our part of the covenant was to live out the Harmony Way and keep our land in a good way. Other First Nations have similar stories.

These stories reflect a "Native American Old Testament" established many thousands of years before the European invasion of America. Many Christians claim to believe the Genesis story of the Garden, but Native Americans understand this as a present-day reality. When Native Americans speak of *living with the land,* the preposition *with* should be understood as paramount. One can live *on* the land and ignore the land, even abuse it. Yet living *with* the land implies a harmonious relationship, a partnership between the human beings and everything else, including soil, rocks, water, wildlife. Living *with* the land means one views the land as much more than mere dirt.

This understanding of the relationship between land and people is the lynchpin that informs our overall framework in developing a Native American theology. Other, more sterile options have been chosen for land views in the past history of the church. These alternative views have seen the land, water, even air as commodities to be privatized and sold to the highest bidder. In such a worldview, the relationship with the land becomes one of subjugator and subjugated.

This view, though consistent with a scientific, materialistic view of land, is unbiblical to its core. Says Brueggemann, "Land is central, if not *the central theme* of Biblical faith."[8] He continues:

> Land is never simply physical dirt but is always physical dirt freighted with social meanings derived from historical experience. A literal sense of the term will protect us from excessive spiritualization, so that we recognize that the yearning for land is always a serious historical power and belonging. . . . Land is always fully historical but always bearer of over-pulses of meaning known only to those who lose and yearn for it. . . . Our humanness is always about historical placement in the earth, but the historical placement always includes excess meanings both rooted in, and moving beyond literalism.[9]

As a Native American, I view the land given to my people through covenant with the Creator as sacred. We have developed ceremonies, stories, and traditions that aid us in living a sacred life on the land. Living this life is one that is reminiscent of the original covenant with human beings in the garden. It can be characterized as a "shalom sense of place." Because our land was stolen, the nonindigene must find it difficult to feel the same congruity with the land. Yet the apparent sense of loss and incongruity felt by nonindigenes cannot be avoided until the issue of stolen land and missing relationship with America's host people is worked through.

The solutions will not come easily. There will be more pain and loss to be sure, and it will likely span several generations. Yet God's shalom kingdom demands that the issue of land be addressed. The issue must be addressed if Native Americans are ever to come back from marginality and into wholeness. It must be addressed if nonindigenous peoples ever hope to recover the missing sense of place that God has always intended for all human beings to experience to gain integrity, congruence, and wholeness in their lives. Seeking out and establishing relationships between the emerging church and indigenous people is paramount to finding shalom and providing a secure future for the next seven generations.

AFTERWORD

This Is Just the Beginning: Living Our Great-Grandchildren's History

Doug Pagitt

It is not a misplaced assumption that a manifesto would be the start of something, that there is a plan for the future being communicated in such a bold endeavor. I mean, who goes on a journey without a destination? Who articulates a preferable future without a picture of that reality? So it is a fair question to ask, What is the future of this *Emergent Manifesto of Hope*?

Well, my answer is, it depends on our grandchildren and their children.

Here is what I mean. Movements of consequence are tested not only by their contributions to the participants but by their value to those who follow in decades and centuries to come. Movements have their meaning when they lead to a world of possibilities in the future that were not available at the time of the initial innovations.

It is important for those of us on the front end of hopeful promise to know that it is quite likely that our grandchildren will look at our time as the "good ol' days." They'll be interested in how we lived faith in our day when things were so much simpler and straightforward, when the answers didn't need to be so nuanced and specialized. They will look to our faith, not to repeat our actions, but to be encouraged to find their way through the mountain vistas of hopefulness and the badlands of sorrow in their world.

We must remember that, just as we reflect on the past and the faith handed to us and live the *future* of our predecessors' hopes, we are also living the *histories* of those who will follow us.

We are certainly living in a unique time in history. Many of us take for granted aspects of our lives that were simply inconceivable in past ages. Imagine that only a century ago most people never traveled more than one hundred miles from where they were born—it was only a small minority who could travel to another land or become immigrants in a new homeland. With the idea of the automobile just developing, the thought of traveling from one end of the United States to another just for fun was on no one's mind. The notions that now make up the bases of physics, chemistry, and biology were only the imaginations of "crazy people" at the end of the last millennium. The global dreams of our day—world peace and justice, medications for all people who need them, turning lands and water that are not currently part of the food system into farms of nutrition, having a voluntary distribution of power from the strong to care for the weak, creating hopeful global and "outer space" life—will be carried to extremes beyond our control by our grandchildren.

These wondrous times are just the beginning. Even as many of us realize our call to be brave pioneers who find answers needed for our day, we can rest assured that those who will follow us will have the same burden, but it will be greatly multiplied. They do not need answers from us but a faithful story to follow. So just as we have lived the hope of faith from the early disciples to the founders of the early expressions of Christianity, from the creed-conceivers to the faithful during the Dark Ages, from the Reformers to the reuniters, from the fighters to the peacemakers, from the pioneers to the historians, from the abolitionists to the full-rights activists, may we accept our call to join the long line of the faithful. May our current faithfulness not only be for ourselves and our times, but may it serve as a helpful guide in a long line of faith.

The knowledge we have is fantastic and grows each day. Even so, understanding is nowhere close to its end. And it is possible that our grandchildren will consider our deep, important conclusions and knowledge to be quaint notions of a far more innocent time. So we must live in humility.

Many of us know more about our neighbors around the world than people of other times knew about nearby villages. And as much as we have needed to consider the implications of knowing people from different cultures, this global interaction will be even greater in 2090, when world engagement may be even more consequential. The intercultural friendships many of us are learning from today may only be the start of a dream to be realized by future generations. So we must engage and overcome bias and bigotry as forerunners of a time to come.

The ability of technology to assist human development and relieve suffering today will seem elementary in a half century, and the way that we live faithfully today may be only the building blocks for the road of faith at the dawning of the twenty-second century. So we must do the hard work of integrating our theology and practices with the important ethical issues of our day to give a picture of a way forward at the start of this technological era.

While no one can manage their own legacy well, and those who try often lose the vitality needed for their own time by looking too far ahead, let me try to outline a few areas we will need to give effort to if we are to be a helpful part of this faith family line.

We can't count God's friends as our enemies. Anyone who is a friend of God must be a friend of ours. Then what do we do with our enemies? Love them because God loves them. The ways we love our neighbor and enemy may comprise the most important example we can set.

We can't allow our knowing to stop growing. We all live with a version of the world that works for us, but we need to be sure that we do not isolate ourselves with those who know as we know.

If our grandchildren speak of our time as characterized by a cultural niche expression of faith specially formulated for Gen-whatever, we will have left them very little. No one in 2140 will need examples of trendy cultural tricks masquerading as missional innovation. But hopefully our grandchildren will be able to speak of us as those who followed our own way with faith, understanding, and passion and who embraced the ways of others with wonder and respect. Without wonder for the other (persons and ideas), we will become focused on ourselves rather than on the life of God unfolding in our world and time.

We can't forget the poor or the past. If our grandchildren are overly burdened with our bad memory of the poor, then our efforts of faith may be in vain. If we forget the poor and do not work toward freeing people from the oppression of others and from systems of abuse, we will fail to claim the mandate of Isaiah and Jesus for our day, and we will not be seen as helpful in the future, for our grandchildren may have to deal with a kind of economic and global imbalance beyond our imagination. If we do not find a path forward in caring for the needy, future generations may need to forge new paths in their efforts to live the faith of Jesus.

But we also must not forget the past. There are two ways to be confined by the past—replaying it and forgetting it. This can be true for the individual and for entire cultures. We do not want to be the traumatized amnesia victim who can't remember from where we came, nor do we want to be the former high school star who can't live beyond the "glory days." Our past—the good, the bad, and the ugly—must be remembered and integrated into our story. This will be especially true in the aspects of our past that seem least like our present. Increasingly this will be the situation for future generations—when the present world will seem to be less and less like the past.

We must know and tell the story of God. We need to be people of the whole story—the full counsel of Scripture and present working of the Spirit. We need to tell of all that the Lord has done and not just our selected sections. We live in a time of unprecedented dialogue. We have the privilege of knowing how others see faith and read the Bible and interpret the times. We need to take advantage of opportunities to understand better what God is doing and has done in the world. If we live stuck in our version of faith and do not have a growing understanding of the Bible, we put at risk our ability to live the hopes and dreams of God through Jesus.

We must see the world as hopeful even when it is hurtful. For God so loved the world. . . . We need to love the world too. We need to be people of faith who love as God loves. We must be a *crucified-hopeful* people in our day, who speak blessing even in the midst of death. If we allow our struggle, pain, and even destruction to drive out our hope, our grandchildren will need to look to others for hope that lasts.

We must exist for the benefit and blessing of all the world. The gospel of Jesus is a fulfillment of the blessing of Abraham—"You will be a blessing to all the world."

If our grandchildren are forced to speak of our day as a time filled with those who saw faith as the prized possession of the insider with member benefits, we will have failed. If we leave a version of the gospel that is ultimately for the benefit of the faithful and not the whole world, we have missed something. Our grandchildren must be able to say about us: "They did not see themselves as end users of the gospel. Faith was not value-added living, but life-giving to all the earth."

The long and short of all this is to say that we need to be faithful in the little things of our day so that our grandchildren will be encouraged and compelled to be faithful in the big things of their day.

May we be a people not only of a faithful life but of a faithful legacy.

AFTERWORD
TO THE PAPERBACK EDITION

TONY JONES AND DOUG PAGITT

For our part, we couldn't be happier with the reception of *An Emergent Manifesto of Hope* thus far. It has provoked conversation, sparked controversy, and furthered the imaginations of those of us involved with the emergent phenomenon.

Authors, editors, and publishers have a couple of options when titling a book. On the one hand, they can get cute and pick a title that is an enigmatic metaphor, then get down to explaining that metaphor in the opening chapter. On the other hand, the title can be a straightforward descriptor.

Or one can choose the path of boldness, make a significant claim in the title, and then spend the book trying to justify that claim. This is the path we chose with the book you hold in your hands. So we were delighted to hear the criticism, "It's a great book, but it really isn't a 'manifesto.'" Or, "How is this more *hopeful* than other versions of Christianity?" Those criticisms mean that people are paying attention, that they're reflecting critically on the thoughts expressed in this *manifesto*.

We've said it *ad naseum*: we desire the books with the Emergent Village leaf on them to be conversation *starters*, not conversation *enders*. To that end, we're thrilled several of the *Manifesto* essayists have been invited on radio programs to defend their ideas, and that others have been pursued to write books on the ideas first presented herein. But most of all we are thrilled that so many people have found the ideas in this book connecting with the dreams of their hearts. Not only did readers find the ideas instructive but also confirming of what is happening in their situation. We have heard so many times of those who, while reading, said "That is just what I have been thinking about." Readers have wanted to pass the book on, and many have wanted to jump in. They put the book down not satisfied with the ideas but encouraged to keep looking for friends on the journey. For us this result is beyond our control. When a book becomes not only helpful but hopeful, all one can be is grateful.

It's not lost on us that many in the emergent conversation are particularly interested in quantum physics, wherein to hold something down long enough to measure it is to then not be able to see anything in it but that measurement. Or else the thing does the unthinkable and shows up in two places at once. So it is with the still virginal emergent movement. Taking its temperature may not tell us what we need to know, for its frequently changing manifestation may be the most important and difficult to record.

Like any authors, we're curious, reader, about what you think of this book. And right now, we're talking to you, the guy who just picked up this old, tattered paperback off the clearance rack on the sidewalk outside a used bookstore. What is "emergent" now? Did it make any difference to the faith we wanted to live at the start of the twenty-first century? Do the ideas in this book have any legs? Did these ideas contribute to a beautiful faith that is beneficial to the world?

Pondering questions like these is particularly interesting in our era of rapid change. When those of us who started what would become Emergent Village began meeting ten years ago, it seemed like an exclusively evangelical conversation. But recently, as many evangelicals have become uncomfortable with the theological adventures of emergents, we've experienced great interest from "mainline" Protestants (and, increasingly, Anabaptists, Roman Catholics, and Orthodox). Where exactly this is going, of course, is anyone's guess, which is thrilling.

Regardless of where this emergent thing goes, this book has marked an important point on the journey, for it represents the great variety of background and opinion that makes up the movement. In fact, a prolific book reviewer recently told us, "Sorry I didn't review the *Manifesto*, but I'm just tired of telling people how diverse the emerging church is. The diversity of the movement," he continued, "is an established fact."

We're thrilled he thinks so, but there is no end game when it comes to diversity. As a conversation among friends, Emergent only gets stronger when more people, with more opinions, come to the party. So we'll continue to press for more voices in our books and behind our microphones, even if those voices occasionally contradict one another. May we be people who have the eyes to see the beauty in diversity.

NOTES

Introduction Friendship, Faith, and Going Somewhere Together

1. LN is primarily an evangelical group, and as such, the early years of Emergent (then called the Young Leaders Network) was predominantly white and male—honestly, it was a weakness that we were immediately aware of and that we have done much to amend. The diversity represented in this book is, I hope, another step in that direction.

2. Aristotle, *Nicomachean Ethics,* 1.1.

3. Alasdair MacIntyre, *After Virtue* (Notre Dame, IN: Notre Dame University Press, 1984), 187, italics added.

Chapter 2 Meeting Jesus at the Bar

1. Brian McLaren, *More Ready Than You Realize* (Grand Rapids: Zondervan, 2002).

2. Dallas Willard, *Divine Conspiracy* (New York: HarperCollins, 1998).

Chapter 5 The Art of Emergence

1. A delightful book of short essays on this process of embodied learning through "accidents" is Richard Feynman's *The Pleasure of Finding Things Out* (Cambridge, MA: Helix Books, 1999).

2. Walter Brueggemann, using the work of Paul Ricoeur and Peter Berger, points to the ways that our lives are mirrored in and by the Psalms, "that our life of faith consists in moving with God in terms of (a) being securely *oriented*, (b) being painfully *disoriented*, and (c) being surprisingly *reoriented.*" The psalmists themselves, he argues, are "driven to such poignant prayer and song as are found in the Psalter precisely by *experiences of dislocation and relocation.*" He continues: "the Psalms are . . . in a history where we are dying and rising, and in a history where God is at work, ending our lives and making gracious new beginnings for us." Walter Brueggemann, *Praying the Psalms* (Winona, MN: Saint Mary's Press, 1986), 16, 17, 24.

3. The theology of the incarnation is artistically explored in brilliant ways by Jeremy Begbie and a collection of contributors in Jeremy Begbie, ed., *Beholding the Glory: Incarnation through the Arts* (Grand Rapids: Baker, 2000).

4. Note two helpful surveys of "story" from the point of narrative theology and missiology. George Stroup describes one of narrative theology as providing "a foundation for theology by unit-

ing experience and reflection in a way that recent forms of systematic theology apparently have been unable to do. . . . Narrative theology does recognize . . . that the Christian faith is rooted in particular historical events which are recounted in the narratives of Christian Scripture and tradition, that these historical narratives are the basis for Christian affirmations about the nature of God and the reality of grace, and that these historical narratives and the faith they spawn are redemptive when they are appropriated at the level of personal identity and existence." George W. Stroup, *The Promise of Narrative Theology: Recovering the Gospel in the Church* (Eugene, OR: Wipf and Stock Publishers, 1997), 17.

Steven Bevans summarizes what he has called the "Countercultural Model" of missions (à la Newbigin, Guder, Lowes-Watson, and the Gospel and Our Culture Network) to be rooted in the narrative character of the gospel of Jesus Christ: "The gospel, rather than being a list of doctrines or moral principles, is conceived as a story to be told and witnessed to rather than something to be argued for abstractly." The church's story is simultaneously the "story about one man who incarnated God's presence" and "something that engages one in the same vision as that of Jesus." "It is because of this second meaning that the gospel story is not complete. It is a story that is a clue to the entire story of humankind: it does not know *where* that story will end, or *how* it will end but where it is going." And so Christianity is then, by nature, politically and historically engaged with culture. Steven Bevans, *Models of Contextual Theology* (Maryknoll, NY: Orbis Books, 2002), 121.

5. Here are two helpful discussions on practice from the points of ethics and phenomenology. Alasdair MacIntyre defines *practice* in terms of its relationship to virtues as "any coherent and complex form of socially established cooperative human activity through which goods internal to that form of activity are realized in the course of trying to achieve those standards of excellence which are appropriate to, and partially definitive of, that form of activity, with the result that human powers to achieve excellence, and human conceptions of the ends and goods involved, are systematically extended." MacIntyre, *After Virtue*, 187.

Dallas Willard describes the relationship between practice and belief this way: "You don't have to [accept] anything you don't want. We have to help people understand that belief is something that comes along as you experience. You don't have to fake anything. The way faith works is this: you put into practice what you believe. If you're attracted to Jesus, what do you believe about him that you can act on? Experience shows again and again that when you allow people to act on the little that they do believe, the rest will follow." "Apologetics in Action," *Cutting Edge Magazine*, Winter 2001, http://www.dwillard.org/articles/artview.asp?artID=14.

6. Diana Butler Bass offers this "mosaic": "Christian practices are both individual and corporate. Christian practices embody belief, and, conversely, beliefs form practices. Christian practices are the constituent parts of a larger Christian way of life, as revealed, modeled, and taught by Jesus Christ. Christian practices necessarily involve reflection, imagination, repetition, attention, and intentionality. Practices imply practice, repetition, craft, habit, and art. Christians engage these actions for their own sake—because they are good and worthy and beautiful—not because they are instruments to some other end (like increasing membership or marketing the congregation)." Diana Butler Bass, *The Practicing Congregation: Imagining a New Old Church* (Herndon, VA: The Alban Institute, 2004), 65.

7. Anthropologist Frank Tannebaum in *Slave and Citizen* (Random House, 1946) tells how sacraments such as baptism participate within the socio-economic context of slave trade. Slaves were captured by Portuguese and forced to be baptized before being taken overseas. Slaves were often baptized on the shores of Brazil as they were taken into the Americas. And some anthropologists suggest that baptism even inspired acts of manumission. In these cases sacraments shaped the context in which they were practiced actually reinforcing incomplete understandings of the story of God.

8. Lesslie Newbigin, *The Gospel in a Pluralist Society* (Grand Rapids: Eerdmans, 1989), 227.

9. This illustration of three-cornered relationship expounds on Lesslie Newbigin's theology of cultural plurality. George R. Hunsberger, "The Newbigin Gauntlet: Developing a Domestic Missiology for North America," in George R. Hunsberger, ed., *The Church between Gospel and Culture: The Emerging Mission in North America* (Grand Rapids: Eerdmans, 1996), 8–9.

10. Ibid.

11. This is not to diminish the value of "tracing" the old patterns or learning the symbols and field of classical theology. What I am pointing to is the assumption that classical theology, or symbols bound in prior contexts, are sufficient substitutes for the theological task of equipping ourselves to navigate life's ambiguities today as witnesses to the emerging hope of the resurrection. Having tried out life at different points as both a conservative evangelical and a mainline liberal, I have noticed the divorce of story and practice playing into desires to manage and control the church's future. And so our control issues contribute to our own blind spots regarding the openness of the very story and practice meant to put our own creativity into play.

12. This is from a helpful discourse on the shared transitory relationship the children of God have with nature as described by Paul in Romans 8. Moltmann writes, "Nature becomes in a positive sense the 'sister' and traveling companion of hoping, searching human beings" (31). Jürgen Moltmann, *A Passion for God's Reign: Theology, Christian Learning, and the Christian Self* (Grand Rapids: Eerdmans, 1998), 31–32.

13. Walter Brueggemann, *Texts under Negotiation: The Bible and Postmodern Imagination* (Minneapolis: Fortress, 1993). "The church is only an anticipation of the full, promised community of the whole world . . . the church itself is not a goal of God's creation" (46).

14. David Bosch, *Transforming Mission: Paradigm Shifts in Theology of Mission* (Maryknoll, NY: Orbis, 1991), 510.

15. Newbigin has also been critical of the separation between theory and practice in modern Western Christianity. This can be seen in his work with the theology of the Cappadocians—two brothers, a sister, and a close friend who left behind the new privilege granted Christians by Constantine, consequently readapting Christian practice into what would become Eastern Monasticism. These early innovators of Christian theory and practice argued vigorously for the meaning of the incarnation (*logos* theory) in their Greco-Roman culture. To insure that Christian innovation would proceed from a Christ center, they argued first that *creation* did not emanate from God (as Greek myths claimed), neither was it bound in determinism, but it was relatively free and open, able to be changed by new, surprising events. Second, they argued that everything was material, not even the astrological world was a separate "heaven" where the gods lived. These two points sharpen the reason for seeing the incarnation as a model for integrated living. Lesslie Newbigin, *Proper Confidence: Faith, Doubt, and Certainty in Christian Discipleship* (Grand Rapids: Eerdmans, 1995), 7–9.

16. Elizabeth O'Connor, *Eighth Day of Creation: Discovering Your Gifts and Using Them* (Waco: Word, 1971), 48–49.

17. Walter Brueggemann, in his address to the Emergent Theological Conversation, 2004, taught that the "ministry of the church, and the precise location of the Holy Spirit's new gifting, is to manage the ambivalence between the subversive script of the Gospel and the dominant script of technocratic, therapeutic, militaristic consumerism."

18. Moltmann, *Passion for God's Reign,* 54.

19. Mihaly Csikszentmihalyi, *Creativity: Flow and the Psychology of Discovery and Invention*, (New York: HarperCollins, 1996), 6.

20. See Dave Tomlinson, *The Post-Evangelical (Revised North American Edition)* (Grand Rapids: Zondervan, 2003); and Frie.

21. Csikszentmihalyi, 11.

22. Henri Nouwen, "Moving from Solitude to Community to Ministry," *Leadership* 16, no. 2 (spring 1995): 81–87.

23. This insightful comment was offered by a participant during an early emergent YS convention workshop.

24. Moltmann has put it this way: "If theology takes the church seriously, then it—like the church itself—must become a function of the kingdom of God in the world." Moltmann, *A Passion for God's Reign*, 51. Theology and its practice, then, require *emerging theo-practical environments* to be engaged in the wider scope of creation mediated through cultures.

Chapter 6 An Ever-Renewed Adventure of Faith

1. Joel B. Green, *Salvation: Understanding Biblical Themes* (St. Louis: Chalice Press, 2003).

2. Walter Brueggemann, *To Build, to Plant: A Commentary on Jeremiah 26–52,* International Theological Commentary (Grand Rapids: Eerdmans, 1991), 32.

3. Wendell Berry, *Sex, Economy, Freedom, and Community: Eight Essays* (reprint, New York: Pantheon, 1994), 168.

4. Ann Morisy, *Journeying Out: A New Approach to Christian Mission* (London: Morehouse, 2004).

Chapter 8 The Existing Church/Emerging Church Matrix

1. In *The Journey of Existing Churches into the Emerging Culture* (Grand Rapids: Zondervan, 2006), I offer some detailed descriptions of these differences and the terminology on this chart. See especially chapters 2–4.

2. The descriptions are certainly nonexclusive generalizations. My point here is to demonstrate the magnitude of potential differences between the two traditions. One should also remember that both the existing church and emerging churches are not monolithic expressions. For example, the existing church I served for fifteen years had some emerging church characteristics (right column).

3. Brian Walsh and Sylvia Keesmaat, *Colossians Remixed: Subverting the Empire* (Downers Grove, IL: InterVarsity, 2004).

Chapter 9 The American Catholic Merger-Church

1. B. T. Froehle and M. L. Gautier, *Catholicism USA: A Portrait of the Catholic Church in the United States* (Maryknoll, NY: Orbis Books, 2000), 1.

2. The term *religious*, when used as a noun, refers to those in a religious order or community.

Chapter 12 Church Emerging

1. The article is available at www.anewkindofchristian.com.

2. For a vigorous conservative evangelical polemic against the dangers of postmodernism, see D. A. Carson's *The Gagging of God* (Grand Rapids: Zondervan, 2002) or *Becoming Conversant with the Emerging Church* (Grand Rapids: Zondervan, 2005).

3. The quote is from www.wikipedia.org, s.v. "Colonialism" accessed July 2006. I am not equating colonialism with capitalism. There can be socialist or communist colonialism, for example, and there can be noncolonial capitalism.

4. Adam Hochschild's *King Leopold's Ghost: A Story of Greed, Terror, and Heroism in Colonial Africa* (New York: Mariner, 1999) provides a highly readable history of colonialism in the Congo. Dee Brown's *Bury My Heart at Wounded Knee* (New York: Holt, 2001) provides a history of colonialism closer to home in America. The classic movie *The Mission* conveys some of the issues of colonialism in Latin America.

5. Mabiala Kenzo's article, "Evangelical Faith & (Postmodern) Others" (Sept. 15, 2005), is available at http://anewkindofconversation.com (a blog-book) and will appear in a book edited by Myron Penner, *A New Kind of Conversation*.

6. One thinks of postmodernism's inability to propose a coherent response to terrorism, for example, or the way postmodernity so easily plays into consumerism. See Ken Wilber's *Boomeritis* (Boston: Shambala, 2003) or David Korten's *The Great Turning* (Berrett Koehler, 2006).

7. Kenzo, "Evangelical Faith."

8. For more on the Emergent conversation, see www.emergentvillage.com.

9. Kenzo, "Evangelical Faith."

10. See Jim Wallis, *God's Politics: Why the Right Gets It Wrong and the Left Doesn't Get It* (San Francisco: HarperSanFrancisco, 2005), for more on left-right polarization and paralysis.

11. My book, *A Generous Orthodoxy* (Grand Rapids: Zondervan, 2004), explores this convergence in more detail.

12. See Randy Woodley, *Living in Color* (Downers Grove, IL: InterVarsity, 2004) and Richard Twiss, *One Church, Many Tribes: Following Jesus the Way God Made You* (Ventura, CA: Regal, 2000) for two Native American perspectives on the way ahead.

Chapter 13 The End of Reinvention

1. George A. Lindbeck, *The Nature of Doctrine: Religion and Theology in a Postliberal Age* (Louisville, KY: Westminster John Knox Press, 1984), 16.

2. N. T. Wright, *The Challenge of Jesus: Rediscovering Who Jesus Was and Is* (Downers Grove, IL: InterVarsity, 1999), 17.

3. Lindbeck, *Nature of Doctrine,* 16.

4. The most famous of these queries in recent times was H. Richard Niebuhr's *Christ and Culture* (New York: Harper & Row, 1951).

5. Newbigin, *Gospel in a Pluralist Society*, 222.

6. Lindbeck, *Nature of Doctrine*, 18.

Chapter 14 Converting Christianity

1. Douglas Coupland, *Hey Nostradamus!* (London: Bloomsbury, 2003).

2. Karen Armstrong, *A History of God* (London: Heinemann, 1993), 402.

3. Dutch theologian Mieke Bal has written extensively about the traces of Christian faith on the landscape of the West. In her opinion, Christianity is one of the religious structures that informs the cultural imagination, and any talk of faith in the postsecular era requires consideration of the influence of Christianity on the West. I recommend her essay "Postmodern Theology as Cultural Analysis" in *The Blackwell Companion to Postmodern Theology*, ed. Graham Ward (London: Blackwell, 2001), 3–21.

4. Peter Harrison, *"Religion" and the Religions of the English Enlightenment* (Cambridge: Cambridge University Press, 1990).

5. John Drane, *Cultural Change and Biblical Faith* (Carlisle, UK: Paternoster Press, 2000).

6. Marxist theory seeks to undermine the authenticity of religion by highlighting the dynamics of culture in the practice of religion. While I do not agree with the conclusions of Marx, Feuerbach et al., I do believe that religion is always a contextual and cultural experience. We cannot avoid who we are, where we are from, and all the other social dynamics that shape us as individuals and peoples and how we understand and define the nature of faith.

7. Gianna Vattimo, *After Christianity*, trans. Luca D'Isanto (New York: Columbia University Press, 2001), 1.

8. Christopher Partridge, *The Re-Enchantment of the West* (London: T&T Clark, 2004), 1:4.

9. This comment from Du Bois was taken from David Chidester, *Authentic Fakes: Religion and American Popular Culture* (Berkeley, CA: University of California Press, 2005), 8.

10. Quoted in John Drane, *Do Christians Know How to Be Spiritual? The Rise of New Spirituality and the Mission of the Church* (London: DLT, 2005), 105.

Part 4 A Hopeful Way Forward

1. Thomas Armstrong, "Multiple Intelligences," www.thomasarmstrong.com/multiple_intel ligences.htm.

2. Ibid.

Chapter 15 Leadership in a Flattened World

1. Margaret Wheatley, *Finding Our Way: Leadership for an Uncertain Time* (San Francisco: Barrett Kohler, 2005), 4, 28.

2. The Starbucks "third-place" concept: home is first place, and work, second.

3. Margaret Wheatley, "Goodbye, Command and Control," *Leader to Leader,* July 1997, 1.

4. James Surowiecki, *The Wisdom of Crowds: Why the Many Are Smarter than the Few and How Collective Wisdom Shapes Business, Economies, Societies, and Nations* (New York: Doubleday, 2004), 16.

5. Jeffrey Pfeffer, "Why Employees Should Lead Themselves," *Business 2.0,* January/February 2006, 76.

6. Surowiecki, *Wisdom of Crowds,* xiv.

7. Ibid., 160–61.

8. See www.theamericanchurch.org.

9. Richard Florida, *The Rise of the Creative Class* (New York: Basic Books/Perseus, 2002).

10. Surowiecki, *Wisdom of Crowds,* 31.

11. The term "big-box church" refers to suburban churches (most often dubbed "community" churches) with over a thousand in attendance.

12. Carol Gilligan, as interviewed on the Dick Gordon Show, *The Connection,* WBUR Boston, May 10, 2002.

13. Thomas Friedman, *The World Is Flat: A Brief History of the 21st Century* (New York: Farrar, Straus and Giroux, 2005).

14. Peter Senge, *Presence: Human Purpose and the Field of the Future* (Cambridge, MA: The Society for Organizational Learning, 2004), 131.

15. William Bergquist, *The Postmodern Organization* (San Francisco: Jossey-Bass, 1993), 113.

16. Malcom Gladwell, *Blink: The Power of Thinking without Thinking* (New York: Little, Brown and Company, 2005).

17. Carol Gilligan, *In a Different Voice: Psychological Theory and Women's Development* (Cambridge, MA: Harvard University Press, 1982).

18. Carol Gilligan, *The Birth of Pleasure: A New Map of Love* (New York: Vintage, 2003).

19. John Eldredge, *Wild at Heart: Discovering the Secret of a Man's Soul* (Nashville: Thomas Nelson, 2001).

Chapter 16 The Sweet Problem of Inclusiveness

1. This scene is from the 1991 movie *Black Robe.* Father Laforgue (Lothair Bluteau) and chief Chomina (August Schellenberg) are characters from the novel by Brian Moore that was adapted for the movie. The story is historical.

2. See the chapter "Postlude: A Conversation with a Skeptic" in Miroslav Volf, *Free of Charge: Giving and Forgiving in a Culture Stripped of Grace* (Grand Rapids: Zondervan, 2005).

3. See www.wikipedia.org., s.v. "Christianity."

4. Pastor Timothy Keller from Redeemer Presbyterian Church in New York City has developed this idea of religion as "self-salvation" and conversion as a "trust transfer" better than anyone I know.

5. The notion that Christianity cannot possibly be a candidate for idolatry has been recently expressed by D. A. Carson, whose argument hangs on an assumption that sins of Christianity are always a departure from true Christianity (*Becoming Conversant with the Emerging Church*, 201–202). However, evil done under the banner of Christianity cannot be dismissed by declaring, "That was not *true* Christianity." Christianity is what it is. To dismiss Christianity's sins by appealing to a Platonic idea of some "true Christianity" is both dishonest to other religions and unhelpful to Christians. We simply never had and will never have pure, true Christianity.

6. I paraphrase Kierkegaard here. His books brought me into Christian faith and I recommend *Either/Or* (New York: Penquin/Putnam, 1992) and *Fear and Trembling/Repetition: Kierkegaard's Writings*, vol. 6 (Princeton, NJ: Princeton University, 1983). He manages to criticize Christianity in a way that compels the reader to become a Christian.

7. Ernest Becker, a Pulitzer Prize–winning author for his book *Denial of Death*, writes about this in his last book *Escape from Evil* (New York: Free Press, 1975). He says: "Each person nourishes his immortality in the ideology of the self-perpetuation to which he gives his allegiance; this gives his life the only abiding significance it can have. No wonder men go into rage over fine points of belief: if your adversary wins the argument about truth, you die. Your immortality system has been shown to be fallible, your life becomes fallible" (64).

8. Inclusivism, a view about the destiny of the unevangelized, holds that all people have an opportunity to be saved by responding in faith to God based on the revelation they have. In contrast to restrictivism on one side and universalism on the other, inclusivism affirms the particularity and finality of salvation only in Christ but denies that knowledge of his work is necessary for salvation. Inclusivists believe that the work of Jesus is ontologically (in substance) necessary for salvation but not epistemologically (in name) necessary. Among adherents to the inclusivist view are Justin Martyr, Zwingli, John Wesley, C. S. Lewis, Wolfhart Pannenberg, and Clark Pinnock. In the twentieth century, of all traditions, Roman Catholic theology had most decisively embraced inclusivism, with Karl Rahner's "anonymous Christianity" as the most celebrated presentation of it. Presently, among evangelicals, inclusivism is beginning to challenge restrictivism for supremacy. For key biblical texts and a solid treatment of all three views see John Sanders, *No Other Name* (Grand Rapids: Eerdmans, 1992).

9. Examples of this include Jesus's parable of judgment in Matthew 25:31–46 and the report about Peter's encounter with Cornelius in Acts 10:23–48.

10. For numerous examples of these dynamics from the Bible, history, and the writings of authors like C. S. Lewis, see Sanders, *No Other Name*, chapter 7.

11. Volf, *Free of Charge*, 223.

12. I discovered this obvious teaching of the New Testament while reading Brian McLaren's *The Last Word and the Word after That* (San Francisco: Jossey-Bass, 2005). One needs only to look at any discussion of judgment or works in the New Testament to see this truth.

13. For a condensed discussion of this concept, see chapter 23 in Abraham Heschel's *Between God and Man* (New York: Free Press, 1997).

14. This phrase from the Christian hymn "This Is My Father's World" is often used to express the teaching of "common grace," grace that God gives to *sustain* all the world, differentiated from grace that *saves*. In contrast, inclusivism (see n. 8) argues that all revelation is saving revelation and that any grace God extends to us is not just to sustain the world, but to save it.

15. Buddhism and Alcoholics Anonymous have already proved the point.

Chapter 17 Orthoparadoxy

1. Roy Sorensen, *A Brief History of the Paradox: Philosophy and the Labyrinths of the Mind* (New York: Oxford, 2003), xii.

2. Jürgen Moltmann, *Theology of Hope: On the Ground and the Implications of a Christian Eschatology* (Minneapolis: Fortress Press, 1993), 337.

3. Søren Kierkegaard, *The Journals of Søren Kierkegaard : A Selection*, ed. Alexander Dru (London: Oxford, 1938), no. 206, s.v. 1838.

4. Lesslie Newbigin, *Gospel in a Pluralist Society*, 183. The reference to Song's work is found in C. S. Song, *Tell Us Our Names* (Maryknoll, NY: Orbis, 1984), 114.

Chapter 18 Humble Theology

1. You can read more about what began specifically to cause me to rethink theology and its relationship to methodology in the chapter I wrote in Robert Webber, ed., *Listening to the Beliefs of Emerging Churches* (Grand Rapids: Zondervan, forthcoming).

Chapter 19 Leading from the Margins

1. Brian McLaren, *A Generous Orthodoxy* (Grand Rapids: Zondervan/Youth Specialties, 2004), 9.

2. H. Middleton, *Precious Vessels of the Holy Spirit* (Protecting Veil Press, 2003).

3. Conversation with Benedictine monk Father Adam Ryan, June 2004.

4. Daniel Pink, "The Revenge of the Right Brain," *Wired*, February 13, 2005, http://www.wired.com/wired/archive/13.02/brain.html.

5. Ibid.

Chapter 20 Digging Up the Past

1. Eberhard Busch, *Karl Barth* (Philadelphia, PA: Fortress Press, 1976), 81.

2. Ibid., 97–98.

3. Ibid., 89.

4. Karl Barth, *Church Dogmatics*, vol. 1 (Edinburgh, Scotland: T & T Clark, 1975), 1:76–77.

5. Busch, *Karl Barth*, 426.

6. Barth, *Dogmatics in Outline* (New York: Harper & Row, 1959), 7.

7. Ibid., 9.

8. Busch, *Karl Barth*, 362–63.

9. Ibid., 418.

10. Ibid., 418–21.

Chapter 21 A Pound of Social Justice

1. See Tim Keller, *Ministries of Mercy: The Call of the Jericho Road* (P & R Publishing, 1997); John Perkins, ed., *Restoring At-Risk Communities: Doing It Together and Doing It Right* (Baker, 1995); John Perkins, *Let Justice Roll Down* (Regal, 2006); and Orlando Crespo, *Being Latino in Christ: Finding Wholeness in Your Ethnic Identity* (InterVarsity, 2003).

2. John Perkins, *With Justice for All* (Ventura, CA: Gospel Light, 1981).

3. Ibid., 23.

Chapter 22 Emergent Kissing

1. Larry B. Stammer, "The Times Poll: 15% Identify as Gay or 'on Homosexual Side,'" *Los Angeles Times*, October 20, 2002, sec. A.

2. David Carder, "High Risks Factors in Pastoral Infidelity" (seminar, Pasadena, CA, May 5, 2005). For more on this study, see David Carder, *Torn Asunder: Helping Couples Recover from Affairs* (Chicago: Moody, 1995), 26ff.

Chapter 23 Our Report Card in the Year 2057

1. Amy Caiazza and April Shaw, ed., *The Status of Women in the States* (Washington, DC: Institute for Women's Policy Research, 2004). Bureau of Justice Statistics Crime Data Brief, *Intimate Partner Violence, 1993–2003* (February 2003). The information was culled from these sources.

2. Edward N. Wolff, *Changes in Household Wealth in the 1980s and 1990s in the U. S.* (New York: The Levy Economics Institute and New York University, May 2004), 31, table 2.

3. Anup Shaw, "Behind Consumption and Consumerism," http://www.globalissues.org/TradeRelated/Consumption.asp, accessed October 5, 2006.

Chapter 24 Practicing Pentecost

1. Kenneth Leech, *Race* (New York: Church Publishing, 2005), 107–8.

2. Charles West et al., *Stormfront: The Good News of God* (Grand Rapids: Eerdmans, 2003), 21.

3. Darrell Guder, a leader in the missional church movement and one of the authors of *Missional Church: A Vision for the Sending of the Church in North America* (Grand Rapids: Eerdmans, 1998), describes being missional as: (a) The church as a body of people sent on a mission in contrast to the church as an entity located in a building or in an institutional organization. (b) The church as a community of gathered people brought together by a common calling and vocation (sent people). (c) A shift from a church-centered view of mission (mission is about building a church) to an emphasis on the mission of God (mission is about the kingdom or reign of God). The founding voices of this movement are normally held to be Bishop Lesslie Newbigin (*The Open Secret: An Introduction to the Theology of Mission*, Eerdmans, 1995) and David Bosch (*Transforming Mission: Paradigm Shifts in Theology of Mission*, Orbis, 1991).

4. A general definition of the Enlightenment: The scientific and intellectual developments of the seventeenth century (the discoveries of Isaac Newton, the rationalism of René Descartes, the skepticism of Pierre Bayle, the pantheism of Benedict de Spinoza, and the empiricism of Francis Bacon and John Locke) fostered the belief in natural law and universal order and the confidence in human reason that spread to influence all of eighteenth-century society. Currents of thought were many and varied, but certain ideas may be characterized as pervading and dominant: a rational and scientific approach to religious, social, political, and economic issues promoted a secular view of the world and a general sense of progress and perfectibility.

The major champions of these concepts were the *philosophes*, who popularized and promulgated the new ideas for the general reading public. These proponents of the Enlightenment shared certain basic attitudes. With supreme faith in rationality, they sought to discover and to act on universally valid principles governing humanity, nature, and society. They variously attacked spiritual and scientific authority, dogmatism, intolerance, censorship, and economic and social restraints. They considered the state the proper and rational instrument of progress. The extreme rationalism and skepticism of the age led naturally to deism; the same qualities played a part in bringing the later reaction of romanticism. The *Encyclopédie* of Denis Diderot epitomized the spirit of the Age of Enlightenment, or Age of Reason, as it is also called.

5. D. Stephen Long, *The Goodness of God: Theology, the Church, and Social Order* (Grand Rapids: Brazos, 2001), 199.

6. Cornel West, *Prophesy Deliverance: An Afro-American Revolutionary Christianity* (Louisville, KY: Westminster John Knox, 2002), 49.

7. Long, *Goodness of God*, 134–35.

8. Dietrich Bonhoeffer, *Life Together* (San Francisco: Harper, 1978).

9. Howard Thurman, *Jesus and the Disinherited* (Boston: Beacon, 1976).

10. The best treatment of Pentecostalism I have read thus far is by Amos Yong, *The Spirit Poured Out on All Flesh: Pentecostalism and the Possibility of Global Theology* (Grand Rapids: Baker, 2005).

11. One of the few white theologians I have read that practices what I believe to be Pentecost is James Wm. McClendon. His trilogy (*Ethics, Doctrine,* and *Witness*) on a narrative systematic theology is a classic, especially the third book in the set, *Witness*. In *Witness* he explores the various cultures in our North American context.

12. *Sarx*, Greek word meaning the flesh; denotes mere human nature, that aspect of our humanity that capitulates to and partners with sin and injustice.

Chapter 25 Restoring Honor in the Land

1. George Russell, *American Indian Facts of Life: A Profile of Today's Population, Tribes and Reservations* (Phoenix: Native Data Network, 2004), 35, 54, 68, 101.

2. Ward Churchill, *Kill the Indian, Save the Man: The Genocidal Impact of American Indian Residential Schools* (San Francisco: City Lights Books, 2004).

3.Leander McDonald, Richard L. Ludtke, and Alan Allery, *Long Term Health Care and the Health Needs of America's Native American Elders: Part 1*. Testimony submitted to the US Senate Committee on Indian Affairs (Center for Rural Health, University of North Dakota School of Medicine and Health Sciences: National Resource Center on Native American Aging, 2002), 3.

4. Ibid., 4.

5. Richard Twiss, One *Church, Many Tribes: Following Jesus the Way God Made You* (Ventura, CA: Regal, 2000).

6. Churchill, *Kill the Indian, Save the Man.*

7. Walter Brueggemann, *Peace: Living toward a Vision* (St. Louis: Chalice, 2001), 14.

8. Walter Brueggemann, *The Land: Place as Gift, Promise, and Challenge to Biblical Faith* (Philadelphia: Fortress, 1977), 2.

9. Ibid., 3.